THE PELICAN LATIN AMERICAN LIBRARY
General Editor: Richard Gott

THE SHADOW:
LATIN AMERICA FACES THE SEVENTIES

Sven Lindqvist was born in Stockholm in 1932 and received his Ph.D. from Stockholm University in 1966. The author of *The Myth of Wu Tao-tzu* and ten other books, Sven Lindqvist is considered one of the foremost Swedish writers. In the early sixties he lived in China for two years, studying Chinese, and has since then travelled extensively in Asia, writing several books on third-world problems. In 1967-9 he spent fourteen months in Latin America collecting material for *The Shadow*.

The Shadow:

LATIN AMERICA FACES
THE SEVENTIES

Sven Lindqvist

Translated by Keith Bradfield
with an Editorial Foreword
by Richard Gott

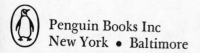
Penguin Books Inc
New York • Baltimore

Penguin Books Inc
72 Fifth Avenue
New York, New York 10011

Penguin Books Inc
7110 Ambassador Road
Baltimore, Maryland 21207

Slagskuggan: Latinamerika inför 70-talet first published in Sweden
   by Bonniers 1969
This translation first published in Pelican Books 1972
Reprinted 1974

Printed in the United States of America

Contents

Editorial Foreword 9
Preface 15
Preface to the English Edition 16

CHORRILLOS 1967 17

Jacinta Vegas 19   Rinaldo Rivas Loude 20
Víctor Li Mau 22   Lucía Rojas Centeno 24
Ana Castañón Ormeno 27   Her father 27
Marina Pérez 29   Miguel Barranichea 31
Felicita Salva Plácido 34

LATIN AMERICA FACES THE SEVENTIES 37

The Growth of the Slums 39
The Middle-class Myth 49
A Hundred Million Mouths 63
The Debt 77
The Rise of Violence 95
The Race Problem 107
The Church 123
The Military 139
The Reformers 151
The Revolution 168
Cuba 194

8 Contents

PERU – A CHECK-UP

The starting-point 211   The government of
generals 212   The real power 215   The fumes of
La Oroya 219   It all depends on how you count 224
Risks and risk premiums 231   Invasion in the
desert 236   The poetry of figures 240   What the
fight is about 253   Who owns the oil? 257   The
'Paris award' 262   From Leguía to Belaúnde 264
General Velasco 266   Postscript, August 1971 267

CHORRILLOS REVISITED

Jacinta Vegas 275   Rinaldo Rivas Loude 276
Víctor Li Mau 277   Lucía Rojas Centeno 278
Ana Castañón Ormeno 278   Marina Pérez 279
Miguel Barranichea 280   Felicita Salva Plácido 281

Bibliography 284

Editorial Foreword

This book is a classic. It is a must for anyone concerned with Latin American affairs, and it should be read by all those concerned in any way with the problems of development and revolution in the dependent world. Both a work of literature and of scholarship, it is extremely easy to read, for the writer's skill masks the effort that has gone into the composition.

In his house outside Stockholm, I have seen the author at work – an electric calculator looking rather out of place on a philosopher's desk. Here he dissects the mystery of 'the adjustment of the banana', the 'depletion allowance', and the fate of coffee futures. With infinite care he reveals the nature and extent of dependence and corruption. Each apparently random encounter illustrates a point or illuminates the drift of the argument.

All the time he is deflating illusion and debunking myths – about the middle class, or the radical church, or the guerrilla. Violence will increase in the Seventies, he has no doubts on that score, but have not the forces of conservatism got the upper hand, and can the revolutionaries get anywhere without stirring up racial consciousness which they are reluctant to do?

I first met Sven Lindqvist in the lift of the Sucre Palace Hotel in La Paz towards the end of September 1967. Bearded, pipe-smoking, with a merry twinkle to relieve an otherwise rather severe expression, he seemed almost put out when I exclaimed: 'Not *the* Sven Lindqvist?' A typically reticent Swede, he could hardly believe that his name would ring a bell with someone in a Bolivian hotel.

Years before, I had read some articles he had written from China that had been published in the *Guardian*. What, I wondered, was he doing in Bolivia? It soon transpired that he was doing what every second European seemed to be doing that year – converging on Latin America, specifically Bolivia, to discover what on earth was really happening. The Havana Tricontinental Congress of 1966, Che Guevara's guerrilla expedition of 1967, and the Organization for Latin American Solidarity's conference in Havana in August 1967 – which Lindqvist looked in on – all served to awaken a new European interest in Latin America which, fortunately, has proved lasting.

Lindqvist was at the beginning of a mammoth tour that was to take him all over Latin America, together with Cecilia, his wife, and Aron, their infant son, all unceremoniously bundled together with an oxygen cylinder in an aged Volvo shooting brake. For a few days I travelled with him, on an unforgettable expedition to the Bolivian tin mines – Oruro, Huanuni and Siglo Veinte.

These mines are spectacular at the best of times – 500 miles of tunnelling in Siglo Veinte alone and all well over 10,000 feet. But in the middle of 1967 they lay at the heart of the Bolivian – and continental – political crisis. The tin miners are a crucial force in Bolivian politics, and the army, anxious to have no second focus of insurrection to parallel the activity of Guevara in the east of the country, had moved in to crush incipient rebellion and to intimidate anyone who felt stirrings of sympathy and solidarity for the guerrilla.

The soldiers and the miners outstared each other in perpetual confrontation. Both from the same poor and exploited stock, both victims of the same system, one group worked in the mine all day, the other lounged about outside fingering their rifles.

Sven Lindqvist is the most percipient and painstaking observer with whom I have ever travelled. Long after I had put my pencil down in sheer exhaustion – especially at 12,000 feet – he would go on probing and questioning, seeking the elusive fact that would complete the puzzle he had set himself. Beware the commanding officer who pleaded another engagement: Lindqvist would be outside his door the next day. Beware the public relations man with a line in fudge and flannel: Lindqvist would truss him up like a chicken and pluck the feathers.

No fact or figure seemed too unimportant to him. 'Come on, Sven, let's go back' would be my insistent call as evening fell and Sven would still be verifying the prices in the miners' *pulpería* with the list he'd been given by the company. Not content with calling it a day, we would then stumble on through the night, looking for dissident union leaders or rebellious priests.

Lindqvist calls himself a writer – a profession that has all but disappeared in Britain. He is not by inclination a journalist – though he contributes regularly to the *Dagens Nyheter* – nor is he an historian or a novelist. He is a plain and simple writer, by training a philosopher, by force of necessity an economist. And what he saw in Latin America made him increasingly despondent, not so much because of poverty and disease and structural rigidity and all the obvious things that make an ordinary person from a comfortable home in Stockholm, London or Washington angry, but because so few people seemed to be doing anything about it, or bothering to discover the real nature of the problems. Hence his careful arithmetic which, coupled with his gently sardonic prose, illuminates more clearly than anything written elsewhere the subtle ways in which outside economic interests rob and plunder the continent and mystify those who seek to uncover their activities.

You cannot read it elsewhere because, as Lindqvist explains (exploding) at one point, no one else has done his homework. Investigating the activities of the Marcona Mining Company in Peru, he finds doors shut in his face when he visits the company town of San Juan:

'This isn't my job,' I thought furiously, as we left. 'This is a job the economists and contemporary historians should have done for me. I'm a writer.' . . .

Every minor poet these days qualifies for a biography. But who will write a biography of the Marcona Mining Company? Who is currently studying the influence of the Southern Peru Copper Corporation? Who is researching the history of the Cerro de Pasco Corporation? These giant companies that move mountains, create towns and level them once more to the ground, that intervene in the lives of millions, and whose influence extends over centuries and continents – what makes them so uninteresting from the scientific point of view?

At most they have been the subject of a commissioned work to commemorate some anniversary, or a romanticized brochure from the company's public relations department.

There must be something radically wrong with research, when it turns its back like this on the great questions in economics and contemporary history – leaving it to the writers to dig for the most elementary facts about the world we live in.

Gently grumbling to himself, Lindqvist then does the necessary digging.

The message that emerges is bleak, but who is to travel through the dependent world and remain optimistic? Lindqvist has had long experience of India and China and, as he writes here, 'I came home from India in 1964 with a feeling of hopelessness and despair. I did not believe that any economic or political system had the answer to India's problems.' He learnt from India's example that an increase in misery is no guarantee of revolution. His last book, *The Myth of Wu Tao-tzu*, ends on a note of deepest pessimism :

> Is social and economic liberation possible without violence?
> No.
> Is it possible with violence?
> No.

Here and again when travelling through Latin America, this old pessimism returns. 'You can't keep a whole people down for ever,' a kindly foreman in Brazil tries to reassure him.

'Perhaps not for ever,' Lindqvist muses, 'but it has worked for 400 years, and the ruling classes reckon it will work for a while yet.'

He admits, though, to being marginally more cheerful when coming back from Latin America :

> Returning from Latin America, my mood was entirely different. The misery there is great, but not so deep and all-embracing as that of India. Latin America is not sunk in religious lethargy; in places, religion is actually a spur to social reform. The injustices are frightful – but not so institutionalized as in India. The corruption and waste of resources is striking, but in Latin America a change seems at least possible.

And Cuba, he argues, still exists as a symbol of the possibility of change. His underlying argument is that liberation from political and economic dependence on outside influences is a necessary condition for progress in Latin America. But he would readily acknowledge that it is not the only one.

RICHARD GOTT
17 September 1971

Preface

This book is the result of two years' work. During this time I have spent a total of fourteen months in Latin America – from July 1967 to August 1968, plus a further visit in March 1969. I have driven over 20,000 miles from Tierra del Fuego in the south to Caracas in the north, visiting all the countries of Latin America apart from a few minor states in Central America.

My investigation of the Latin American situation in the late Sixties has led me to make a series of forecasts for the coming decade. I only hope they will be proved wrong.

Why then make them? For the sake of clarity. A description of the present will be much clearer if it contains some sort of prediction. Above all, our views of the future constitute an important part of the present; and Latin America, like a pregnant woman, is already carrying its future.

This does not mean that the future is predetermined. The future is our own work, we can change it. So what information could help more to change the future than a cold, clear statement of what we already believe ourselves to know of it?

Believe ourselves to know. We cannot claim more than this, largely because the underlying statistics are incomplete and often misleading. I have spent a great deal of effort checking the reasonableness of the statistics included in this book, but I am still bound to warn the reader from the start that my margins of uncertainty are often wide.

However, the tendencies evident in the statistics are so marked that the shortcomings of individual figures need not jeopardize my conclusions. Political developments are more difficult to foresee, as is shown particularly by events in Peru. I have therefore discussed the situation in Peru in a separate section.

Latin America is not a single country. It is a continent, consisting of more than twenty states which differ widely from one another. I have tried to make this clear, but the very structure of this book emphasizes the similarities at the expense of the differences. This the reader should bear in mind.

At the same time, there is one circumstance that unites all these countries. They live in the shadow of a great power. It is almost impossible to overemphasize the position of power enjoyed by the United States in Latin America. It is perhaps possible to overestimate the ability of the United States to retain its power – after all, liberation from the Spanish and Portuguese empires once seemed equally inconceivable. It is certain, at any rate, that the United States throws a dark shadow over Latin America's whole future.

SVEN LINDQVIST
Stockholm, May 1969

PREFACE TO THE ENGLISH EDITION

The Swedish edition of this book appeared in the autumn of 1969. Subsequent developments in Latin America have dictated certain cuts and an additional section discussing some of the steps since taken towards economic independence, above all in Peru and Chile. The reader will find this additional material on p. 267.

Stockholm, August 1971

Chorrillos 1967

Chorrillos 1967

JACINTA VEGAS

'I come from the district of Piura in northern Peru, and I have lived in Lima for sixteen years, almost half my life. It is difficult living here, but I have got used to it and my children, after all, were born here. I have no money in Lima, but then I wouldn't have any money in Piura either.

'The father of my eldest boy was a good-for-nothing, he denied paternity. But the boy bears my present man's name. We aren't married. We met here in Lima, but he is also from Piura.

'My eldest boy wants to be an engineer or doctor. He'll go to night school, he says. He is twelve years old now, and in the fifth grade. The eldest girl is five, and she goes to kindergarten for a dollar 20 cents a month. She gets food there and they look after her while I work. The two youngest I take with me.

'I work at the Regatta Club down by the beach. It's a very exclusive club. I clean the toilets and work as a cloakroom attendant, looking after people's cases and clothes while they bathe. I work for two days a week, and make two dollars a day. For three months during the summer I have work every day, and on top of that I get an annual bonus of twelve dollars. That's when I buy school things for the boy, he gets a big writing book with over 100 pages.

'We moved to this shed four years ago, and we own the site, it's a good shed, very solid, fresh bamboo mats in the walls. And two rooms! Everything looked fine, but two years ago I got a sore on my foot, and had to stay in bed for a month. Then my man fell sick, and was in bed for six months. And then the boy got appendicitis. The operation cost 120 dollars. We took the money we had saved to build a proper house, and borrowed the rest.

'Three months ago it happened. My man is a driver, he got mixed up in a traffic accident, hit someone in the dark and the police took his papers away. He was supposed to pay 200 dollars in damages, so he had to go underground. He ran away, and I haven't heard from him since. I have to manage on my own. We spend about twenty or forty cents a day. We eat porridge made from pea-meal or oatmeal. On Sundays, we eat porridge made with flour. Sometimes we manage rice and stewed vegetables. Never meat.

'I've never voted. I don't have a birth certificate. I went to the authorities, and asked for dispensation. It cost twelve dollars, I took my annual bonus and paid. But I got a paper that was no good, the signature was wrong and the stamp. My employer went back with me, and the man was sent to prison. But I never got my money back, and I still have no birth certificate. So I've never voted.'

RINALDO RIVAS LOUDE

'I work for Manufactura de Calzado Glenny, España 211, Chorrillos. I'm the one who sews on the uppers. I get a dollar 30 per dozen, and I do a dozen to a dozen and a half a day. I don't get more work than that until Christmas, then I get as much as I want and can work all round the clock.

'I support a wife and four children, and my two brothers, aged fifteen and eight, all with this machine. I had a bit of luck when I picked it up second-hand eight years ago. Then it cost 72 dollars. Today a new one would cost 480 dollars. I also work as guard for the Leasehold Association, which means that I can live in this house for two dollars a month. Of course, this means that one of us – my wife or I – must always be at home. But I sit here all day in any case, at the machine.

'There are fifteen guards here altogether. We have to sound the alarm if there is an invasion. Yes, you see, those who have leases here don't want other people to come and settle and build huts. Four years ago, this was one great rubbish heap. The Association, they say, paid 4,000 dollars to get the rubbish away, and in the end the members had to come and move it out themselves. Now everything has been cleaned up, and they don't want anyone else moving in.

'I was born in Lima, just near here in Barranco, in 1933. My parents rented a room in a *barriada* [slum town]. I started early as an apprentice, and I have worked for six years since my training ended.

'Better pay? Well, I could take an extra job. Or look for some other job. More than a dollar 30 per dozen? I never thought of it. No, I'm not a union member. It's just not worth it. The factory is owned by Juan García and Víctor Glenny. They decide. There are ten of us working for them. The factory provides the leather, I buy my own thread, needles, whetstone and other bits and pieces. It makes a bit of a change to go into Lima on business.

'My eldest brother is in the *primaria*, in fifth grade. I think he can go on to the first or second year of the *secundaria*. I can't support him any longer than that, the secondary school is more expensive. Then he can start in the police school or join the army if he wants to go on studying. But my brothers are not big enough yet to understand what a burden they are to me.

'When did I last eat meat? On Sunday. We have meat on Sundays. Otherwise we have soups and porridge. The worst thing is that the children never get milk. The cinema? I get round to it every other week, I suppose. And every other week some friends come over, and we have a few drinks. Otherwise, I have the transistor here on the machine.

'Yes, I've voted. I voted for the present mayor. I believed in him, he grew up in a *barriada* himself. He has promised water, street lights, sewerage, pavements, everything. So far there's only lighting on the main road over there, it's still a long way to us. But he's got two years to do the job.

'Fidel? I've read the newspapers. He's done some good things. But here in Peru, well, we have Hugo Blanco of course, but I don't think he's the sort of man who could fight a guerrilla war in the hills, like they're doing in Bolivia.

'What I fear most is eviction. What I want most of all is a safe site, where no one can put us out, and a house of sun-dried brick. Also, of course, I can fall sick. I have no insurance, and the factory doesn't do anything for you if you are ill. It should, of course. I must try to find out a bit more about it.'

The whole time we are talking, I can hear a whining sound as if from a dog that has been shut in. It comes from a little cubicle by the door. A small boy is lying there, in the rags of the family bed. Lying absolutely silent in the darkness, perfectly still, with fright in his eyes. The new baby is on the earthen floor, smeared with faeces. Flies are crawling round his eyes. The whining is from him.

VÍCTOR LI MAU

'I'm twenty-nine years old, an electrical engineer. After university, I worked for a year and a half in the *sierra*, at a cement factory. Then I was at a cable factory in Lima. I've been a voluntary social worker here in Chorrillos for two years now. We collect rags and scrap. We sell on Wednesdays and Saturdays.

'What I want to achieve is a new sort of understanding. Obviously, I could be of more use as an engineer, they need all the engineers they can get in the *sierra*. But I don't want to become part of the hierarchy. I don't want a mass of paperwork. I want contact with the poor, and that I get here.

'My father came from China, he rented a little *hacienda*, 80 hectares, from a relative. He grew rice. He had ten to fifteen families who worked for him. Each of them got half a hectare, and a small wage. He supervised the work himself. My brothers are carrying on the *hacienda* on the same terms. They would like to buy the land, but they can't pay the 8,000 dollars needed.

'I sympathize with the Acción Popular, but I have no great political interests. I'm simply not the political type. I do my job, and get on with it.

'Things have come to a head now that the *sierra* is moving down to Lima. Previously, the problems were at a comfortable distance. Now the authorities are terrified, but no organization actually functions. Theoretically immigration and transfers of domicile are controlled, theoretically some sort of records are kept, and there is a Census. Only it doesn't work. The boys come down to the coast when they do their military service, and they see a different sort of life. The schools mean a lot, too. And the radio. They think life is easier here. There is no industry in the *sierra*. There they have handicrafts and giant foreign companies – nothing in between. The land reform has hardly begun to touch the problems of the landless.

'There is a great difference among the *barriadas*. The oldest are the worst, the newer ones are better planned, not so dilapidated and overcrowded. The best *barriadas* are the ones where a lot of building workers live. Here in Chorrillos, which has been a *barriada* since the earthquake twenty years ago, there live all sorts of people. The mixture of classes means less solidarity. There are traditions and prejudices here, a terrible struggle to maintain the differences. All in all

Chorrillos is one of the bad *barriadas*, but there are many worse.

'Since the economic basis of a community like Chorrillos is so weak, a lot depends on how the money is used. A lot depends on the mayor. Is he any good? Even as a politician, he is a businessman. He thinks in money, in a way that gives a pretence of social progressiveness.'

'What should he do?'

'Try to get people to take part in what is done. Divide up the *barriada*, organize it into small groups that can discuss and decide. The *municipalidad* should simply be an office that coordinates the proposals of the people, and is at their service. But only two years ago it was the government that appointed mayors. That the community should also serve the people – that is too much to ask. In this *barriada*, about 60 per cent live in extreme poverty, 30 per cent are a bit better off, and 10 per cent fairly well off. The candidates in the election were all from the upper class. I don't really think anything will get done.'

LUCÍA ROJAS CENTENO

'I came to Lima thirty-six years ago, when I was born. My parents were from Ayacucho. They are dead now. I have been to school for five years, and I can read and write. My eldest daughter makes sixteen dollars a month and can support herself. The other seven, I support.

'I am a washerwoman. Usually I have work two days a week, sometimes four. I make two dollars 40 a day. It's a doctor's family and an architect's family. I don't have much contact with them, they have a mass of servants. The doctor has a major domo, a cook, cleaner, errand-boy and then me. The doctor's wife? No, she doesn't work. She's always out for walks, and invited to places. They have a large garden, and a house in two storeys. Apart from the bedrooms, they have seven rooms. I don't understand what they do with them all.'

'How does it happen that a woman who doesn't work can have so many rooms, while you only have one?'

'They have money.'

'Is that fair?'

'If they have enough money to run the house, what can you do?'

'Is there no political party that can do anything?'

'No. The doctor's wife may give money to the poor, how should I know? But they own their things, and there is nothing any political party can do about it.'

'So the rich will always be rich, and the poor poor?'

'That's how it's been all my life, and that's how it always will be.'

'What do you hope for?'

'I hope to manage – as long as I can go on working all my life, and get a helping hand from time to time.'

'Are you ever afraid?'

'I'm afraid for my arm. It hurts sometimes, and I am afraid of it getting worse so that I have to stop work.'

'Are you afraid of getting more children?'

'No, I don't live with my man any longer. But I often used to be afraid.'

'Have you voted?'

'Yes, I voted for the Acción Popular.'

'Why?'

'You get fined if you don't vote.'

'Isn't the party any good then?'

'If you have relatives and friends, the party will help you. I've never had a thing from them.'

'How long have you lived in this house?'

'One year. I'm a guard, but I don't know how long they will let me go on. I'm afraid they may force me to move. I need 40 dollars for a site where I can build properly. These stones are only temporarily put together, with clay.'

'Who decides in the Leasehold Association?'

'The President and Board.'

'What about the members?'

'Us, you mean? The President has his group of ten or twenty people, and he's the one who decides. For three years we had a President, that was while I was living with my man. We paid two dollars a month, three times we paid eight dollars, and extra for the engineer, altogether we spent over 120 dollars. The President bought himself a truck, and ran away with the money. Altogether, there was 8,800 dollars missing. The police caught him, and the trial is still going on. But he worked as assistant to a lawyer, he'll always get by. He did the same thing before, in other *barriadas*. We'll never get our money back. Take the first President of the association. He got away with 1,800 dollars. We took him to court, it cost 280 dollars. We got nothing back, and he was never punished. There were no papers.'

'You mean the court is on the side of the criminals?'

'I expect we could have put him in prison, but it costs so much to pay the judge and lawyers, and he can pay too. Both sides pay and pay, there's no end to it. Take my own case – I am legally divorced, with the right to maintenance for my children. But to get hold of my husband and force him to pay would cost more than the maintenance.'

'But surely you don't pay the judge?'

'Oh, yes. There was some trouble with our meeting-rooms here. The President put a lock on the door, so that we couldn't get into our own place. We tried to get it opened legally. The judge wanted 120 dollars to come. We could have tried to tell him he has his salary – but where would that get us?'

'Have you heard of Fidel Castro?'

'No' (firmly). She holds her child tightly against her breast.

'Is it dangerous to talk about him?'

'No ... My youngest brother is a communist. He gets a mass of books and paper. I don't have time to think about things like that.'

'Have you ever thought of moving from Lima?'

'I don't know anyone. I can't just appear with eight children and say "Here I am".'

ANA CASTAÑÓN ORMENO

'I've lived in this house for two years. Or is it five? I don't really know. I wash and iron for a captain's family in Pueblo Libre. I go there two days a week, and I get four dollars 80 a week plus money for the journey.

'There are eight of us living in this room – I and my four children, my mother, my father and brother. That's my mother lying there in the bed, she's been ill for a long time now. The nails on her big toes are gone, her liver is bad, she has giddy turns when she gets up. She lies in bed all the time. My brother is seventeen. Sometimes he gets work as a painter, then he makes a dollar and twenty to forty cents a day. My father is in business. That's him coming now.'

HER FATHER

Suit. Negroid features. He comes towards us along the twenty yards long and one yard broad passageway between the clay walls. Some eight or ten families each occupy a room along this passageway. This particular room is fairly large, and well lit by an electric bulb in the ceiling. We sit down at a modern kitchen table, with steel and plastic chairs. Otherwise the furniture is worthless. The father sits down on the bed, beside the mother.

'We come from Ica. We had a large house, where I lived

with my brothers. We had a fishing boat with an engine. But the engine broke down, we couldn't get it repaired. That's 24 years ago now. During the war you could get work with the rubber, up in the jungle. I was there for two years. Then we moved to Lima, and I became a caretaker in the port. I worked there until 1960. Then I decided to go back to the jungle, and left the job. Only I never got away. Now I am 48, and can't get my job in the port back. I got 480 dollars from the pension fund when I finished, and I used the capital to start up in business. Of course, I haven't got a licence, and my capital is finished. I'm just a middle-man, and I take a commission.

'My income is very uneven, of course. It's difficult to say just how much. Ana here gets four dollars 80 a week. Perhaps we make eighty dollars a month ...' (At this, the mother and daughter express violent disagreement.) 'The food for a big family like us costs over three dollars a day. No, we can't make ends meet – we seldom have milk for the children, on ordinary days we don't have enough food to go round.

'The rent? We pay to a lady who lives not far away, one dollar 40 in charges and sixteen dollars a month rent. But it's not certain who owns the house. I don't think she has the papers. If you've got enough cheek, you can take the money. And *francamente*, señor, I don't like this *barriada*. Too many people come here from the *sierra*, people who don't belong here, and just settle down and take land. We want to get out. We have bought a site. That is to say, we didn't pay anything and the man who sold it didn't own the land, and anyway it was just a rubbish heap. If the real owner comes, we will lose the ground.

'I'm not interested in politics, but one of my brothers is. He supports APRA. I voted last year for our present mayor, not for the party's sake but because he seemed the best man. He was born in a *barriada* like this himself.'

'Has he got anything done?'

'He has asphalted a street, and put up street lamps. I'm satisfied enough, it's nice and quiet here.'

'Fidel Castro?'

'He's a good man. He governs according to what he believes, and doesn't let other countries interfere. And then there's freedom to write, democracy. Everyone can't be equal, of course, but it's right to divide up property the way he's done. Nothing like that can happen here. It seemed a good move recently with the 30- to 40-per-cent tax on luxury goods here – but everything else is going up too, even the price of oatmeal.'

'And Hugo Blanco?'

'There was a man who wouldn't leave the government alone to work in peace. Guerrilla fighting is all right if it's constructive, but you mustn't upset people in their work. Best let those in power run the country, and see what happens. The important thing is that we get water and drains.'

MARINA PÉREZ

An Indian woman, twenty-two years of age. Lives in a hut made from bits of wood and corrugated cardboard. Furnished with a bed, a barrel, and a few wooden packing-cases, nothing more. On the walls some pictures from magazines, including one of a machine-gun. The buzzing of flies. A sand floor. The house is three yards by five, and a single careless gesture might knock it down. But she goes in and makes the beds up with rags before letting us in, and apologizes for the mess round about.

'I am so glad that you came. I had just cleaned up, but the children made a mess again and I told them "don't do that, someone might come" and so you did. Just like I said.

'I came to Lima as a baby. My father was from Ayacucho.

I have talked to people from there, and they say that it's more beautiful than Lima. I wouldn't know.

'I've lived in this house for eight years, no, wait a minute, three years perhaps. I thought we could build a proper house here, but it's impossible. If I had the money, I would move back to the old *barriada* in central Chorrillos. But a room there costs twelve to fourteen dollars a month, and I can't pay that.

'There are no jobs, and if I get a job I can't find the right bus, and even if someone helps me to the bus I can't find the address. There's nothing I can do about it.

'What I do is take the bus down by the road, and go on until it stops. That takes me to the market in Lima. A blind man could do it. There I buy a sack of sweet potatoes for fourteen cents, then I come back and sit in the market here by the road and sell them. What do I earn? It's impossible to work out. I pay forty cents a month market fee, plus eight cents a day. For holidays they take between eighty cents and a dollar 20 extra; you have to pay – otherwise you lose your place. And then there's the bus fare. And we eat the potatoes all the time, I don't know how much we eat. Also, I'm not very good at prices and quality, I often get cheated; sometimes I only get ten cents for potatoes that cost me fourteen. I try to get enough together to go in and buy a new sack, that's all.

'I have four children, nine, six, four and two years old.' (The two youngest are on the floor, covered in the sweet potato that she peels for them the whole time.) 'Yes, I had the oldest child when I was fourteen. He's just started school, together with the six-year-old. Their father has only just signed the birth certificate, he couldn't start before. Also they have to have a school uniform, and of course they haven't got one. They haven't been able to go to school this week, they haven't got shoes or exercise books.

'Their father isn't much of a man, otherwise he would

have straightened out the poles of this house. He works with garbage, makes a good wage, eighty dollars a month. But he doesn't live here. He comes here when he's drunk. Then I wash for him. He's not father to all the children, but he's signed for the eldest two and promised to sign for the youngest. It would be a good thing if the oldest boy could go to school. He wants to be a doctor.

'Last summer he worked as a gardener's boy for a rich lady. We were very worried, as he didn't get any money. But when he finished he got twelve dollars, and we bought two small pigs at seven dollars 20 cents each. They are outside in the sand. The boy wants us to eat them, but of course we'll have to sell them.

'I have never voted, because I'm illiterate. Also, you have to have a birth certificate. I don't even know if I've been baptized. Which party is best? I'm a Peruvian. It's typical for a Peruvian to think mainly of himself. Am I an Indian? Yes, all Peruvians are Indians. Fidel Castro? I've heard the name, but I don't know anything about him. What I fear most is thieves. I've lost several jumpers and skirts, and three times they've stolen the blanket. Even if the door is locked, you can put your hand in anywhere. The police – even if you got murdered, and went and complained, they wouldn't lift a finger. A woman in the neighbourhood was buried yesterday, she went to the police I don't know how many times. But no one took any notice until she was beaten to death by her man when he came home drunk. That's why I want to move back to the centre of Chorrillos.'

MIGUEL BARRANICHEA

'I have been in Lima for a year and a half. I come from El Carmen, in the *sierra*. I am forty-five years old. My birth certificate is up here under the roof.' (He shows it to me, and then carefully pushes it back in place.) 'My wife is forty-one. We have seven children living.

'We live here free, with relatives.' (He points to the hovel around him.) 'Only it's impossible to get the site leasehold. It costs forty dollars to enter the Association. And then you have to have a paper. We were going to get it from an engineer, but he never came.

'My wife goes down to the road at four every afternoon, and puts up the stand. She sells roast hearts of cow and fried potatoes. There are four or five stands in a row, she has to fight for customers. She usually makes about eighty cents, sometimes up to two dollars, at best. She pays twelve cents in tax on weekdays, and twenty cents on Sundays.

'I am a building worker, I get a dollar 60 cents a day, plus forty cents for the bus. But it's always a gamble. I put down twenty cents on going there, and there are usually a lot of people. About 200 men usually turn up, and only one in ten gets a job. Three times a week I have been there in vain. Each time I have lost forty cents on the trip. Today I didn't dare take the risk. It's getting more difficult for me to get work since I hurt my eye. I don't see very well any more, and I'm afraid of heights.' (His left eye has fastened yellow and bloodshot in its socket.)

'I didn't vote last autumn, because I'm still registered in El Carmen. But next time I'm going back to vote, cost what it may. I'm a member of Acción Popular. I signed up with them, they paid my travel down here. That was how I came to Lima.'

'What's good about the AP?'

'They've built a school in El Carmen, and they're busy on a road. What I hoped above all was that the party would give me work, but I didn't get any. I would like to be a watchman or something like that, something safe and steady. I went to the mayor here in Chorrillos and said: "I worked with AP, I'm a member, get me a job." He didn't have one.

'I've got a friend at the police house, I went there and asked to go round the market and collect the tax. He wanted four dollars to give me the job. I hurried home and asked my wife for the money, but she didn't have any. What a time it took to borrow it! Then I ran all the way back! By that time, someone else had got the job. Tomorrow I'm going into Lima, I'd thought of talking to party headquarters. There must be a job somewhere.

'What I would really like would be to get back to the *sierra*. But my brother and sister want to sell. My sister is already here in Lima. And my brother, who is still in the *sierra*, is going to try to get down. They both want to sell. We own altogether three-quarters of a hectare of land. It's not land that gives anything. There are no potatoes or bread in the *sierra*. While we wait for the harvest, we work on a nearby *hacienda*. On land that belonged to my grandmother, in fact. We used to earn twenty cents a day, and up to seventy cents at harvest time.'

'Can the land reform help you?'

'Yes, of course, if only the land of the *hacienda* is divided up. But it has never happened yet. All my brother and sister and I really want is to get back the land they took from my grandmother. The owner of the *hacienda* produced some papers, there was a trial. His lawyers won, of course, and our grandmother lost the land. It would be enough, if I only had two hectares I could live on it.'

'What are you most frightened of?'

'I'm not afraid of anything. Of course, if I fell sick or got run over. ... No' (very determinedly) 'if you fall sick you have to get well again! I'm not afraid of anything.'

'So your problem is quite simply land?'

'That's it. If I had land I could live in peace.'

FELICITA SALVA PLÁCIDO

'I come from northern Peru, I moved to Lima in 1947, and I've lived in this house since 1958. I can't afford to move, the rent here is only two dollars a month. There's an agent who collects the rent, and sends the money to the nephew of the original owner. I think he lives in the United States.

'I have seven children, and live here with them alone. The boys are called Dante and Eliot, those are the names of great poets. They have the same father, he chose the names, he had great plans for them when they were born. Now he pays two dollars 80 cents a week for them.

'I make twenty dollars a month from domestic work. Mondays to Fridays 9 to 4, on Saturdays I finish at 12. For a building engineer in Miraflores. I've worked there for nineteen months now. It's not a big wage, but I can eat as much as I like and get home in time. If the wage is higher, the food is worse – every house has its way. They treat me well. Though when I've got up early, made the children's food, and sent them off, and get to Miraflores all out of breath dead on 9, and then the lady tells me to come back at 12 so she doesn't have to hear the vacuum cleaner while she lies there in bed. ... Well, sometimes it makes me angry.

'My mistress is well off. All three of her children are grown up. She has a servant who cleans the four rooms upstairs, another who does the four downstairs rooms and cooks the food.'

'How does it happen that a woman with only three children and no job can have eight rooms, while you work and have seven children but only one room?'

'It's the money difference. Her husband has a job, and a wage. He can pay. But just to get a job at an office, you have to go in fine clothes and have a different manner.'

'Is it fair?'

'It's not right. Being rich makes people selfish. Here in Lima there are many people who don't eat, many who are sick. But the rich don't take a humanitarian attitude.'

'What can be done about it?'

'We can only beg them. We can't force them.

'I believe in APRA. But I can't vote, my birth certificate was stolen.

'Financially, of course, we can't make ends meet. I have to buy on credit. Sometimes my bill in the shop at the end of the month takes my whole wages. The children have to have shoes, to go to school. I buy them on the instalment system, twenty cents a week. Then of course they are more expensive – I pay over five dollars for shoes that cost about three dollars cash. If I go to the money-lender he takes ten per cent. The same interest whether I borrow for a week or to the end of the month.

'My father still lives in the *sierra*, but I have never thought of going back. Here you can at least get work, you can eat and have a little money. In the *sierra*, when the harvest is bad, you starve, and the following year you have no seed and things just get worse and worse. There's hardly anyone still living in my village now.

'My great hope is to be able to build a house of my own. I have a site, which I have fought to keep for eight years. I've paid all the fees, the engineers, measurements and charges. A week ago I got the registration certificate – here it is. It feels wonderful to have this paper at last. Now I have to start building within two years, and I have absolutely nothing to build with. I tried to borrow fifty dollars from my mistress, but her husband refused.

'And now I have another worry. My eldest boy, who is sixteen, lives with my grandfather up in the *sierra*. I haven't seen him since he was a baby. Now I've had a letter. He is only in the third grade, and they haven't any money for the books.

'The cinema? Excuse me for laughing. I haven't been for several years. Even going to someone who has a television costs too much, besides by the time I've got home, made food for the children, and put them to bed I'm very tired. I've never watched television. And I've never had any friends here for a party.

'Sometimes I get so depressed, particularly when I have my days. I get beside myself, sort of, and sometimes I'm afraid I may do the children an injury. When the big girl was small, I had nothing I could do with her while I went to work. I had to lock her in here every day, until she was five. When I came home from work and she stood there howling in the dark, and couldn't say a sensible word, I thought sometimes I would go out of my mind. And when I hear that eternal whining' (Dante lies ill in the rags behind us, heavily, his face down, complaining quietly the whole time), 'I'm afraid of what I might do. But ... things will work out in the end. I'll go and get them to say a spell over him tonight.'

Latin America
Faces the Seventies

The Growth of the Slums

Every year, 75,000 Peruvians move to Lima. The majority end up in districts like Chorrillos. They are part of one of the greatest migrations in history – the Latin American flight from the countryside. Between 1960 and 1975, the urban population of Latin America will increase by 100 million.

In the mid-Fifties, Lima had a population of one million, ten per cent of whom lived in slums. By the early Sixties the population had doubled, and 20 per cent lived in slums. At the time I talked to Miguel, Marina and the others, the official population of Lima was 2·6 million, half of whom lived in condemned housing and over 30 per cent in downright slums.

Immigration has been faster, the spread of slum areas more brutal, in Lima than in most other places. But this is a continental phenomenon. One of the safest forecasts we can make about Latin America is that the urban slums will spread and grow worse during the Seventies.

The towns of Latin America are growing at a rate of five per cent per year. Their population doubles in 15 years. Many of them are growing faster than this. Lima is one example. Chimbote, also in Peru, has been growing at a rate of 13 per cent a year since 1940. The towns of Venezuela grew by 80 per cent during the Fifties, and the rate is still very high. Otherwise, the rate of expansion is most rapid in Central

America, least in southernmost South America – in the Argentine, Uruguay and Chile.

What causes this great migration to the towns? People blame national service, which is supposed to give the country boys a taste for city life. They point out that transistor radios are carrying the siren tones of the city out to the hill villages. They say that better roads are making it easier to get into town. They describe how irresponsible politicians excite the crowds at election time with visions of a paradise offering both food and education, visions that cannot possibly be realized. All this is true. But the real point is different. The landlessness, the stagnation, the low wages, all the unbearable aspects of life in the country districts, have always been a direct or indirect condition for the affluence of the upper stratum in the cities. For centuries, the Latin American rural proletariat has been kept at a comfortable distance from its exploiters. This is no longer possible. The crowds are on the move, flowing in the direction traditionally travelled by the profit of their labour – to the big cities. They are taking their slums with them.

There are different sorts of slums.

The climbing slums of Caracas or Rio de Janeiro, where the water in the rainy season pours down the mountainside, washing through the huts and hovels. The marsh slums of Recife or Chimbote, where the children grow up like creatures of the sewers.

The rented slums, in which huge families with screaming children and sick old people crowd into their rooms along dark winding corridors. The 'owner–occupier' slums, where people have simply squatted on a piece of free ground and hope to be left there.

The old third-generation slums, hardened, crowded and beyond hope. The new slums, sprawling and half-finished, often the result of an invasion organized by some enterprising individual with political connections, to give him a block of votes to sell, a nucleus of customers for a shop and a few bars.

There are many types of slum, but the dwellings are all the same: houses made of old crates and bits of sheet metal, sacking or rush mats, unplastered stone; houses without floors or sanitary arrangements, shrouded in the acid stench of their own waste.

2

Since the housing situation is the most striking aspect of the misery of the slums, the problem has been regarded simply as a shortage of housing. The towns, it is said, have simply grown too fast for the production of houses. The object is to build the slums out of existence. Countless politicians have gone to the people on programmes like this. Almost every country has at least one official or semi-official body to deal with the 'housing problem'.

It would be an exaggeration to say that these bodies are efficient. Housing policy directly affects the incomes of one of the society's most influential groups, the property-owners in the towns. Latin American legislation gives them practically unlimited rights *vis-à-vis* both their tenants and the community – except in Argentina and Uruguay, where the slums are least extensive. They see to it that the state organization is poorly financed, and lacks the right of expropriation. The field is then free to apply all kinds of pressure, and the end result is a practically total paralysation of state activities.

During the Sixties, the situation was to some extent altered by the quite large loans made available by the United States for residential construction. It is hardly probable that these loans will continue in the Seventies, since the Latin American burden of debt will by then have reached astronomical figures. And as American money has flowed in, building prices have rocketed. Rubén Utria, housing expert on the U.N. Economic Commission for Latin America, calculates that speculation in land prices has put the price of new housing up by 20 to 30 per cent. The administrative costs of the over-bureaucratized government body add a further 15 to 20 per cent, and fees to planners and architects roughly the same again. Interest charges are between 6 and 24 per cent on between 50 and 80 per cent of the capital. A chain of middlemen puts up the price of building materials by 20 to 30 per cent. And the industrialization of building has often meant increased costs owing to the lack of standardization, idle capacity, and a *de facto* monopoly on the part of the big companies, which add a profit of around 20 per cent on top of the price increases mentioned.[1]

With two results. Too little is built, and those who most need housing cannot afford to pay for it.

In 1961, the United Nations estimated the housing shortage in Latin America at 20·3 million dwellings, of which 6·6 million in the towns and 13·7 million in the rural districts.

It was stated at the time that to prevent this deficit from *increasing* it would be necessary in the 15-year period 1960–75 to build 23·5 million dwellings, of which 18·7 million in the towns and 4·8 million in the country districts. In other words, housing production had to reach levels noted only in the Soviet Union, Sweden and certain other highly industrialized countries, in order to *maintain* an already untenable situation.

During 1960–65, the deficit rose by 6 million. To hold the 1965 deficit, it would be necessary according to Dr Utria to build during the rest of the Sixties and throughout the Seventies an average of 2·45 million dwellings a year.

'How much is actually built?'

'About 400,000. The rest are shacks.'

1. Rubén D. Utria: 'The Housing Problem in Latin America in Relation to Structural Development Factors', *Economic Bulletin for Latin America*, 2/1966.

'Is there any solution?'

'The housing problem cannot be solved in isolation. We can't build the shortage out of existence, since those without housing cannot pay even a fraction of what real housing costs. The housing problem will only be solved by eliminating unemployment, and radically changing the distribution of income.'

'So it's pointless to build housing at present?'

'No, but my personal opinion is that the capital could be better used. Residential construction ties up capital, without making it productive. It only creates job opportunities during actual construction. And the money that is in any case put into housing should not be spent on isolated projects as it is now, a few expensive drops in the ocean; it should be used to assist and organize the spontaneous building that takes place the whole time. In other words better shacks.'

'Has this not been tried in Peru?'

'Several countries have tried something of the kind, but interest fell off very quickly.'

I met Rubén Utria early on in my journey. His analysis of the situation was subsequently confirmed in town after town. In Caracas, Venezuela, we saw people from the Workers' Bank pulling down a slum district on the desirable land along the Autopista del Valle. At the same time, the bank was building three tall blocks containing 970 flats, which cost over 500 dollars in key money and more than 40 dollars a month in rent. None of the slum people wanted to move to them. In spite of everything, the slum is a functioning society with both services and opportunities to make money on the side – laundry, sewing, shops, small repairs. The high rents of real housing put up the prices of such services to a level at which no one can use them. They then disappear. The women refuse to move into a building from which they could be evicted if the husband, the breadwinner, abandoned them. The men, of whom only one in ten has a regular income, refuse to commit themselves to a fixed, high rent. The result is that those driven away from the slum take their compensation and build a new slum a bit farther away. Middle-class families move into the flats.

In Recife, we visited a project where centrally situated slums with a high ground-value had been cleared, and the population moved to newly-built small houses on cheap land outside the town. This, however, meant that they were an eight-cent bus journey away from all job opportunities. Also, the transport costs put the prices of goods up, so that turn-over fell and prices shot up even higher – those who were moved out pay about 20 per cent more than the same goods cost in town. They are simply unable to manage. They start by selling the door, and go on to sell windows, roof, tiles, door frames and the toilet seat. When nothing is left, they sell the actual right to live in the house and move back to town, to some other slum.

Great sums of public money are spent on ill-conceived projects of this kind. But still larger sums of private money are spent on projects that are not even intended to help the housing shortage, and function entirely as a source of income, a capital investment, a speculative enterprise and status symbol. The luxury villas are spreading in the big cities, from Mexico City in the north to Buenos Aires in the south. This is easy to see but difficult to quantify – most countries seem to have no interest in assessing the proportion of residential construction claimed by the upper classes.

I obtained the clearest information from the Institute of Development at Bogotá University, where the class structure of residential construction had been studied in connection with work on a new town plan. Of the capital invested in housing in 1960, about 20 per cent was for workers' dwellings. This figure had fallen by 1966 to 18·6, while construction for the upper middle class and upper class claimed 64·1 per cent of the available capital. The figures suggested that the proportion spent on workers' dwellings would fall still further in 1967 to 17 per cent.[2]

There is reason to believe that these results are fairly representative of Latin America as a whole. It should also be remembered that 'workers' dwellings' is often an erroneous description of buildings in which workers cannot afford to live. 'Luxury villas', on the other hand, is a very adequate term. The more desirable districts of English and Swedish towns have few counterparts to the modernistic palaces with which rich Latin Americans mark their status.

However, it is not above all the expensive housing of the rich in Latin America that claims the community's resources. Private motoring involves still greater investments.

There are about 200,000 cars in Caracas. About 60,000 of them are used to carry 15 per cent of wage-earners to and from their jobs in the heart of the city. The others are served by 1,300 buses. These are always crowded to bursting point, and edge their way with painful slowness through the traffic jams created by private cars. Traffic difficulties are not helped by the fact that both slums and luxury dwellings are spacious forms of building, which sprawl over wide areas. To solve the problem, enormous investments have been made in a system of city motorways and flyovers that makes those in Stockholm or London seem naïve.

It is grotesque to see these giant spiders' legs of steel and concrete stretching out over the slums. But 'progress' is forcing town planners further in the same direction. Unrestricted private motoring means poor public transport services, and this in its turn increases private motoring. At a very conservative estimate, Caracas will have 600,000 cars by 1990, which will entail the investment of many millions of dollars in new traffic apparatus that will still not be able to provide an efficient transport system.

2. Centro de investigaciones para el desarrollo: *Bogotá, política urbana y alternativas de desarrollo*, Bogotá 1968, Table XI-5.

Underdevelopment traditionally suggests a somewhat Arcadian picture. I had not exactly expected to find Latin America populated entirely by peasants plying wooden ploughs in the fresh mountain air, and glowing girls posed by pure springs of cold water – but what perhaps surprised me most was that the continent, in addition to its awful poverty and stagnation, was plagued by exactly the same diseases of civilization as we are.

When it comes to car queues in the rush hour, Bogotá or Mexico City have nothing to learn from Europe. The air pollution in Lima is worse than in any other town I have visited: bad engines and low-quality fuel make the city's 200,000 motor vehicles a formidable source of fumes; and the permanent cover of cloud that lies packed over the roof-tops is charged with a steadily stronger concentration of pollutants as winter progresses. Other grave problems are the noise and death on the roads. The beaches around the town, of course, are horribly polluted by waste water.

The only Arcadian capitals in Latin America are Quito, La Paz and Asunción – and to make up for them there are numerous second, third and fourth cities with fully developed urban problems. When people speak of 'progress', they often mean precisely the growth of these problems. Modern Latin Americans announce with a sort of perverse pride that they are struggling with the same difficulties as the industrialized countries.

Increasing numbers of Europeans are realizing that the investment preferences of our type of society are inane. In the Latin American context, they appear downright criminal. The surface problems of the modern city are being solved at the expense of the poor, who are deprived of the most elementary necessities of life.

They suffer not only from lack of housing, but from a whole series of shortcomings in the societal organization and distribution of resources. The accounts given me in Chorrillos are revealing. Let me just sum up a few main points.

One or two of the people I spoke with would have had difficulty managing in any society. But in another society, they might perhaps not have become what they were. And the majority of the slum inhabitants are – or at least have been – ordinary able-bodied people, continually on the hunt for temporary jobs in a disorganized and hostile society.

Disease declasses you mercilessly. Miguel has his bad eye; the hard life of the slum means that most people sooner or later acquire such a handicap, and the inevitable downward slide begins. Jacinta's boy got appendicitis, the operation cost 120 dollars – and their hopes of rising from the slums were dashed to the ground.

The next greatest misfortune is to lose 'the papers'. There is almost always a document missing. 'We were going to get it from an engineer, but he never came.' Miguel's story crops up, in different versions, with practically everyone you talk to. Illegitimate children, which, since their parents can seldom afford to marry, means the majority of all children in the slum, are particularly hard hit; the father has to admit paternity for them to get their birth certificate, and start school. The need for clothing, books and shoes is another effective obstacle to schooling – Marina's children couldn't attend school by reason of her poverty. The same pressures drove Felicita to ruinous instalment deals – she paid five dollars 20 for children's shoes that cost 2·80 – or to the money-lender, who takes ten per cent on money lent for a week.

They have practically no rights whatsoever. Marina isn't alone in living in terror of thieves and assault; Lucía is not the only person to have been cheated by smart 'lawyers'. The law had never protected Jacinta, but suddenly it crushed her entire family, forcing her husband to flee to the hills.

The majority have no vote. Many of them 'believe' in one

or other of the populist middle-class parties – only they are hoping not for any basic changes in society, but for small local improvements and personal protection within the prevailing power structure. The people have practically no political consciousness or will to fight.

'Best let those in power run the country, and see what happens.' (Castañón.)

'No, I'm not a union member. There's no point in it. It's Juan García and Víctor Glenny who own the factory.' (Rinaldo.)

'The rich don't take a humanitarian attitude. We can only beg them, we can't force them.' (Felicita.)

Their anger is turned inwards instead; persisting states of deep depression are common. Felicita didn't believe you could force the rich, but sometimes she got, as she said, 'beside herself', and was afraid of doing the children an injury. She associated these states of desperation with her menstrual periods, and above all with the situation of the children. The eldest girl had to be locked in every working day until she was five years old. 'When I came home from work and she stood there howling in the dark, and couldn't say a sensible word, I thought sometimes I would go out of my mind.'

She is not alone in this. Many millions of Latin Americans live in districts like Chorrillos. With the present social system, this form of existence – and this is one of the safest prophecies we can make about Latin America in the Seventies – will both spread and deteriorate.

The Middle-class Myth

'I have been going around this past week here in Chorrillos, talking to people about their lives. Many of them seem to have great hopes of you as mayor. Why are they so confident?'

'If their hopes lie in me, it is because I myself have lived the same sort of life. I came to Lima when I was eight years old. My mother and I lived in an ordinary *chosa* until I was nineteen. By then I had already worked seven years as an errand boy in a firm that sold car tyres. In the evenings I went to school, and in the daytime I tried to pick up as much as possible about the paper work at the office. At the age of twenty-one I was employed in the office, and five years later I was senior clerk.

'Meanwhile, my brother had opened a firm of his own, also in tyres. We bor owed 240 dollars from a relation and I helped with the accounts. Things went well, and after two years we obtained the Goodyear agency. I resigned my job, and we put everything into our own firm. My brother and I did all the work ourselves, and we worked late into the night. The secret of our success, I think, was that we went in for a lot of publicity.

'Now I have a two-storey house in Chorrillos, six bedrooms, five children, four servants and two cars. For all this I have God to thank. A lot of people come to us and my wife has a little charity. I have been a member of the Acción

Popular since it was founded, and since the firm has run itself for the past ten years I have had the time over to run for mayor. People believe in me, because I represent the chance of rising from the slums to the middle class.'

'What can you do for them?'

'There is not much I can do. Everything moves at a snail's pace. As a private individual I hand out a few pills if anyone comes to me and is sick. As mayor, I don't have very much more at my disposal. My firm's turnover is 800,000 dollars a year, the turnover of Chorrillos is about half that. We have no right to tax people, and we get only a very small government grant. We take a charge for cleaning and for the market, we have a "Chorrillos Week" with a fairground and fireworks which gives 2,000 dollars. Our biggest revenues are from the beach in summer. All in all about 400,000 dollars.

'Most of these revenues are tied to fixed expenditures, only about 70,000 dollars is available for improvements. I've got three years. In that time I hope to get asphalt, electricity, water and sewerage in this part of the *barriada*.'

'How big a part?'

'It's difficult to say. Perhaps 20 per cent, if the total population is 30,000. But it may be 45,000. No one knows. I'd like to do more, but I haven't got the money. That's why I'm going to try to get the army to build a multi-lane road down to the beach. Private capital could then be invited to construct a *plaza* down there, with exclusive restaurants and clubs. It could be done. I calculate that we would take 6,000 dollars a month in ground rent and charges for three months of the year, altogether 18,000 dollars, to be used for roads and sewerage in Chorrillos. That's one of my more ambitious plans.'

'So you first invest millions down on the beach, in the hope of getting streets and sewerage up in the town later on. Isn't that rather a circuitous approach? I mean, scraping money together for the necessities of the poor via the pleasures of the rich?'

'That's because the pleasures of the rich pay their way. In the present situation, I can't see any other way out.'

2

'It's terrifying to see how the guerrilla dominates the news from Latin America, in both the United States and Europe. The myth of the guerrilla draws attention from what is really happening. It's not the guerrilla that is taking over Latin America, it's the middle class.'

This was said to me by a Colombian sociologist. But I heard much the same thing hundreds of times, in different countries. It's true – the place occupied by the Latin American guerrilla in our consciousness has very little counterpart in reality. A guerrilla myth exists. But there is also a middle-class myth, which is far more dangerous.

The number and influence of the Latin American middle class will continue to increase in the Seventies. This is an almost automatic consequence of urbanization, so that it can be foreseen with some certainty. The middle-class myth is that this will be the salvation of Latin America.

The middle class, it is claimed, is a product of education, social mobility and technological progress. It represents a new spirit in Latin America, rational, efficient and full of initiative. It stands for nationalism, an active government economic policy, reforms and social justice. It will pursue a moderate, foresighted policy that will neutralize the extremists on either side and prove that stability can be combined with progress.

Obviously, the growth of the middle class does mean an improvement on the traditional social structure, in which a ruling aristocracy of landowners and officials stood in isolation against the proletariat. Politics were decided by the '*caudillos*', or strong men, or by votes taken within a closed circle of people in power. The struggle was between 'conservatives' and 'liberals', but both were right-wing parties divorced from the people.

This upper-class rule was shaken to its foundations by the Mexican revolution of 1910. In the Thirties it began to totter in countries like Argentina, Uruguay and Brazil. Only in the past decade, however, have modern, 'democratic' mass parties with a middle-class basis really begun to break through.

Typical examples are Venezuela since 1958 and Chile since 1964. Much less definite breakthroughs occurred in Peru in 1963, and Colombia and Guatemala in 1966. In Brazil and Bolivia since 1964, in Argentina since 1966, and in Peru since 1968, middle-class rule has taken the form of a military régime. The established revolutionary party in Mexico has become ever more deeply conservative.

It is quite impossible to say what this constellation of governments will look like by the end of the Seventies, because to begin with, Latin American politics is largely a question of personalities. What we can say perhaps is that countries like Guatemala, Venezuela and Colombia are on the threshold of a process of development, of which the Big Three – Mexico, Brazil and Argentina – represent a later stage.

Schematically, the course of development is as follows:

• A middle-class government is swept into power by the discontent of the masses. It is allied with organized labour, which has been promised wage increases and social security. It is nationalistic, and promises economic independence. It has a large-scale programme of social reform.

• The government apparatus, however, offers no constitutional means of rapidly and radically breaking the power of the old upper class. To be able to start its programme the middle-class government is therefore forced to compromise with the traditional holders of power. Reforms are watered down, and tend to benefit only the middle classes. The workers feel cheated, and demand more action.

• The middle-class government obtains generous loans from the United States, and support in its struggle against the traditional upper class. Loans mean debt, and increased dependence. The terms of these loans are political compliance, and free play for foreign capital. The object is to create a 'favourable investment climate'. Middle-class nationalism is pared down to the bone, which is protectionism – protective tariffs for domestic industry. The workers pay for this in the form of high prices for poor goods. In spite of subsidies, industrialization fails to pick up speed and the level of wages remains low, apart from in individual sectors. The discontent of the workers grows. New middle-class groups not yet in power prepare to saddle this discontent. Disturbances begin. The army officers, primarily sons of the middle class, become an increasingly important power factor.

• The middle-class government starts a new round of reforms to calm the masses – but who is to pay for them? The upper class still refuses and is supported in this by the top stratum of the middle class, which is now well established. The government is forced to finance its programme by inflation, which puts the burden on the wage-earners. Discontent grows, the chorus of demands swells, the rule of the middle class is threatened from below. Military forces then take over as the representatives of law and order. The upper middle class, foreign capital and the old upper class – all graciously agree to a stabilization of the economy that places the entire burden on the workers and small earners. Opposition is kept down by violence.

This, briefly, is the road of the Latin American middle class from democratic reforms to class dictatorship.

3

My best contacts with the Latin American upper class were in Arequipa, one of the most 'feudal' towns in Peru. As a Swede of good repute, without visible negroid or Jewish features, I gained entrance to the town's aristocratic club. The thankless task of the landowner is there regarded as a patriotic duty. And I began to understand why no major conflict had ever arisen between 'feudalism' and 'capitalism' in Latin America.

The landowners did not deny that the land had once belonged to the ancestors of their land workers. In theory at least they could agree that ownership rights based on previous state charters were poorly established. They were quick to point out, however, that the factories in the towns were also in a way 'gifts' from the state – they had been built with state loans at negative interest, tax remissions, high protective tariffs and other privileges.

It may seem unreasonable that 100,000 landowners should control the best land in Latin America at the cost of 30 million poor peasants and landless families. But now that even agriculture is organized in company form, many landowners regard themselves simply as big businessmen. They point out that the concentration of property is even higher in industry.

They do not deny that a lot of good land is lying 'idle' on their estates. But is the percentage of utilization higher in industry? Surely both machinery and markets are 'lying idle' when the factories prefer to produce a little expensively, rather than a lot cheaply. In many sectors, Latin American industry is working to less than half capacity.[1]

And if agriculture has failed in supplying the country,

1. United Nations: *The Process of Industrial Development in Latin America*, New York 1966, pp. 72 ff.

then the manufacturing industry has failed in its exports. This is the trump card of the landowners – they answer for foreign currency revenues, while the products of industry are usually unsaleable outside the country.

In other words, industry cannot demand land reforms without, by an extension of their own argument, pleading for 'industrial reforms'. This the industrialists are careful not to do. Instead, the leading middle-class group of industrialists has silently adopted the vices of the upper class, putting much of its profit into buying land. This has emerged quite clearly when middle-class governments have tried to introduce land reforms.[2]

4

I have used the term 'middle class' as if its meaning were entirely clear. This, of course, is not the case. The term means different things in different countries, and to different people.

The concept of the 'middle class' can be quantified with the help of the income distribution studies performed during the Sixties by the U.N. Economic Commission for Latin America. The results are shown in Table 1.

According to the same source, the share of total income claimed by corresponding groups in the United States is 5, 19, 31, 25 and 20 per cent. This gives some picture of what extreme class differences exist in Latin America.

But what is the 'middle bracket'? What differences between different countries underlie these average figures for the whole of Latin America? Are there not countries in which the middle class occupies a much stronger position?

In Table 2, I have taken four different definitions of the 'middle bracket' – 60, 45, 30 and 15 per cent of the population – and shown how the results are distributed in three

2. cf. Raúl Prebisch: *Towards a Dynamic Development Policy for Latin America*, United Nations, New York 1963, pp. 44 ff.

countries in which the middle class is considered to be very dominant.

The italics indicate such values as lie *above* the average for Latin America as a whole. These deviations gradually shift towards the higher brackets as we travel from Argentina via Mexico to Venezuela.

In Argentina it is 'the poor' who occupy a comparatively good position, whether you let this group cover 20, 50 or 80 per cent of the population. The poorest 20 per cent in Venezuela, on the other hand, lie well below the average, and this group does not reach the average level for Latin America until you extend it to cover 80 per cent of the population. It then claims something over half of its 'just' share of income.

Table 1

LATIN AMERICA:
DISTRIBUTION OF INCOME 1965

Income group	Share of total income	Mean income (LA=100)
The poorest: 20 per cent	3·5%	18
The poor: 30 per cent	10·5%	35
Middle bracket: 30 per cent	25·4%	85
The rich: 15 per cent	29·1%	194
The richest: 5 per cent	31·5%	629

Source: *Estudio Económico de América Latina* 1968. Naciones Unidas E/CN. 12/825 March 1969.

In Argentina, on the other hand, it is the 'middle bracket' that must be given a very broad definition, 60 per cent, for its share of income to exceed the average in Latin America. The distribution profile in Argentina is thus that most in line with the United States and Europe – there is a large lower middle class, the primitive sector of the economy is negligible, and the unions are comparatively very strong.

In Mexico and Venezuela the 'middle bracket', whatever definition we choose, is stronger than in the rest of Latin America. In both cases, the difference is most marked when the middle bracket covers 30 per cent of the population. This group claims in Mexico somewhat less, in Venezuela somewhat more, than its 'just' share of total income.

However, the overwhelming impression is still made by the economic status of the rich, and the richest. The 20 per cent at the top of the Latin American income scale enjoy more than 60·6 per cent of income, while the 20 per cent at the bottom of the scale claim 30·5 per cent. The poorest half of the population have less than half of the income claimed by the richest 5 per cent. Even such 'middle-class countries' as Mexico and Venezuela show only minor deviations from this pattern.

Table 2

LATIN AMERICA: THE 'MIDDLE BRACKET'
IN 'MIDDLE-CLASS COUNTRIES'

Income group	Argentina	Mexico	Venezuela	Latin America
1.				
The poor: 20 per cent	5·2	3·6	3·0	3·5
The middle bracket: 60 per cent	40·7	37·9	39·0	35·9
The rich: 20 per cent	54·1	58·5	58·0	60·6

Table 2 – continued

Income group	Argentina	Mexico	Venezuela	Latin America
2.				
The poor:				
50 per cent	20·5	15·4	14·3	14·0
The middle bracket:				
45 per cent	48·3	55·6	59·2	54·5
The rich:				
5 per cent	31·2	29·0	26·5	31·5
3.				
The poor:				
50 per cent	20·5	15·4	14·3	14·0
The middle bracket:				
30 per cent	25·4	26·1	27·7	25·4
The rich:				
20 per cent	54·1	58·5	58·0	60·6
4.				
The poor:				
80 per cent	45·9	41·5	42·0	39·4
The middle bracket:				
15 per cent	22·9	29·5	31·5	29·1
The rich:				
5 per cent	31·2	29·0	26·5	31·5

Source: *Estudio Económico de América Latina* 1968, Tables 1–8 and 1–10. Concerning Latin American statistics, see Preface. The Table shows tendencies rather than reliably quantified facts.

5

Which of these income groups is meant when people speak of the 'middle class' in Latin America? It depends on the context. Among this group's own champions, one frequently notices a shift between different senses of the term.

When they speak of the size of the middle class, they mean almost all people who are not wealthy land barons or poor peasants and slum dwellers. All those who have some education, and do not perform unskilled manual work. All those in contact of some kind with the 'modern sector' of the country's economy. They include both the office girl who has to go on the streets at least once a week to eke out her pay, and her boss who drives home to his villa in a new Mercedes.

When they talk of the power of the middle class, they are thinking instead of a minute group of politicians, factory-owners and businessmen. And when they speak of the middle class as a progressive class by comparison with the old parasitic upper class, they are thinking of another group, which does not coincide with that in power.

When I try to imagine to myself the middle class as the salvation of Latin America, I see before me some of the highly qualified technicians at the Telecommunications Administration in Venezuela, who have reduced the price of Ericsson telephones from 200 to 145 bolivars – thanks largely to the training they had received from the Ericsson company. I think of the road haulier in São Paulo who started with a broken-down old truck and gradually worked his way up to a Scania. Or an enterprising timberman in Bogotá who has become a building contractor but continues to work himself. Of the welfare worker in Quillabamba who lies shivering from malaria in a basement lined with rags of plastic. The government had been forced to cancel his funds, but he refused to give up.

It is people like this who give the myth of the middle class its meaning. They do exist. But the middle class in Latin America is dominated by very different people.

The middle class are the 'middlemen', the entire stratum of buyers, speculators, agents and sub-agents who lower prices for the producer and raise them for the consumer – perhaps the heaviest single burden on the Latin American economy today. And the most rapidly growing.

The middle class are the bureaucrats, all the petty tyrants who man the chaotic, swollen apparatus of state. This sector of the middle class is also multiplying. Everyone agrees that its inefficiency and corruption constitute one of the most serious obstacles to progress. In Brazil, the state has made a mass offer of advance pensions equalling two-thirds of previous pay to get rid of these people.

The middle class are the property jobbers and slum profiteers, who feed on urban growth. The turnover of capital in Latin America is dominated by their transactions. They make the fastest, greatest and least taxed profits. Ask Víctor Delphin, in charge of state land purchasing in Venezuela, how much land prices in eastern Caracas have risen in the past 20 years! By between 50,000 and 120,000 *per cent*! Fortunes are made, while every investment by the state – as President Leoni has said in his fourth message to Congress[3] – pushes up the price of land to a level that almost prevents further state investments.

The middle class are the entrepreneurs, the people who profit from corrupt central and local government contracts. The middle class are the officers, bribed with clubs, official residences and a labyrinth of privileges, not to meddle in politics – until the middle class is threatened from below. The middle class are the factory-owners, who never find the climate sufficiently 'favourable' for investments. And the middle class are many who are prevented by the backward-

3. *IV Mensaje al Congreso Nacional*, pp. LIX f.

ness of industry from doing a productive job, and are assigned to the artificially-growing services sector.

Among the middle class we must count also the worker aristocracy, the small groups of contented workers who have succeeded in obtaining disproportionate benefits. And those who profit from the slow pace of reform, exploiting the tiny education and minimal social security that distinguishes them from others, to ensure that they will have the lion's share also of future benefits.

The middle class includes also all the wavering politicians who should be dealing with all this – but who must first feather their own nests. In 1967, when Uruguayan congressmen lost the right to import duty-free luxury cars, the last Cadillacs were brought into the country by air. To retire from a political post other than as a rich man excites not admiration, but contempt. 'The man's a fool.'

Finally, the Latin American middle class includes all the frustrated intellectuals who have seen through the myth and are powerless to do anything – except, perhaps, to form a guerrilla in the hills.

6

I would have liked to meet the mayor of Chorrillos once again. It is impossible for everyone to get rich by selling one another American tyres. This is why he represented so splendidly the dream, the illusory dream of personal success that the rise of the middle class has revealed to the masses of Latin America.

He proved, however, corrupt to a degree that attracted attention even in Peru. When I returned to Chorrillos six months later he had been fired, and a new mayor was installed – younger, keener, even perhaps more honest. But with the same programme as his predecessor. The only way of obtaining money for the poor was still to do something profitable for the rich. First millions for the motorway and clubs on the beach, then a few thousands for asphalt and water in the slums. The only road forward runs via the pleasures of the rich.

This is the road of the Latin American middle class, which has advanced its position step by step before and after the war. Shaken by the revolution in Cuba, menaced by the migration to the towns, it has made during the Sixties a feeble attempt at reform. It has failed. And it has failed because the growth of the middle class, and the power of its leading stratum, are directly tied to some of the most severe obstacles to economic development.

The dominion of the middle-class leaders will further increase during the Seventies. It will become perfectly clear that they are as parasitic as the old upper class, and that they are incapable of leading the continent out of its stagnation. That they are incapable of liberating Latin America, and that they are in fact leading their countries into ever deeper dependence.

The myth of middle-class salvation will be exploded.

A Hundred Million Mouths

1

From my work notes:
Three interviews today.

1. I visited first de Morais, the cement king. The nucleus of his group was a little textile mill, acquired in 1935. There was chalk on the site, and he began to make cement. In 1938 the firm was still worth less than 200,000 dollars. No foreign capital has been invested. Today, the group is worth at least 75 million dollars.

I asked about wages, and was given the official figures from 'The Association of Brazilian Manufacturers of Portland Cement'. Only on a few occasions have the real wages of the workers been higher than in May 1940, when statistics began to be kept. Today they are 30 per cent lower than this.

2. I then went to a meeting with Walter Ahrens, chairman of the Estate Agents' Association. São Paulo has expanded explosively, from a population of half a million in 1924 to five million today. How has this affected real-estate prices? They have risen still more rapidly. Ground that could be bought in 1924 for one dollar costs today about 200 dollars. The price increase has been steepest in the centre of town, from one dollar to 1,000. The tendency has always been the same, but the really big increases started in the Forties. There used to be a tax on land-property gains, but it was abolished after the military *coup* in 1964.

3. In the afternoon, I talked to industrial magnate José Matarazzo. I wanted to hear his views on the population expansion, and the problems of the poor parts of Brazil. Giant strides were being made here in São Paulo, but what was to be expected in north-eastern Brazil? He was an optimist.

'The market will come,' he said, 'don't you worry. In ten years every Brazilian, wherever he lives, will be our customer.'

It is evening now, and I am summing up the day's results.

The prices of real estate in São Paulo have risen by between twenty thousand (20,000) and a hundred thousand (100,000) per cent, mainly since the Forties. The value of the Cement Group has risen by at least thirty-seven thousand five hundred (37,500) per cent since 1938. The wages of workers in the same industry have fallen by thirty (30) per cent.

And Matarazzo believes in a future mass market. He is another of these big businessmen who stare in fascination at the growing population figures, and see in their mind's eye as many potential customers. I have met them in Brazil and Mexico, in Chile and Colombia. They sit waiting for a market suddenly to emerge from this sea of poverty. In the meantime, they rationalize their workers into redundancy, cut their wages, resist taxation, and give their whole-hearted support to any government that promises to stabilize the currency at the expense of the workers. And year after year, decade after decade, the giant market always glimpsed below the surface fails for some reason to appear. The land elevation they all hope for never occurs. Instead, the sea of poverty stretches wider and wider around them.

Needs without purchasing power – no market, only want.

2

When we left Lima and started our journey by car around South America, I did not entirely realize that 2,400 miles of the Pacific coast of Latin America are sheer desert. This is a paradox. The world's greatest water area washes the coast, the clouds roll in, heavy and dark, dripping with moisture – and the ground below lies barren and dry, mile after mile of dunes and fine, light sand, crossed by dark ripples. Not a blade of grass grows there.

At intervals of hours you see a tree screwed into the sand, a low shrub of a tree guarding its water like a dragon. Around Ica, where we spent the first night, grow a few scattered palms. Otherwise it is all desert, the classical cartoon picture. Yet the humidity is everywhere. You feel the mist from the sea coming in, you feel it on your face, see it on your windscreen – but not a drop on the ground.

This sea-scented desert stretches from the fifth to the thirtieth parallel. It contains the occasional agricultural oasis, and a few harbour towns that have grown up around foreign mining companies. But you can drive for days and see no other traces of men than the abandoned churchyards of closed saltpetre factories. Or small fishing villages – the desert is populated mainly by fishermen. Their houses consist of a hole in the ground and a little heap of stones, no larger than a kennel. The cracks are caulked with wads of paper, and a rag hangs in front of the entrance. Five or six of these houses form a little village, where the children teem and the nets are laid out to dry.

Passing through the densely populated heartland of Chile, the road continues south through the Patagonian wastes of Argentina. We travelled it in December, the summer evenings were long and bright. On the road to Perito Moreno, we met in the course of the day only one vehicle, a road scraper. Herds of guanacos sped gracefully away over the land. Ostriches lurched unattractively past. Otherwise you see only sheep-scarers, strange little riders on the grinning carcasses of horses, surrounded by fluttering rags. The *estancias* are marked like the boundaries between provinces; several of them bear the name 'Siberia'. Every hundred or hundred and fifty miles we tanked up at some lonely general store, selling concertina boots, preserves, flour and lassos. Cowboys in an old car, with a cowhide filled with water as a radiator. Midsummer and deathly cold.

On the frontier between Argentina and Chile, we travelled through vast areas blackened by forest fires that had raged for months – until the rains put them out. Who else was there to put them out? On the pampas we passed through a wheat fire that burned for days and laid waste 6,000 hectares. A few farm workers were trying to beat out the fire with their shirts, their horses reared up screaming in the smoke and the *contratista* ran about in the road trying to stop the traffic to hire men:

'I'll pay! I'll pay!'

Even the pampas, one of the most fertile agricultural areas in the world, are very sparsely populated. The *estancias* are enormous; they were originally intended to offer their owners a reasonable livelihood as *hunting grounds*.[1] Today, the miles and miles of wheatland are harvested by *contratistas*, who travel the roads with harvesters and caravans. And actual farms? At long intervals you see a sheet-metal silo, a wind pump, some fast-growing poplars, and a provisory dwelling that gives no greater impression of permanency than a tent. There are no farms here, only small stations along the wheat trail, where paid employees handle the harvests.

3

Latin America is a continent of solitude. Historically, its problem has always been underpopulation. Lima became the centre of the Spanish Empire in South America because there were Indians there to enslave. The *'encomienda'* system on

1. James R. Scobie: *Argentina – A City and a Nation*, Oxford University Press 1964, p. 70.

which the power of landowners is grounded originally meant the right to not land, but labour. Until machinery came, both land and mines were valueless without forcibly conscripted Indian labour.

When the Indians ran out, the problem was solved by importing four million Negro slaves. Then came the policy of immigration which predominated during the period 1850 to 1950, particularly in Brazil and Argentina. 'To govern is to populate' runs the classical slogan of the age. This goal has not been seriously questioned until recently, in the late Sixties.

It is not easy to make the switch. The leaders of Latin America can fly by jet for hour after hour over unpopulated wastes – it is difficult for them to realize that their countries are overpopulated. For centuries they have maintained that only a larger population can create progress and riches; now they have to do an about face and say that birth control is the only hope.

By 1980, the population of Latin America will have grown by 100 million people.

This is as much as the increase during the entire first half of this century. Or the increase throughout the centuries up to 1925, when the population of Latin America was 99 million. Today it is 260 million. By 1980 it will be 360 million. These are the figures given by the Alliance for Progress, while other sources give considerably higher figures for both the present and the future population. The year 2000 lies within my own normal life-expectancy, and that of the majority of Latin Americans now alive. At the present growth-rate, the continent will by then have a population of over 700 million.

Governments have woken up a bit in the past few years. Guatemala and five other Central American republics have just started to introduce birth-control clinics. In Colombia two per cent of all women of fertile age have been treated, in Venezuela 0·7 per cent. In Chile and Costa Rica, the official health services have included birth control for just over a year now (1969). In most other countries the authorities close their eyes while a few courageous doctors try to save the country on the quiet.

People often avoid the politically dangerous subject of overpopulation, and speak instead of the increasing abortion rate. In Chile, according to the official figures, there are 130,000 discontinued pregnancies to 300,000 normal births; for every 100 normal deliveries, the state health services receive 67 women with injuries from abortions; 27 per cent of the blood available in the emergency clinics goes to the victims of abortions. Even a very cautious application of the Chilean statistics, which are the most reliable, to other countries gives ridiculous figures : between 20 and 30 million abortions in Latin America during the Seventies. In Peru I spoke to doctors who spent their entire days looking after the night's harvest of injured abortion cases, and who do not have the right to instruct these women in birth control.

Resistance to birth control is mainly from the Catholic Church. It has been heightened by the Pope's latest encyclical on population. It is nourished, particularly in Brazil, by military dreams of becoming a great power. It attracts also the support of the ruling classes, who traditionally see a growing population as a guarantee of cheap servants, cheap labour and a growing market. The left, which one would expect to be a natural counterweight to these groups, also opposes birth control.

The revolutionaries point out that it is the United States which finances birth control in Latin America. They see the pill as a cheaper alternative to napalm in the American arsenal, and believe it better that a Latin American should fall with a gun in his hand than dying in the womb. Francisco Prada, the Venezuelan guerrilla leader, reminded me that the war of liberation against Spain cost Venezuela one-third of its population; revolutionary students in Paraguay quoted the War of the Triple Alliance, which killed off 90 per cent of the country's male population. They have no reason to believe that their countries will be overpopulated by the time they come to power.

This is the background to the slogan of the OLAS conference: 'WE CAN NEVER BE TOO MANY.' In Cuba, however, I talked to demographers who – almost in a whisper – admitted their fears. Cuba, very quietly, is also running what is probably the largest-scale state birth-control programme on the continent – the official object, as usual, being to keep down the abortion rate.

Cuba, like several other Latin American countries, has requested Swedish assistance with birth control. This is something we should provide, whatever suspicions this may provoke. Only we cannot expect miracles. The population increase is bound up with social and economic conditions: it will be difficult to hold back even if mass efforts are made and this still seems unlikely. In the Seventies, any results achieved are likely to disappear in the margin of error surrounding the forecast increase of 100 million mouths.

4

How are these mouths to be fed?

It is estimated even now that 180 million Latin Americans suffer from a lack of protein and other nutrients, while 50 million live at or below starvation level. For this deficit not to increase, agricultural production must be stepped up by 40 per cent before 1980. In the past ten years it has risen by an average of 3·2 per cent a year, but the increase has been mainly in export products.

According to F.A.O. experts, the measures necessary to overcome the crisis in the Seventies are a determined switch of food production to domestic needs, a radical change in the structure of land ownership and a capital investment of about 50,000 million dollars, which is twice the level of investment to date.[2]

These goals will not be achieved, partly because of political resistance and partly because they conflict with other important aims (such as paying the interest on Latin America's growing debts to the United States and Europe). We can therefore expect hunger and malnutrition to increase in Latin America. The great catastrophe, however, will probably not occur in the Seventies – such acute crises as arise are likely to be limited, and possible to control.

5

What about the schools?

The situation here varies greatly. At the top, as usual, lie Argentina, Chile and Uruguay – while countries like Brazil, Guatemala and Bolivia are well down the scale.

However, all the Latin American countries (except the Dominican Republic) can show clear improvements in their official statistics during the Fifties and Sixties. Between 1956 and 1965, the number of pupils in all types of school rose from 13·3 to 17·1 per cent of the population, an annual increase in number of pupils by 7·2 per cent. The increase was sharpest in the intermediate schools and at universities, where the middle classes answer for the pressure, but great progress has been made also at the primary level. In 1960 there were 24 million children attending primary schools in Latin America; by 1967 the figure was 36 million, an increase of 50 per cent.

It is uncertain whether this trend can continue during the Seventies. According to a rough calculation (ECLA), Latin America spends 3,000 million dollars a year or 3·5 per cent of

2. Inter-American Development Bank: *Agricultural Development in Latin America: The Next Decade*, Washington 1967, pp. 45 ff., pp. 205 ff.

its national product on education. If the present trends are to be maintained, education will cost about 11,000 million dollars by 1980, which would mean between five and seven per cent of the national product. Few countries will be able to manage this.

It is also uncertain how far the upward trend in the official statistics is reflected in real improvements. The rising figures relate to numbers of pupils *enrolled*.

No similar increase has been noted in the opportunities of pupils actually to attend school, or in the time they continue at school.

The children of the poor 'start late, are frequently absent, fail their tests, and leave school after a year or two of half-hearted attempts'. The majority of Latin American children still have only two years' schooling, and less than 20 per cent complete the primary school. The number of children of school age *not* at school increased from 26 million in 1960 to 27 million in 1967.

The situation will probably improve slightly during the Seventies, but by no means in step with the demands currently being made by practically all sectors of the Latin American community.[3]

6

What will happen to employment?

The object will be to find work for another 50 million people. *These people are already born* and will reach able-bodied age in the Seventies.

There is no room for them in agriculture. The agricultural labour force increased between 1925 and 1960 from 20 to 32 million. It was estimated then that this entire increment of

3. ECLA: *Economic Survey of Latin America 1967*, pp. 1–106 ff. C. Véliz: *Latin America and the Caribbean – A Handbook*, London 1968, pp. 712 ff.

labour was superfluous to the existing latifundia-minifundia system. The result was corresponding underemployment, unemployment and mass emigration to the big cities.

Since then, the population growth of ten years has further stepped up the pressure on the mini-farms. On the big estates there has been a tendency to switch to extensive animal farming and increased mechanization – particularly in production for export. Within the framework of the system, this is a necessary development which will mean increased profit for the landowners and in time, one hopes, a more decent life for those workers who are left. Above all, however, it means increased unemployment.

Nor can industry provide the work. The 400,000 factories of Latin America employed, in 1969, about ten million people. Between 1925 and 1960, the labour force in the towns grew by 23 million, only five million of whom could be absorbed by industry. If mass unemployment in the towns is not to deteriorate in the Seventies, employment in industry must be at least doubled. This is inconceivable.

In actual fact, the proportion of total employment ascribable to industry has been steadily falling since the Forties, as Latin America has adopted techniques created by the industrialized countries that have a shortage of labour and a surplus of capital. Industrial expansion means not only the opening of new markets, but above all the replacement of crafts by factory goods, with on the average eight job opportunities lost for every one created; or else, out of date factories are replaced by modern, in which on the average one worker can replace a previous two or three. Again, this is a necessary and laudable development within the framework of the system. But it means that industry cannot help to absorb the surplus manpower of the Seventies.[4]

4. International Development Bank, op. cit., pp. 256 ff. United Nations: *The Process of Industrial Development in Latin America*, New York 1966, pp. 35 ff., 57, 74 ff.

In all probability, the greater part of this surplus will go to the service sector. You get an idea of what this will mean even today if you sit down for a beer in the centre of Recife. While emptying my glass one evening I recorded the following offers:

(1) Fresh mackerel, (2) rag monkey on a string, (3) toy television set showing the Holy Family, (4) a pair of brown indoor shoes, (5) smuggled scent and ditto cigarettes, (6) wooden mortar and pestle, ditto beaker and mugs, (7) lottery tickets about ten times, (8) blessing by beggars three times, (9) the same newspaper as I was reading, five times, (10) shoe-shine, 15 to 20 times (in spite of immaculately gleaming shoes), (11) plastic flowers, (12) tropical fish of unfamiliar species, (13) American raisins, (14) gilded statuette of the Buddha, (15) doll's bed of steel wire, (16) plastic clothes hangers, (17) gaslighter, (18) comb, (19) peanuts, (20) pocket torch, (21) automatic plastic toothpick stand, which shot up a toothpick at the touch of a button – etc.

I had not yet finished my beer. The military police – another strongly expanding service occupation – moved in against a group of priests and theological students, and I had to leave.

7

If the population problem were a matter of inhabitants per square mile, Latin America would be underpopulated. If the population problem relates to number of inhabitants per unit of available capital, the continent is overpopulated. And still would be, if another economic system could be introduced today.

If you also take into account the use of available capital, and the relations between capital and labour within the current system, then the degree of overpopulation is catastrophic.

I was a bit surprised that Cheddi Jagan, the radical opposition leader in Guyana, could go out among the sugar workers and describe to them how the Chinese build dams 'with their bare hands'. Was this really an advertisement for socialism? But he repeated this particular phrase 'with their bare hands' again and again, to the growing enthusiasm of his audience. I understood better on the way home, when our car was stopped time and again by workers wanting to talk to Jagan. One stretched out a thin bony hand:

'I am sick.'

'What do you lack?'

'Food.'

I saw starvation shining in his eyes.

'And you?'

'A day's work last week.'

A third:

'I have only had work *once* this month. I got a dollar for 25 yards of ditch.'

One of them sat where he was, without getting up:

'These are days of starvation.'

'What are you doing?'

'Sitting and wondering.'

'What about?'

'How to live without work.'

I experienced similar scenes from Argentina in the south to Santo Domingo in the north; in the sugar districts unemployment is the normal thing, work an exception, a benefit. But the same thing happens not only in particularly vulnerable industries, or stagnating countries. In Ecuador I saw the craftsmen standing in queues outside the ironmongers', skilled workmen begging for work, their little tool bags in their hands. In Venezuela, whose economy is flourishing, SENTAB advertised for new workers. Such a crowd formed that the police had to be called to drive away with machine-guns those who could not get work and who refused to leave.

'It's terrible,' another Swede told me in Venezuela. 'It's terrible to see them collecting in their hundreds when there has been a false rumour we're going to expand. However much we deny the rumour it doesn't help, they stand there for days outside the factory gate just *hoping*.'

Until a day comes when they cannot even hope. I have seen them outside the mines and mill gates on pay day, these outclassed ancients – perhaps slightly older than I am. They do not beg. It would have been easier if they had. The beggars of India had a sort of power in their appeals that made you first afraid, then cold. They were professional beggars exacting a toll of misery, and when you passed them without paying, you sometimes felt a sort of twisted pride, as if you had succeeded in smuggling a bottle of brandy through the customs. In Latin America it is different. Embarrassed, unaccustomed people, too shy even to hold out their hands, made still more desperate by receiving than by hunger itself. Cilla, my wife, asked if they needed something, and only then did they dare look at us, nod, and accept. One hurried limping away, almost with a cry, as fast as the sinews could drag his emaciated body.

8

I think that unemployment will be the most explosive problem of all in Latin America during the Seventies. It should not be. There is, of course, no *real* surplus of labour. The idle capacity of the factories could be used to fill the most elementary needs of the people. The underexploited land on the big estates could be cultivated intensively to feed a hundred million new mouths. Housing, schools, hospitals, roads, dams – all these are still lacking for this new hundred million generation. The job to be done is overwhelming.

And yet mass unemployment is the most immediate problem.

The inadequacy of the political and economic system could hardly reveal itself more clearly. Obviously, the ruling classes of Latin America must be overthrown. The only question is how and when it can be done.

So far, both parties have put their faith in the growing population. The rulers believe that it will create a growing market, production increases, progress – so that they will not have to share their riches. The revolutionaries hope that it will increase the misery until an explosion is inevitable – so that they can get into power.

The latter hypothesis seems more likely, but it is far from certain. A rapid population increase naturally cannot guarantee progress. But neither does it guarantee revolution. Otherwise we should not have India. The terrible thing that can happen in Latin America is for opposing parties to go into a clinch, incapable of winning over each other – while the population continues to grow towards a catastrophe that will render even a revolutionary government powerless. This is the most terrifying prospect. And the most likely.

The Debt

1

For a couple of centuries, Potosí was one of the biggest cities in South America. It was here that the Spaniards mined the silver which the East Indiamen carried with them to China – Europe had nothing to offer the Chinese that they wanted except silver, which came from Potosí. This city, then, was the necessary condition for early European trade with the Far East.

The highland Indians worked as slaves in the Potosí mines. It was their silver that made possible the transition to a monetary economy through the 'common market' comprised by the Spanish empire in Europe. Potosí laid the foundations of modern capitalism.

Today, Potosí is the poorest city in the poor country of Bolivia. Its population has dropped to 50,000, and yet the streets are thronged with unemployed. The majority of people have only rags and tattered cloths with which to protect themselves against the bitter mountain cold at an altitude of 4,000 metres. Cerro Rico, the 'rich mountain', is now a gutted ruin.

The mines around Oruro created some of the biggest fortunes of our age. The cheap tin from these mines made possible the triumphant spread of the European canning industry, it created a new market situation for European agriculture, and contributed to the liberation of European womanhood. For half a century the tin king Patiño skimmed off the cream from the mountains round Oruro, and when the mines were nationalized in 1952 there remained only worn plant, low-grade ores and a population of miners who could at last put forward the wage claims that had been held back for centuries.

The road between Potosí and Oruro crosses a mining landscape in ruins. Abandoned smelting furnaces, rusty conveyor belts, the relics of the exploitation of centuries. The land pierced by trenches and craters like some ancient battlefield. Everywhere, the traces of former wealth. Left is simply a land of extreme poverty. It is only along the road between Potosí and Oruro that children stand with outstretched hands, screaming for bread. Someone had been there, taken what he needed and decamped.

But there is hope yet. Suddenly, in the midst of this plundered desert landscape, at the bottom of an apparently dried-up river-bed, is one of the biggest dredgers in the world.

It was put there by Peter Grace, whose grandfather started a small import firm in Callao, Peru. The grandson heads one of the biggest financial empires in the United States, one that operates throughout Latin America. In this valley, he has joined Chase Manhattan, Lockheed and U.S. Steel in operating the dredger.

True the dredger is more than a quarter-century old, and already out of date in California where it was built. But here it is a miracle of technical capacity. Poor people have always extracted tin in this valley, and they still do with the help of ladles and barrels. But the dredger eats its way through 500,000 cubic metres of river-bed a month, taking the tin ore.

One man operates the automatic machinery from the bridge. Seven other men have to be in place. But with twenty-two men the dredger can be operated in three shifts, all round the clock. Add repair and maintenance personnel, and various storage functions. With a total strength of 150 men, this undertaking will produce 150 tons of pure tin a month.

This is one ton per worker per *month*. In Siglo XX, the largest of the traditional tin-mines, a worker fails to reach even half a ton *per year*.

And so technology progresses. The Spaniards consumed great volumes of slave labour in Potosí – the average life expectancy was very low. Tin king Patiño needed tens of thousands of workers, none of whom lasted more than five to ten years in the mine; the same is still true. Grace needs only 150 men, and has no widows and orphans to look after.

So he can pay good wages. His workers make on the average 46 dollars a month, and their social benefits cost the company some 32 dollars a month. The best paid can afford to keep servants, whom they pay two dollars a month. They live in dwellings like row houses, with three rooms plus kitchen, running water, and electricity all round the clock. They are far too satisfied, claims the local manager, to want to join any union.

The state of Bolivia also profits, making at full production about 500,000 dollars a year in taxes and charges.

And what does Grace make?

'We've invested 5.5 million in this valley,' says the local manager. 'And we reckon on getting our capital back within five years.'

That would be 20 per cent a year. But when I mention this figure to foreign businessmen in Oruro, they laugh at me.

'Not a day over two years, otherwise Grace would never have made the investment. And then they have 20 years to just go on making money.'

A mining engineer in our party added:

'There's ore in the valley worth over 50 million dollars, that's been proved. If they can take out the ore at the rate they think, they'll recoup their capital once a year for ten years. It's a beautiful operation.'

As they admitted, they had not studied the question in detail. That, however, had been done by a group of students in Oruro, under the leadership of Father Tim. I went through the figures with them one evening in the Dominican parish centre. The American priest said:

'I came here as a Christian Democrat, and found that the students were almost all communists. There was nothing real in it though, they were just spouting slogans. The best way to get them away from communism seemed to be to give their radicalism a more objective slant, to give them some concrete problem to try their teeth on.

'We took Grace's investment as an exercise. We've worked on it now for three months. The results terrify me. Our calculations may be wrong, I only hope they are. But it looks as if Grace is making a profit of 18 million dollars a year. More than three times the capital he put in!'

He went on:

'And this is Peter Grace, one of the most pious Catholics in the States, well known for his donations to cathedrals, and his charities. I'm flying to New York the day after tomorrow. I'll go straight up to Peter Grace, tell him it's not right, and ask him to give the money back.'

'And what do you think will happen, Father?'

'I don't hold out much hope,' he answered tiredly. 'But I may get enough for a sportsground for the boys.'

I returned to Oruro a month later. Father Tim was still in the United States. He had still not met Peter Grace.

Out by the dredger in the valley, I asked the local manager what he thought about the guerrilla.

'They've already done untold damage in Bolivia,' he answered. 'They scare off the foreign capital. Capital is the only thing that can help this godforsaken country. You've seen the kids down by the road, standing there screaming and holding out their hands. It's a terrible sight. Without outside capital, they haven't a hope of a better life.'

2

'The whole time I was scared half to death. Guess what I had in my brief-case? *The New York cables*!'

This was in one of Brazil's coffee ports. We had been walking around all day among the sacks, in the heavy silence and semi-darkness of the great coffee warehouses. The atmosphere of a cathedral under the great vaults, among the wooden pillars of the chutes, and the organ pipes of the cleaning machines. Submissive bare-footed men carried sacks around on their heads. The silence was broken only by a tremendous rattle whenever the sorting machine upstairs suddenly discharged a stream of green coffee through one of the wooden conduits, with a sound like tropical rain.

Now it was time for lunch with this amiable businessman, the agent of a big European purchasing organization. He tossed his first spoonful of soup back against the taste buds of his palate with the characteristic gesture and sharp smacking sound of the trained coffee taster. Laughter, amiability. And a succession of cheerful anecdotes. Could we, for instance, guess what had happened one night last week? He had been arrested on his way home from the office, and forced to stand there in the street with his brief-case under his arm while the police searched through every inch of his car. Finally, they had triumphantly shown him the result, a little razor-blade case for a razor with an automatic blade exchange. Here was the evidence! A spy camera! They took him off to the police station, his brief-case still clutched to his chest. Three hours later and many 20-dollar bills poorer, but with his brief-case intact, he was allowed to leave the station with the apologies of the inspector.

'The whole time I was scared half to death. Guess what I had in my brief-case? *The New York cables*!'

Our wondering faces brought him suddenly down to

earth. A boo-boo. An awful boo-boo! He was not sitting among his buddies in exporting and importing. He was with us, who did not know about New York and should never have found out; people who might even be irresponsible enough to give it publicity. But the damage had been done and he could not stop now without its seeming even more suspicious.

Well, this was how it was. Only we must never let on to a living soul. Even if you could not really call it dishonest, because *everyone* did it. It was a public secret that not a sack of coffee is sold in Brazil at the invoice price. About ten per cent of the real purchasing price was never put on paper, but was credited to the seller's office in New York. Eight out of ten of the big coffee exporters in Brazil are foreign firms. And the Brazilian firms are equally interested in having dollars in New York.

'And I was taking the New York cables with me home, right? There I stood with enough evidence in my brief-case to put me in prison for ten years – while the Brassies were looking for cameras in my razor case!'

Ha. Ha. Ha. A joke never goes down quite so well when you have to explain it. The atmosphere was spoiled, and in any case he had to get to court. Some landworkers on the little place he had bought were refusing to accept notice, the bastards had sued him. It would not take long to fix, but just now he had to rush.

We went back to the hotel.

Ten per cent then, in this business. Yet another case to add to the list. Better check it of course, as usual. (Yes, it was true. Everyone does it. The authorities, of course, know about it and try to limit the traffic by legislation on minimum prices.) Ten per cent of the purchasing price of Brazilian coffee never gets to Brazil. What was this in terms of money? In the five-year period 1962–66, Brazil exported coffee to a value of over 3,600 million dollars. If my informants were right, it should have been 4,000 million dollars instead, a difference of 400 million.

This of course is a very rough estimate; the real figure could be higher or lower. But even a much smaller sum would have meant a lot to Brazil, which was struggling at this time with a constant shortage of foreign exchange. Every dollar was needed. And at the same time hundreds of millions of dollars were disappearing in the form of undeclared and untaxed profits to bank accounts in New York. And they still are.

And the fish-meal? The mineral, the meat, the cotton, the bananas, the oil? I was beginning to understand something of the picture.

This was not the first time.

3

On my first evening in Latin America I met a European businessman who when I asked how his firm was going explained that 'the profit, old boy, you take at home, not here'. It was taken by over-invoicing, by salting the bills for goods sold by the parent company to the Latin American subsidiary. Practically every businessman I met in Latin America gave me a new insight into this game.

Latin America officially exports to a value of about 12,000 million dollars a year, and imports for about 11,000. These figures are largely fictitious, since they are based ultimately on the companies' own doctored accounts. The value of Latin American exports is in fact greater, the value of its imports less. The difference is the invisible profit.

At San Carlos University in Guatemala I met Professor Piedrasanta, Dean of the Faculty of Economics. We discussed the undervaluation of Latin American exports, and he referred to a study performed by his Institute in the late Fifties, in reply to an American study in the series 'United States

Business Performance Abroad'. The results are summarized in Table 3.

Table 3

THE UNITED FRUIT CO.'S UNDERVALUATION
OF BANANA EXPORTS FROM GUATEMALA

Institute for Economic and Social Studies, San Carlos University, Guatemala.

	1955	1956	1957
1. Mean price to wholesaler in United States port, dollars per quintal bananas	7:50	7:59	8:04
2. Loading, discharge, insurance, transport by sea. Dollars per quintal bananas	1:20	1:20	1:20
3. Railway freight, dollars per quintal	0:36	0:36	0:43
4. Mean price on the plantation (1 minus 2 minus 3), dollars per quintal	5:95	6:03	6:41
5. United Fruit's banana exports from Guatemala, minus loss in transport, millions of quintals	3·1	3·4	3·1
6. Value of exports (5×4), millions of dollars	18·3	20·6	19·8
7. United Fruit's expenditure in Guatemala, millions of dollars	10·4	11·1	12·0
8. Company profit (6 minus 7), millions of dollars	7·9	9·5	7·8
9. Profit declared by the company in Guatemala, millions of dollars	2·3	1·8	1·5
10. HIDDEN PROFIT (8 minus 9), millions of dollars	5·6	7·7	6·3
11. Declared profit (9) in per cent of the company's stated capital	7·6%	6·0%	5·0%
12. True profit (8) in per cent of stated capital	26·5%	31·8%	26·1%

Sources: (1) Bureau of Labour statistics, U.S. Department of Labour. (2) Current tariffs. (3), (5), (7), (9) The company's own information in 'Datos Cía Agrícola de Guatemala', bulletins 1949–57.

Look at this carefully! What is Piedrasanta calling 'company profit (8)'? Is it not the gross profit? While what he calls 'declared profit (9)' is the taxable net profit, after the permitted depreciation and allocation to reserves. A fairly wide gap between gross profit and net profit is nothing unusual, and thus does not prove that United Fruit had undervalued their exports to evade taxes.

I therefore went to the Banco de Guatemala and asked what they thought of Professor Piedrasanta's study.

'Ah,' they said, 'that's the "adjustment of the banana".'

'The adjustment of the banana?'

'Yes, that's what we call it. To make it possible to use our export statistics on bananas in international comparisons, we adjust the figures given by exporters every year. The sales figures given by the exporters are consistently too low, so we quite simply correct them on the basis of import prices in the United States. We have done this since 1951.'

'But the companies still pay tax according to their own evaluation of exports?'

'Yes, but that's none of our business. We are concerned with the export statistics.'

'Should Guatemala not get some part of the hidden profit created by undervaluation?'

'Possibly. But by the terms of United Fruit's contract with Guatemala, the state must accept the company's own evaluation of exports.'

'Is there nothing you can do?'

'Not within the present system.'

Together we compared the results of Piedrasanta's study with the bank's figures. The bank had somewhat lower figures for the entire banana trade than Piedrasanta had for the dominating company – mainly because they had ascribed some of the price discrepancy to the parent company in the United States, probably with good reason. Table 4 column (1) presents the bank's more cautious estimate of the banana companies' undervaluation of exports 1951–67.

Table 4
'THE ADJUSTMENT OF THE BANANA'

Bureau for Economic Statistics, Banco de Guatemala

Year	1	2	3
1951	8·2	8·2	8·6
2	3·3	11·5	12·5
3	3·3	14·8	16·6
4	9·1	23·9	27·0
5	5·8	29·7	34·4
6	5·8	35·5	42·2
7	5·0	40·5	49·6
8	4·5	45·0	56·8
9	4·7	49·7	64·6
1960	4·0	53·7	72·0
1	2·5	56·2	78·3
2	3·3	59·5	85·6
3	2·4	61·9	92·4
4	5·0	66·9	102·3
5	2·0	68·9	109·5
6	4·3	73·2	119·5
1967	6·0	79·2	131·8

Source: Banco de Guatemala. (1) 'The adjustment of the banana.' Figures for 1952 and 1955 were not available; I have used the smaller of the two surrounding figures. (2) The cumulative value of (1). (3) The cumulative value of (1) plus 5 per cent compound interest. The interest figures have been calculated by Sveriges Kreditbank.

Column (2) gives the total figure, which by 1967 had reached almost 80 million dollars. At ordinary bank interest,' the current discounted value of the underassessment is over 130 million dollars, as shown by column (3).

This since 1951. It is probable, however, that undervaluation had continued for some time before they had started estimating it. United Fruit have operated in Guatemala since the Great War, and exports in the Twenties, Thirties and Forties were considerably higher than now. If undervaluation bore the same relation to exports then as in the Fifties and Sixties, which is not improbable, then the figures at compound interest would be very, very large.

It is difficult to say how this sum should be regarded. It seems reasonable to see at least the tax revenues lost on the hidden profit as a compulsory loan from the state of Guatemala to the American banana companies. Or an involuntary 'investment' made by Guatemala in these companies.

Guatemala, of course, will never see a cent of all this money. On paper, it is Guatemala that is in debt to the United States, or more particularly to EXIMBANK, BID, Bank of America, First National City Bank, Bank of California, American Trust Co., etc. Interest and amortizations amounted in 1963 to 35·2 million dollars, or 19·4 per cent of Guatemala's total export revenues. The costs of the debt have risen every year, and amounted in 1966 to 68·1 million dollars or 25·6 per cent of export revenues.

In other words, more than one quarter of the country's income is spent on keeping the loan afloat. But what United Fruit have 'loaned' in Guatemala does not count.

4

In the seven years 1960–66, Latin America received an annual capital inflow of more than 3,000 million dollars a year in loans, investments and gifts.

This seems a solid contribution to development. Amortizations and capital exports, however, also amounted to a considerable sum, and the annual net inflow was only 850 million dollars.

This figure includes 'foreign aid'. But the inflow consisted mainly of capital attracting costs in the form of profit and interest. The *declared, repatriated* profit on investments by foreign companies rose from 900 million dollars in 1960 to 1,450 million in 1966. The average for the period was 1,165 million. In interest, Latin America paid 390 million a year. Its total capital costs were thus 1,555 million a year.

The end result of the process, capital movements plus capital costs, was thus an *outflow* of on the average 705 million dollars a year (*Economic Survey of Latin America* 1966, Tables 40, 43, 45, 46).

This means that Latin America, in spite of the large loans, was not in a position to import more goods and services than it exported. On the contrary, the continent noted a constant surplus of exports. The size of this surplus cannot in reality be calculated, owing to the artificial pricing I have exemplified. According to official figures, the total export surplus during the period 1960–66 was almost 5,000 million dollars.

This, we would think, must mean that Latin America is paying for a large surplus of imports in previous years. Going back to the period 1946–61, we find that the I.M.F. statistics show a capital inflow of 11,800 million dollars and an outflow of 16,000 million dollars in amortization, interest and profits. This means an outflow of resources to the figure of 4,200 million dollars.

The incomplete figures available for the first half of this century do not suggest any inflow of capital that would warrant the continent's present payment situation.[1] On the contrary, there is reason to believe that the outflow from Latin America has been continuing ever since the Spanish

1. Wendell C. Gordon: *The Political Economy of Latin America*, Columbia University Press 1965, pp. 240 ff.

conquistadores first plundered the wealth of the continent.

In the Sixties the outflow of resources has accelerated, while the burden of debt has reached alarming proportions. We would naturally expect a continent with a large export surplus to be reducing its debts. But the total foreign debt of the Latin American countries actually rose – from 6,100 millions in 1960 to more than 12,000 millions in 1966. It has doubled in seven years. Which will mean in turn increased interest and amortization during the Seventies.

At the same time, investments by foreign firms – which also mean a sort of debt, in so far as they have to be amortized and give a profit – rose probably by an even greater figure, and will produce a devastating outflow of profit in the Seventies.

The figures I have quoted for the Sixties are taken from the U.N.'s *Economic Survey of Latin America* compiled annually in Santiago de Chile. I asked Jorge Ross, one of the men behind this report, what will happen to the burden of debt during the Seventies.

'The situation is dangerous,' Ross says. 'The debt is growing by its own impetus. About 40 per cent of the increase is the result of re-financing old loans. We take new loans to be able to pay off those we already have. Even now, we can foresee that this will be still more necessary in the Seventies.'

The debt roughly corresponds to the value of one year's Latin American exports, about 12,000 million dollars. But it is growing much more rapidly than exports. Interest payments and amortization are growing with it. In 1966 one third of Argentina's exports went to paying interest and amortizations; figures like this will become increasingly common in the Seventies.

Credit that was previously given for five years must now be extended to ten. In the Seventies credits of twenty and thirty years will probably be needed, which means that payments will in many cases far exceed the lifetime of the goods purchased.

What is the answer? In some countries, perhaps, a drastic cutting down of imports. But in Latin America as a whole, no conceivable import restrictions can prevent accelerated growth of the debt. Also, imports now consist largely of capital goods and semi-manufactures, which as Jorge Ross points out cannot be cut down without crippling development.

'To achieve a faster growth-rate, we would in fact have to increase imports. We have calculated that to reach an annual growth-rate of 2·5–3 per cent per inhabitant, Latin America needs an annual *import surplus* reaching something like 5,000 dollars even by 1975. To clear off our debt, we need an *export surplus* on the same scale. The two aims are incompatible. We cannot grow and pay.'[2]

5

The Latin American burden of debt consists to a large extent of short-term loans. This means that governments must continually toe the line for their creditors, who in many cases can directly command currency-stabilizing measures such as devaluation, wage freezes, 'a favourable investment climate', a balanced budget, etc. A greater debt thus means greater dependence, less freedom of action – even in internal politics.

Since the Latin American upper classes refuse to be effectively taxed, Latin America has borrowed money abroad for much that should normally be financed within the country – schools, hospitals, roads, housing, land reform, water and sewerage. Social investments of this kind pay off only slowly, and do not create foreign currency. Loans have largely to be repaid in dollars. The social investments of the Sixties will thus burden the economy of the Seventies. As a result, the

2. cf. ECLA: *Economic Survey of Latin America 1966*, p. 6.

debt will grow and social investments will have to be cut down.

If Latin America had borrowed the money to pay for plantations, mines, smelting plants, factories – investments that fairly soon give an opportunity to pay back loans – the situation would be quite different. It is difficult to borrow money for these things. The lending authorities in the United States are not anxious to help the Latin American countries to compete with North American firms. To exploit its natural resources, Latin America must therefore seek private foreign capital, in most cases direct investments by foreign firms – the most expensive of all loans. These 'loans' usually attract a higher interest than others, and have to be paid back more quickly. Another property of these 'loans' is that the claim remains, however often the money is paid back.

Latin America is burdened with an expensive heritage of foreign investments from the great days of unbridled capitalism. These 'investments' were built up from the giant profits made when the companies themselves could dictate their terms. They are still the property of the company, and still attract a profit even if the initial outlay has been recovered many times over.

'We are trying to live down our past,' an executive of Bookers in Guyana told me.

'We are still charged with the sins of the past,' said Mr Pilgrim, information officer of DEMBA, the bauxite company, in the same country.

Both these gentlemen thought it a little unfair that the sins of the past should be charged against them.

But the *results* of these sins – the ground, the buildings, the machinery, the entire capital – these are sacred private property, and must not of course be touched.

Until the Great War, the land now occupied by DEMBA in Guyana was in the possession of small-holders who naturally had no idea what the ground contained. It was purchased for a song. And since the ore thus became the company's private property, they have never paid (and still do not pay) one cent on royalties to the state for the right to mine their own land.[3]

So the 'sins of the past' continue to give a yield. How much? Neither Bookers nor DEMBA would tell me.

The tax authorities kept their figures on the taxes paid by these two companies in an impressive-looking file labelled SECRET. The facts could not be told, because if you know the tax you can work out the profit. And as Mr Veecock, an official of the Ministry of Finance, said:

'It would only incite ignorant workers to ask for higher wages.'

DEMBA's information officer put it like this:

'It would only cause political disturbances. The people here can't see things yet from the standpoint of the shareholders. But this will come! The small traders and salaried employees own shares in the local brewery, which is doing enormously well. (Annual profit during the Sixties between 40 and 60 per cent.) As shareholders they defend their profit with tooth and nail, and really dig their heels in when the workers demand wage increases. But so far it's only a few of them who see things this realistically.'

When figures on profit are published, they are doctored and misleading; the custom is to declare about 5 per cent. Mr Bears, one of the directors of Southern Peru Copper, made the following comment on current practice:

'To tell the truth, I could give you any profit figures I liked – it all depends how you calculate. In our internal calculations, we have to see that we make at least 30 per cent. Otherwise we have made a bad deal.'

According to the Ministry of Petroleum in Caracas, the profits of foreign oil companies in Venezuela have averaged 21·7 per cent in the past ten years. This figure is

3. DEMBA was nationalized in 1970.

profit after taxation in per cent of invested capital after depreciation. In the past three years, profit has exceeded 31 per cent.[4]

These profits stem from concessions given under Presidents Gómez and Jiménez. Both were military dictators. Gómez (1910–35) passed an Oil Act that the companies themselves wrote for him. He leased the country's oil rights cheaply to his own company, Cía Venezolana de Petróleo, which then sold them to foreign countries on terms that suited Gómez, but were extremely unfavourable for the country. Similar conditions prevailed under Jiménez (1948–58).[5] Since his downfall, the 'democratic' régime has tightened up on the oil companies, which have responded by an investment strike. The capital there now is thus a small fraction of the profits made in the old days of free hand-outs.

I asked Mr Raul Antoni, information officer of ESSO-CREOLE, whether 31·9 per cent profit was not a pretty good yield on capital created in this way. He answered:

'We're competing with ESSO's production companies in the Middle East. Their profit is 60 per cent. Doesn't that put it in a nutshell?'

6

Perhaps it does. Only it is not quite the whole truth. Economists at the University of Caracas believe that the Ministry of Petroleum's figures very much underestimate the true profits, which are exacted mainly in the form of a low price on oil – the companies sell to themselves.[6]

4. Ministerio de Minas e Hidrocarburos: *Memoria y cuenta 1967*, p. I-A-215.
5. Edwin Lieuwen: *Petroleum in Venezuela*, University of California Press 1955.
6. Pedro E. Mejía Alarcón: *'Monopolio y precios del petróleo'*, *Boletín bibliográfico 4/1963*, Universidad Central de Venezuela.

The same applies to bauxite [7] – but I cannot go on and on. I will simply offer a quiet thought to those accustomed to claim that extortion is a myth, since the declared profits of companies are greater in the industrial than in the developing countries. This is hardly surprising, since they systematically *avoid* noting a profit in the latter.

[It is not the *declared* profits of foreign companies (however grotesque these may sometimes seem, in view of the origin of their capital) that has put Latin America in an impossible position. It is the market situation that arises when buyers and sellers are so often identical.]

A succession of reports and interviews has convinced me that the undervaluation of exports and overvaluation of imports are extremely common phenomena in Latin America. This has helped to create an artificial currency shortage, which has to be covered by expensive short-term loans and 'aid'. It creates an artificial burden of debt. In the Sixties, it has been one of the main obstacles to development. In the Seventies it will reach catastrophic proportions.

And the heavier this burden becomes, the deeper Latin America will sink in the morass that is the cause of the debt – economic and political dependence on the United States.

7. H. D. Huggins: *Aluminium in Changing Communities*, London 1965. Norman Girvan: 'The Caribbean bauxite industry', *Studies in Regional Economic Integration*, Vol. 2, No. 4, Institute of Social and Economic Research, University of the West Indies, Jamaica.

The Rise of Violence

The juvenile court in Cuzco, Peru.

Carolina Quisepe Suna, eleven years old, is brought in. Indian features. Hands covered with warts. Arrested for running away. The offence reported by Gregorio Incarroca, the child's godfather. (I.e. employer. When a father cannot support a child he gives it to an employer. The latter is then called the child's 'padrino' or 'godfather'.) Refuses to return to the godfather, who beats her. The parents live in Quiquillana.

Thus far the police report. During the summary hearing, it emerges that the father is a peasant. The girl believes he earns 60 *soles* (a dollar and a half) a month. She is the oldest of three children, and has attended two grades of school. The judge allows me to put some questions.

'Why were you arrested?'
'I ran away.'
'Did anyone tell you to run away?'
'No, it was me.'
'Did you go home?'
'No.'
'Why not?'
'I'm not allowed to go home.'
'Where did you go?'
'To Maldonado's house.'
'Who's he?'

'A relation to godfather. The lady said she would pay me to work for her.'

'Did she?'

'No.'

'How long were you with your godfather?'

'Six months.'

'Did you get any pay?'

'Nothing.'

'What time did you start work in the morning?'

'Six o'clock.'

'What time did you finish in the evening?'

'When it was finished.'

'What time was that?'

'Seven or eight.'

'And on Sundays?'

'The same thing.'

'Where did you sleep?'

She did not understand the question. The judge said it could be taken for granted that they all slept in the same room.

'Did you get the same food, too?'

'No, I only got the soup.'

'It says in the police report that he beat you. How often was this?'

'Always.'

'Every week, you mean?'

'Almost every day.'

After all these questions, of course, she was almost in tears. When her parents were brought in she began to howl. She had not seen them for over six months. She shouted and screamed that she wanted to go home. They tried to avoid her eyes. The father, in a ragged poncho, frightened and tortured, explained to the judge that he saw no way of providing for the girl. In spite of everything, she would be better off with her 'godfather'. There she at least got food. The best thing would be to send her back. The girl wept and pleaded. The mother was silent, looking down at her bare feet. The judge gave Carolina Quisepe Suna into the custody of her parents. They said nothing. The girl too fell silent. They went away together.

2

The first time I walked past an attractive bungalow in Lima and an alsatian came racing over the roof to snap at my face, it scared me half to death. Then I got used to it. Dogs on the roof are a common supplement to the iron bars in the windows in Latin American residential districts. The first time we were invited to one of the 'better class' families, the company, to my astonishment, talked all evening about murders, brutal assaults, friends who had lost their jewels and only managed to save their children at the last moment. The further north you get in South America, the more common this topic of conversation becomes.

The first time I was at a political meeting in Latin America, it surprised me to see the military police packed three lines deep round the whole square, with steel helmets and rubber truncheons. The eternal mist of Lima thickened to a drizzle over the oratory. Suddenly came the attack. A howl of terror rose from the crowd, and everyone began to run. Including me. A moment later the wave had swept past. These were the 'buffaloes', the commando unit of the APRA party, who stormed into the crowd, flailing around them with white-painted lead piping and iron bars. Some of their weapons were left on the ground, together with bleeding and unconscious members of the crowd. The leads to the floodlights and loudspeakers were torn out, and a terrible confusion arose in the darkness as the crowd started to break up chairs and tables to arm themselves. Ten minutes later there was another attack, which was met by a counter-attack. Then the military police moved in, batons flailed behind a wall of soldiers' backs and the meeting was dissolved amid shrieks and prayers.

I met no one I knew except a cleaner from the hotel where we were staying. His entire face glowed when we met in the darkness: 'Are you also of the left?' Six months later we came back to the same hotel. The cleaner had been fired. He had been arrested, and lay in the garrison hospital with severe skull injuries.

3

Violence in Latin America is given a great deal of publicity in Europe, particularly when the guerrilla and students are involved. The flow of information, however, is sporadic and capricious. The massacre of miners in Bolivia in June 1967 was overshadowed by all the fuss about Régis Debray; he in his turn was then forgotten. The student riots in Mexico are noticed only when the Olympic Games are held there; the student revolt in Brazil is noticed, but only in Rio de Janeiro where the foreign correspondents are stationed.

Student resistance in Brazil was triggered when a student was killed and sixty-three others arrested in Guanabara, following a demonstration against increased prices in the student restaurant. On the same day, the following events took place. Four people were killed and many others injured in Maracaibo, Venezuela, during a general strike in the petroleum district. Four people were injured in violent disturbances outside Bogotá University, Colombia. Ten people were taken to hospital after a prolonged struggle between thousands of students and the military police in Quito, Ecuador.

We happened to be in Quito. As usual, information on the background to the trouble was confusing. The clearest picture was given by an ex-army officer who was now an engineer.

'The students are right, the military school of engineering is a scandal. I was there myself. It started in the Thirties as a school of gunnery and engineering. You went there for three years without firing a shot, and read theory on old mortars from the turn of the century. The Yanks, when they arrived in the Forties, told us we were mad. They introduced instead an eight-month practical course in gunnery. Since then the army school of engineering has become more and more civilian, and today it is an exact copy of teaching at the university. The same instructors, the same courses. What's the point of it? It's become part of the military system of privileges. Senior officers and their friends can get their sons a free training as engineers. Look at me! I left the school at the same time as a university engineer with all my education paid, a salary while I was studying, and a separation bonus of 8,000 dollars.'

The students were demonstrating against the army school of engineering. The army put a bomb in their union building. The students answered by attacking the school, whereat the sentry took to his heels – this according to a reporter from the conservative newspaper *El Commercio*. The following day, the paper carried a front-page advertisement, signed by the Minister of Defence and the Chiefs of the Armed Forces, describing the report as an affront to the honour of the services – and also untrue, since it is well known that an Ecuadorian soldier never leaves his post. The newspaper replied: 'With reference to the above advertisement, we can only state that our reporter described the event as he witnessed it.'

This stain on the army's coat-of-arms had naturally to be wiped out. The following day military police in civilian clothes (I saw them being transported to the site of battle in military vehicles) threw themselves into a student demonstration, giving their uniformed colleagues an excuse to intervene. War now broke out in earnest. Evening after evening the tear-gas lay sour and acrid over the town centre, the sirens howled, shouts echoed, the army was threatening to take over power. In other words, the situation was normal.

Meanwhile in Ecuador, the election campaign was taking place that would three months later make Velasco Ibarra president – for the fifth time. I asked what his programme was. He did not have one. 'Velasco is a *man*, not a mass of words.' The 'liberal' presidential candidate Córdova held a meeting in the Square of the Franciscans; crowds and darkness, torches – sturdy wooden sticks with rags drenched in paraffin, formidable weapons. A disorganized chanting of slogans, sudden advances and mass retreats, violence in the air. The police as usual all around us, their hands on their tear-gas shells.

The crowds were even thicker around Ponce, the most conservative of the candidates. We met his caravan up in the *sierra*, fully loaded buses with 20 people on the roof, free booze for everyone; women dragging home their men in the dense mist, shadow-figures under great burdens, hordes of dirty children, opposing groups with stones in their fists, all shrouded in the eternal twilight of the mountain mist, in the primeval darkness of poverty.

What was the campaign about? What were the main issues that caused this tremendous agitation? There weren't any. People were shouting for one or the other candidate as if for Chelsea or Aston Villa.

4

So far as I can see, the outcome of the elections in Ecuador was of no political importance. In Paraguay, where we also experienced an 'election campaign', the result was in any case known in advance. Stroessner, the dictator, looked icily down upon us from every wall; there were other candidates, but you never saw them. Stroessner never dared hold a public meeting, but he did talk on occasion to closed assemblies and praised the stable currency of the country. It really is very stable. He never mentioned the mass unemployment, economic stagnation, or corruption. Or the police state. The state of emergency that was introduced when Stroessner took power in 1954 and which has ever since kept the constitution from functioning was suspended only on the actual day of election. Until that date, and even more important afterwards, the police had a free hand.

Through underground contacts I obtained a list of some thirty political prisoners kept in Asunción itself. In the police station of the Third Commissariat sit Julio Rojas, Antonio Maidana and Alfredo Alcorta, three primary-school teachers with communist sympathies. They were freed by courts of law, 1957–59, but the police are still holding them. They have been held for more than eleven years, for the past five years in dark cells. In the same station is Ignacio Fernández, also accused of communism; he has been kept for more than four years in a cell together with eleven other men.

I went there, playing the somewhat naïve and wondering journalist from a remote country. The Commissar was very helpful:

'By all means look for yourself.'

We went into the inner yard, where he ordered a cell door to be opened. Out flew eleven men and arranged themselves in a perfect line according to height. I was allowed to ask them whatever I liked. As he said, they really had been arrested in the past few days. The cell had no windows, and measured about five by five yards. They were all dripping with sweat in the murderous heat, and two of them had bandaged heads.

'What happened?'

'It was the others that hit us.'

'You hear, it was their fellow prisoners who hit them.

Now you have seen for yourself that there are no political prisoners in Paraguay.'

The same evening I succeeded in locating the wife of one of the prisoners kept at the Third Commissariat. She let me in without question. I took a paper from my pocket and began silently drawing. She at once recognized my plan of the police station, and sketched in her husband's cell. It was on the other side of the inner courtyard where I had stood – probably the men inside had been able to hear the comedy played by the Commissar for my benefit. We spoke together for some time. Suddenly a child began to call persistently from the darkness.

'I have a daughter of five,' she said.

She went away and came back.

'My girl had woken up and heard us. She says I must be more careful. She asked me how I could know you were not from the police.'

During the following days I visited a succession of prisoners' families, and could go to the police stations with fresh, exact information.

At the Fifth Commissariat, the cell doors face a corridor immediately adjoining the waiting-room.

'I know that behind that door are six political prisoners who have not been out of their cell for four years.'

I pointed to it. We were standing not five yards away. Through the little ventilation hatch, the size of a packet of cigarettes, we could glimpse a face in the darkness. The Commissar said:

'There are no prisoners here.'

'Will you let me see for myself behind that door?'

'I'm sorry, that is the armoury. I can't let you in there.'

The Security Battalion lies in a more rural setting. Its commandant was sitting in the shadow of a large tree. Could I meet the prisoners? No, they were *incommunicado*. Could I see them? I could hardly help seeing them, they were just coming back from their work on the land, dirty and sweaty, herded by some ten heavy black dogs. The sharp barking, the panting, the aggressiveness of these dogs, their weight and the number of them – I did not dare to move. The little line of seven prisoners dragged itself slowly back to the cell, followed by their armed guards. Only one of them, an Argentinian revolutionary who was a head higher than the others, looked up and our eyes met. The others kept their eyes on the ground.

María Calendaria Ramirez de Jara is held at the office for Repressive Techniques. Her husband wanted a divorce, and informed on her. She was beaten and raped in her cell, became pregnant, and aborted. She has been held for more than three years. I was naturally not allowed to meet her, but I made another interesting acquaintance. Arturo Hellman is one of Paraguay's three best-known torturers. The interrogation lamp lay unscrewed on the desk in front of him, together with a revolver. In a little alcove behind him he had his private museum of trophies from beaten guerrilla movements. He described, almost with tears in his eyes, how he personally had been forced to crush these revolts against General Stroessner, the father of his country. No one understood him. He alone had to carry on the fight against communism.

'No one helps us. No *one*.'

'Except of course the people,' I suggested helpfully.

'Who's that?'

'The *people*. I mean, it must be a great help to have the people on the side of the father of the country.'

'Oh, the people, yes of course.'

He was annoyed that he had not thought of it himself.

But Arturo Hellman is not entirely alone in his struggle against communism. The following day I visited the U.S. Embassy. Thanks to the law and order prevailing in Paraguay, it lies fully open, with none of the formidable defence arrangements that usually surround U.S. Embassies in Latin America. I was given the usual information sheets, in which I could read that co-operation between the police forces of the two countries is continuing, and growing. 'Between December 1965 and June 1967, 16 Paraguayan policemen underwent various courses in Public Safety at the International Police Academy in Washington D.C. Those who took part are now serving as instructors in a training programme arranged by the local police organization.'

5

You don't have to visit the reactionary dictatorship of Paraguay to meet this sort of thing. The model democracy of Venezuela, the party piece of the Alliance for Progress, contains many of the features of a police state. There are five different police corps: two regular and two 'secret' – the civilian DIGEPOL and the military SIFA – plus 'the holy', who watch over the four others. Even several middle-class people we talked to had friends or relations who had been arrested, and never heard of again. When I asked a student leader if I could talk to some student who had been tortured, he had only to look out over the yard and call to some of those standing nearest. While I was interviewing Professor Mejía, a woman came in and told us that her husband, one of the Professor's students, had been arrested and taken to an unknown destination. This caused no surprise whatsoever in the room. The Professor automatically signed a protest, continuing meanwhile his criticism of how the oil companies book their profits.

Or take Santo Domingo, where the United States intervened with its own troops to save democracy as recently as in 1965. The streets are almost empty. Only steel-helmeted police, in twos and fours. And soldiers with rifles and machine-guns on the street corners. A broken, half-dead town, with a dismal, abandoned, charged atmosphere. Occupied ruins. I visited the PRD party youth club. The flag of the Social-Democratic Youth of Sweden stood on the table. They were touching in their love of Swedish social democracy, which they try in every way to imitate. All of them sitting round the table, a dozen or so, had been imprisoned and maltreated at least once in the past few years. While I was sitting there, a message came by telephone that an officer who was a party member had been found dead in mysterious circumstances. Every week adds to the list of men arrested, killed, tortured.

With the Swedish consul I visited the country's largest sugar refinery, Rio Haina. The area around the mill is called San Cristóbal, and is reached via a pontoon bridge, built and guarded by the army. To enter the area, you pass through a further three check-points manned by military and factory police. The mill itself is entered through long passages of powerful steel-wire netting twice the height of a man, cages through which only one man can pass at a time. The entrance to the office building is still more heavily guarded. It is barred by two systems of heavy steel gates. Every individual storey can be barred off by the same types of gates. Farthest in, behind all these security arrangements, Manuel Gil Fernández, the manager of the mill, sits at his desk with a well-filled cartridge-belt over his stomach and a revolver at his hip.

'Do you have much trouble with strikes and disturbances?'

'Not with the present government.'

'Then why are you so well armed?'

'The wild boar is known by his tusks.'

'How do you mean?'

'The workers have respect for a gun.'

I provoked him by my silence.

'In size, I am a small man. . . . In the United States itself, you have heard what happens there. . . . If I cannot get them to respect me by arms, I am simply a walking target. It is I who cut down this company's expenditure on wages by 30,000 dollars a month. ... So, it is safest to go armed.'

6

The violence I have described is only the visible part of the iceberg, the violence that is so obvious it cannot be hidden; or the violence that is aimed at organizations, and can be made known through them. But what happens under the surface, at the hundreds of thousands of small places of work, in the engineering shops, on the plantations? This silent and unseen violence – represented here only by Carolina Quisepe Suna, with whom I talked in the juvenile court in Cuzco – is probably still more extensive than the political violence. In the courts you can run across it as an irrelevant factor in the case – it was not Carolina's employer who was accused of assault, but the girl who had been arrested for running away. You sometimes catch glimpses of it in the small notices in newspapers. But in the majority of countries, the newspapers give no or highly distorted information about violence to the working classes. The trade unions know a lot. But the great mass of workers, particularly in the rural areas and the slums, are not organized. The priests ought to know. But the majority close their eyes and keep their silence.

You do not have to be a Marxist to see a class struggle in the violence that stamps life in Latin America. The violence is class violence – the direct result of a confrontation between rich and poor, between those with power and those without. This is why violence will continue as long as the confrontation continues, and increase with it. There is every sign that violence will increase in Latin America in the Seventies.

The Race Problem

1

'Your Asian *Indian*,' said the Swedish consul in Georgetown, Mr John Hailwood, 'has a natural preference for hard physical labour. Your *Negro*, on the other hand, is more suitable for commercial and administrative jobs.'

Most people know there are Indians in South America, but *Asian* Indians ... ? Yes, the white plantation-owners in Guyana imported labour from India during the period 1835 to 1917, to replace their former Negro slaves by contract workers. Their contracts, obviously, have long since expired, but the Indians remain and comprise roughly half the country's population – the lower half. It was this difference in social position that Mr Hailwood wished to explain.

'I've just been in Brazil,' I said. 'There, they haven't discovered the administrative gifts of the Negro in this way. In fact, almost all the administrative jobs are held down by Whites.'

'Yes, of course, but by comparison with the *Indian* ...'

'Negroes and Indians live together in East Africa too,' I ventured. 'Are the racial differences as marked there?'

'Hm, East Africa. ... I've been there too, but strangely enough it's the other way round. There it's the Indian who has the commercial ability.'

'Isn't that rather interesting, scientifically? I mean that

inherited racial properties can be so basically altered by crossing the Atlantic.'

'Yes, extremely interesting. ... But the fact is that here in Guyana the *Negro* ...'

And he went on trying calmly to explain the social structure of Guyana by the innate predilection of different races for different kinds of work.

Guyana is the only country in South America where a really explosive racial conflict is just below the surface. There Negroes and Indians are opposed, with a tiny White minority as weighing-master at the top. In most other countries, the Whites together with an intermediate stratum of mestizos and mulattoes dominate the situation so totally that racial conflicts can be suppressed and denied. Officially, there is no racial problem in Latin America. In spite of which it is a very evident reality.

We stayed at the Hotel Arequipa in Peru. Dining in the restaurant were 210 doctors who had come together to discuss malnutrition, an affliction that ravages predominantly the Indian and mestizo populations. *One* of the doctors had Indian features, and I remember how I started when I caught sight of him. That same evening, I asked a Peruvian acquaintance to mention some prominent persons in Arequipa who were of Indian birth. This he found an odd question. Of course, there weren't any. And had I heard the story about the Negro, the Chinese and the Indian who ...

We were travelling through the mountains of Colombia. Large numbers of people lined the road, Indians and mestizos in ragged clothes, and carrying large burdens. Suddenly I saw a white, blonde girl sitting among them. I remember how I started – how had *she* got there? – and felt an impulse to stop the car, and ask if I could help her.

The racial system in Latin America is thus sufficiently imperfect that a white girl *can* sit poverty-stricken by the roadside. It happens. But still the system is sufficiently perfect that I was surprised to see her there. My reaction is revealing. After half a year in the Andes, it had become horridly natural to me that people of another race should live in bestial poverty. I had choked my impulses to intervene. But then a white girl sat there – there must be some terrible mistake, it conjured up subconscious loyalties that automatically carried my foot to the brake.

It's easy to get the habit. We were visiting a Swedish family in Peru. The husband presented himself as a disciple of Tingsten (a Swedish liberal), and Hedenius (the logical positivist). He really hadn't believed in racial differences when he left Sweden. But now he took a more realistic view.

How had this happened? His wife explained.

'We had this maid from the *sierra*, fifteen years old, that we really tried to educate. She arrived in an Indian hat, couldn't look us in the eyes. We gave her some clothes so that she looked really chic, and we told her, you know, about not having a baby.'

'Pills or pessary?'

'No, well, we didn't exactly . . .'

'You mean you simply advised her not to have inter-course?'

'Yes, exactly, we did. But of course she got pregnant, and we said it didn't matter. We really wanted to try with her, and she could have all the clothes our own kids had grown out of if she went on working. *But she was just too lazy.* So she moved to the man's home and lived there with the baby, and of course she got pregnant again. And now they live like pigs, three families in the same room and the children with not a rag to their name. But we wanted her to have one last chance, so I recommended her to a friend and she moved there and worked for three days, but then she just never came back. *That's how lazy they are . . .*'

'And what would you have done?'

She didn't understand.

'I mean, you couldn't imagine wanting to live with the man who is father of your children, if he was badly off?'

'Yes, well, that's a completely different matter. You mustn't romanticize the Indians, usually the girls don't even know who the child's father is, although perhaps that's not true in this case since she *knew* – but she could have met the man on her day off.'

The conclusion, once again, was that it is not racial oppression that keeps down the Indians in Peru. It is their innate idleness and stupidity that condemn them to a subhuman existence.

Another dinner party, this time in Bolivia. During the evening, the boy in the family became violently sick and the Indian girl was sent to fetch the doctor. He arrived, prescribed medicine, and departed. But in the kitchen, the Indian girl sat crying.

'Why are you crying?'

The explanation sat deep down. She had run and run to the doctor, and arrived all out of breath; the doctor left at once, and so she had to run and run again, and it was humiliating ...

'Why? After all, someone was sick. Why was it humiliating?'

'Because the doctor banged the door shut, and told me to show the way and ...'

'Yes?'

But couldn't we understand how it felt to be the person who had to *run in front of the car and show the way?*

She could tell us how it felt. Such contact over the racial frontiers is unusual. What does it feel like for the Indians in Cuzco? How aware are they of their grotesque situation? Cuzco is one of the world's tourist attractions. Plane-loads of American tourists arrive daily – white people coming to admire the ruins of the conquered Indian civilization, to see the genuine descendants of the Incas in their ponchos and embroidered hats. Other white men show them round, and pocket the takings. The Indians, who once built and owned all this, don't make a cent.

The home-woven garments of their poverty hang as decorations in the tourist restaurants. But a human being clad in the same garments wouldn't get in. No notice is even required to forbid this, since it is already financially and socially impossible. They have neither money nor courage. The Indians are only the extras, flowing past outside the windows on sore and naked feet, unreachable and incomprehensible in their own picturesque world.

2

To an even greater extent than other Latin American problems, that of race requires us to distinguish between conditions in different states. Uruguay, which with Costa Rica is the only completely white country, borders on Paraguay, the only country to boast a modern literature in the Indian language. Racial conditions can also vary greatly within different countries: Colombia, for instance, has different racial problems along the Caribbean coast, in the highland of the Andes, and in the jungle area eastwards towards the Amazon.

To start from the south, Argentina has always regarded itself as part of Europe. Its waking up in Latin America came as a shock. It has become a point of honour to explain to visitors how Argentina differs from its neighbours. According to my notes, more than half of all conversations start with some remark about race, often in the form of a leading question:

'What South American country seems to you the most European?'

'Argentina, of course,' is the polite answer.

'So you have already noticed!'

Occasional deviant specimens in one's surroundings can

then be pointed out as Chileans, Bolivians, etc. ('Just look at the cheekbones!') – foreign exceptions that prove the rule.

One should agree, courteously. It is not, on the other hand, good form to ask how Argentina came to be so white. There were in fact some 300,000 Indians in the country, but practically all of them were wiped out in the late nineteenth century.

I remember the abandoned railway station in Gaimán, which has become the local history museum of the Welsh immigrants. The priest's diaries record peaceful exchanges of bread for meat, and acknowledge that the first immigrants would never have survived without the Indians' help. Twenty years later, these same Indians were systematically slaughtered by central government troops. And yet the gaucho legend today surrounds this genocide as compactly as the romance of Red Indian stories around corresponding mass murders in North America.

Where the Indians and Negroes are no problem, people turn against the Jews. A conversation in Montevideo:

'No, it's as my wife says. There are no Uruguayans here, only Jews.'

'I didn't notice. How do you know that they are Jews?'

'One always does.'

'Does it matter?'

'They don't belong to this country, they are foreigners.'

'But who in Uruguay does belong to the country? Everyone comes from Spain or Italy or ...'

'That's another matter. The Jews aren't loyal. When the country was rich, they came here. Now things are beginning to go badly for Uruguay, they move their capital to other countries.'

'You said the same just now about the big landowners. And they, surely, are not Jews, are they? I mean, this isn't a racial question. Rich people are always disloyal, since they have the opportunity to be disloyal.'

'But, you understand, it creates more ill-feeling in the case of a foreign element like the Jews. Look at Argentina, where the Jews collected seven million dollars during the six-day war – just when Argentina was having its greatest difficulty with currency ...'

He looked at me, suddenly doubtful.

'Don't think I mean to pass judgement,' he added somewhat belatedly.

As long as he could tell stories and utter banalities, he was the assured, superior expert. Faced with counter-questions, he had difficulty in speaking, stuttered, got all fat and helpless. I decided to try to inspire confidence, to see where we would end up.

'You say you're not passing judgement. But in all reason we have to admit that there are certain *differences*. As that landowner said to me today – there are people who are trash, and there are people who can carry an *estancia* like this forward. Don't you think?'

I had found the right wavelength. He leaned forward, and spoke with sparkling eyes of the truly dangerous racism of the Jews. We agreed in brotherly concord that South Africa is one of the world's most misunderstood countries. We had just had 'When you see how international communism and international Jewry ...' and were starting on 'Hitler, in spite of certain excesses, wasn't entirely wrong in his ...' – but Cilla kicked me hard on the shin and I stopped in time.

3

In southernmost South America the Indians have been exterminated. In the inner parts of the continent – the enormous jungle areas divided between Brazil, Venezuela, Colombia, Ecuador, Peru, Bolivia and Paraguay – the Indians have had greater opportunities to resist, and an unknown number still survive. These areas are very difficult to penetrate, and less attractive to white conquerors. Yet extermination continues.

On 28 August 1967, a report in the Peruvian *La Prensa* stated that 20 'natives' had been killed and some 100 injured in a brush between the aggressive Amayuca tribe and a group of white oil-prospectors in the jungle. The tribe had attacked to avenge its blood-brothers, who had fallen in an exchange of hostilities ten days previously. On the latter occasion, seven Indians had been killed and an unspecified number injured. Fortunately, these incidents had caused no losses at all among the Whites.

At that time, I was sufficiently surprised over the uneven losses to note it down. Subsequently, I often found similar local news-items in the papers of various countries, always presented as unfortunate mistakes or self-evident aspects of the dangerous life of the jungle.

Fodor's *Guide to South America*, the great North American tourist guide-book, mentions the murder of Indians in passing as a well-known phenomenon: 'Gradually being killed off by land seekers and professional Indian Killers, their numbers are diminishing at a tragic rate' (1967, p. 446).

In Manaus, the jungle town on the Upper Amazon, I visited the SPI office, which covers an enormous area containing about 30,000 Indians. The SPI is a state body, whose function is to protect and assist the original inhabitants of Brazil. Under the office in Manaus were eight jungle stations, with 66 officers. Some twenty of these were Indians, all in subordinate positions. Many of the officials are pensioned military officers, including the head of the office, Alfredo Alexandre de Souza, who at the time of my visit had occupied this position for six months.

His immediate assistant, a civilian with twenty-five years' service behind him, had a sorrowful, experienced face. I asked how much material assistance the SPI had been able to provide to the Indians this past year.

'We handed out goods worth 12 million cruzeiros in all Brazil.'

'And what were SPI's overheads in wages, administration etc. in providing this assistance?'

His face began to light up even as I formulated the question, and his answer came back at once:

'330 million.'

Even if the help provided is thus only a fraction of the overheads, SPI's jungle stations are notoriously badly staffed, with 'teachers' who cannot read or write, and poorly paid 'officials' who live on the trade monopolies set up among the Indians. And at times on plain robbery and murder.

In the spring of 1968, the SPI suddenly made world headlines: according to an investigation, 20,000 Indians had been killed by precisely the state body created to protect them.

How was this possible? And what happened afterwards?

I asked the AFP correspondent in Rio, the original source of this information. He had not seen the inquiry, no outsider had been allowed to see it. No legal proceedings had started. No reliable figures were available on the numbers killed. Details of the inquiry had leaked out from the Ministry for Home Affairs, which was concerned to create an opinion in favour of 'cleaning up' the SPI; this, he thought, was largely in order to get at certain left-wing elements who were considered dangerous out there in the wilds.

Since the murder of Indians had long been a well-known phenomenon in Brazil, the authorities had insufficient fantasy to imagine the reaction it would provoke abroad. To prevent the scandal from growing, the inquiry was made classified information, and the risen corpses of the Indians were buried once more in silence.

4

In the early Fifties, I used to review travel accounts in the Swedish newspaper *Dagens Nyheter*. At that time, books on Latin America were rare. Those published were concerned almost exclusively with the jungle Indians, a fraction of one per cent of the continent's population. During those years, the head-shrinking methods of the Jivaro Indians alone attracted greater attention than any other social and economic problem in Latin America.

The jungle Indians were portrayed as dangerous savages, primitive hunters and fishers who had no contacts with society outside the jungle. Such tribes may exist. But those we encounter in the anthropological and sociological reports from these same areas always have commercial relationships with their environment. Indebtedness and other forms of economic dependence force them to become suppliers to the trading posts on the rivers, or the SPI stations. They work on the periphery of the economic system, but not outside it.

The same is true to an even greater extent of the highland Indians. These rarely appeared in the travel books; at most, one caught a glimpse of Indians in colourful blankets and ponchos at the markets. The explanation is simple enough. The highland Indians are land workers, and live in an unromantic poverty that was considered utterly uninteresting to Western readers. And yet almost half the population in such countries as Guatemala, Ecuador, Peru and Bolivia consists of this Indian proletariat.

The official policy of these countries treats the Indians in much the same way as the travel books. They are regarded as a foreign and primitive race, difficult to integrate into modern society and thus a burden to their respective countries, in fact one of the main reasons for these still being developing countries.

A primitive race? The forefathers of these same Indians created brilliant civilizations, the ruins of which still attract large dollar revenues each year. If the race has grown more primitive since then, it must have been by miscegenation with the Whites.

Difficult to integrate? Originally it was precisely because these Indians were so easy to integrate that it paid to enslave them rather than exterminate them. They were used to organized work, and could be put directly into the service of the colonial economy as miners and land workers. This is where they still are. In fact this social role has so imprinted itself upon the concept of 'Indian' that it is difficult to say whether it is the Indians who are oppressed or simply the oppressed who are called 'Indians'.

A foreign race? There no longer exists any clear biological dividing line between Indians and Whites, only a sliding scale with a greater or lesser preponderance of the two races. On this scale, a lighter colour of skin finds its counterpart amazingly well in higher incomes and a better social position. The 'Indian' is identified not so much by his biological as by his social characteristics – his language, clothing, behaviour. And above all by his poverty and dependence.

A burden to society? It is, of course, 'society' which is a burden to the Indians. For centuries, they have borne up the entire social pyramid that was erected with the surplus from their labour. And this social pyramid is in its turn a severe burden in every attempt towards economic progress.

Serfdom as a legal concept was not abolished in Guatemala until 1945, nor in Ecuador until 1966 – and only then to be replaced by an economic dependence that had very similar effects. The present social structure of the 'Indian countries' is based directly on the old, when the white conqueror could *requisition* Indians for his mines or estates. Just as the social structure of north-eastern Brazil is an inheritance from the time when the white slave-owner bought and sold black labour. These areas were originally the richest on the entire continent, those where the opportunities for prosperity were greatest. But racial oppression dictated the social structure, and the social structure prevented economic progress. Today, these same areas are among the poorest, most retarded in Latin America.

5

Little research has yet been done into the demographic history of Latin America. It is certain that the Indian population has been greatly reduced, particularly during the first century after the arrival of the Whites. Estimates of this reduction vary between 5 and 50 million. Possibly even the higher of these figures is too low; the most detailed studies performed have given the most sharply falling curve.

Table 5

INDIANS IN CENTRAL MEXICO:
POPULATION DEVELOPMENT 1519–1605

1519	25·2 million
1532	16·8
1548	6·3
1568	2·7
1580	1·9
1595	1·4
1605	1·1

Source: Borah, *New Spain's Century of Depression*, Berkeley 1951, as quoted in Mörner, *Race Mixture in the History of Latin America*, Boston 1967.

It remains to make corresponding calculations for the rest of Latin America.

Only a few of the Indians died in battle. The majority fell victim to the diseases brought to America by the Europeans, and to the inhuman working conditions forced upon them.

The history of Latin American revolutions is also largely unwritten. It is certain that, apart from *coups* and palace revolts, there have always occurred popular uprisings, often with strong elements of racial conflict. The best known is the revolt of the Andean Indians 1780–81 under Túpac Amaru. The war of liberation in the early nineteenth century was on the brink of becoming a class and racial conflict, particularly in Venezuela. And since the liberation from Spain failed to change the basic social structure, with Negroes and Indians at the bottom, the attempted uprisings continued during the nineteenth and twentieth centuries. Today they are channelled into Marxist lines of thought, which means a greater emphasis on class struggle than racial conflict.

I remember unheated student premises in Oruro, Bolivia. The students sat wrapped in their overcoats, as in blankets. The majority had markedly Indian features, many spoke Aymará or Quechua in addition to Spanish. I told them about India, where many intellectuals live a double life between English and their native tongue, between Western and Indian civilization. Did they experience anything of this kind?

They denied emphatically any suggestion of cultural dualism. They lived and thought in Spanish, they said. Iberianization was the self-evident path to the future even for the Indians. They felt themselves primarily to be Bolivians, secondarily Latin Americans, but felt no particular bonds with their Aymará- or Quechua-speaking fellow Indians on the other side of the Peruvian frontier. And the revolution for which they worked was certainly not aimed against any race, hardly even against any class, but against American imperialism in Latin America.

The communist land workers' organization in the highlands of Ecuador is named the 'Federation of Indians'. I asked its leader – a lawyer with Indian features, but speaking only Spanish – whether this meant that the Federation was based on racial thinking.

'No. "Indian" is for us not so much a biological as a social concept. There are no sharply defined racial groups in Ecuador. And the cultural process of assimilation is necessary, it is a process of development. What we are trying to create is class consciousness, not race consciousness.'

But in practice this distinction is difficult to maintain, as I soon found out in the week during which I followed the Federation's work. Race and class are so interwoven that social indignation constantly assumes overtones of racial struggle.

'Aren't the social problems in Peru at the same time racial problems?' I asked Hugo Blanco, the revolutionary union leader from the Quillabamba valley, then in prison in El Frontón.

'Of course,' he agreed.

'Is there any race consciousness among the *campesinos*?'

'Only in the form of a suspicion of the "señor". And this is just as much a class concept.'

'Would increased racial awareness be an asset in the work of revolution?'

'The racial theme only needs hinting at. I remember a mass meeting in the Plaza de Armas in Cuzco, where no language had ever been publicly spoken except Spanish. The square was full of *campesinos* in ponchos, and I spoke in Quechua. "WE INDIANS, OPPRESSED FOR CENTURIES ..." No more is needed. I think it would be dangerous to make race a major theme.'

Yes, perhaps it would be dangerous. But if the racial theme only has to be hinted at to prove effective – what would happen if it was not toned down?

In the attempted revolution in Peru in 1965, the guerrilla groups bore the names of Indian heroes. One of the leaders was Héctor Béjar. But when I met him in the prison of the Prefecture in Lima, he said :

'It's easier and more important to create social consciousness; it would be a detour to go via increased racial consciousness. The land workers are very hungry for land. But they hardly ever encounter Whites in situations that they experience as discriminatory on the grounds of race rather than class. Among the radicals, the passion for things Indian is a passed stage. In the Thirties and Forties, people played Indian music and spoke of restoring the Inca civilization. This has come back now as drawing-room politics in Belaúnde. But it no longer fulfils any function in revolutionary practice.'

6

'If you run over anyone, don't wait to be lynched – get out !'

This advice was often given us by our white friends.

As luck would have it I only ran over two small goats. This was on All Saints' Day, by Lake Titicaca, on the way to Puno.

The Indians stood in groups on the dark highland plain, gathered around their graves.

They paint the graves white on All Saints' Day, adorn them with paper flowers and drink themselves paralytic. Never before have I seen so many people so brutally drunk as on All Saints' Day on my way home to Puno.

Everywhere children and wives, trying to overpower and drag home staggering fathers.

Everywhere white graves. Everywhere dark groups.

Everywhere children with bellies like pregnant women.

Beautiful?

Wonderfully, brilliantly beautiful.

The young goats ran headlong over the road, I had no time to brake. They died immediately.

As the crowd approached I did not wait to see who was the

owner – I threw down all the money I had in my pockets, jumped into the car and drove off.

I later found that I had paid more than is customary for running over a human. An Indian costs only 80 pesos, a foreigner told me in Bolivia.

'I know, because two of my friends have knocked off one each. Oddly enough, outside the *same* petrol station.'

I drove on over the *altiplano*, still trembling from the menace and bitterness I had read in the eyes of the Indians.

Nothing suggests that Latin America will see any severe racial conflicts during the Seventies. The Indians of the Andes are migrating *en masse* to the towns, in an effort to avoid the social role that society allots their race. The coloured people of Brazil display as yet no traces of the explosive consciousness of the Negro in the United States. The only open racial conflict is one between Asian Indians and Negroes in Guyana, fanned by the white minority who in this way prolong their power.

Latin America prides itself on the harmony between its races, a harmony more complete than on any other continent. But not a harmony between equal forces. The harmony is based on the subjection of the one party. Racial contempt and racial oppression have naturally created racial hatred; I caught a glimpse of this suppressed hatred when the Indians came rushing at me. Fortunately, such glimpses are rare.

Fortunately? While I drove on towards Puna, I asked myself whether the revolutionary leaders are right to play down the racial struggle in favour of the class struggle. Will the Indians ever gain respect as people, without first winning respect for themselves as Indians? Will their apathy ever be dispelled, without the myth of racial harmony being dispelled also?

The Church

1

What do the revolutionaries of the Church want? Are they trying to save a dying ideology by giving it a new political content? Or are they simply using their priests' robes as a disguise for political activities? How far are they prepared to go?

I went out to Cabo, twenty miles south of Recife, to meet Father Melo. He sat reading the Bible in a little room beside the church. A man of my own age, perhaps younger. He seemed dreamy and mild enough, until I began to speak of Cabo as a future industrial area. The roads were lined with new factories – but where were the workers?

'There aren't any workers!' he almost screamed at me. 'Do you think modern capitalism needs people? The actual construction provides some work, and then it's all over. The technicians and specialists are driven out here from Recife, the local people as poor as ever. Poorer! The old factories that were here before have been forced to rationalize production and lay off labour, and SUDENE's policy gives them the opportunity. Unemployment here is greater than ever.'

'And the peasant leagues you helped create in the early Sixties?'

'Crushed! Or underground. Their only asylum is here in my church. Come tonight at half past nine, and you can talk to their leaders.'

'And MEB, the literacy campaign that you were working at?'

'The bishops capitulated. Here in my parish alone we had forty small places, "schools" we called them. But the movement was under the leadership of the bishops, and they gave in to the army. The schools were closed down.'

'What does the army say about you giving the leagues the use of your church?'

'Here in the church it is I who decide, no one else. Not the bishops, not the army, no one but me.'

'Which means most to you – your work in the Church, or work in the leagues?'

'There is no Church! Obviously, the actual building is there. One person in a hundred goes to church. I can't just sit and wait. When SUDENE capitalism has driven the people into revolution – only then, perhaps, will the church become a Church again. Not before.'

People came and went. Two peasant leaders, Severino and Amaro, sat waiting on the wooden sofa. Thin, hollow-eyed men in ragged clothes. How many of the association's two thousand members had a job? It was impossible to say. Almost no one had a steady job. Work was something you had for a day now and again, three days here, two there. More than half a week's work was rare at this time of the year.

'And the pay?'

'The minimum wage is eighty-four cents a day. But a "day's work" takes at least two days to handle. So what people actually earn is about half.'

Back in Recife I ate the following lunch at a shabby bar-counter in a back street near the centre: a cheese omelet made from two eggs, rice and bread, beer and a cup of coffee. The price was one dollar 20 cents. Almost three days' pay for a land worker.

The following day, a Sunday, I went out to Cabo again.

The leaders of the peasant leagues were still holding their meeting in the schoolroom behind the church. Father Melo's colleagues, five students, led the meeting – analysing, proposing, dividing the men up into groups, drafting motions. The peasants discussed earnestly and heatedly, their faces flushed.

Were the students Catholics or revolutionaries? They maintained that the two concepts were inseparable. The Church or Revolution? Neither – only the revolutionary process that is the meaning of religion. Where the Church opposes this process, the Church is of no value and will fail to survive.

They admitted to reading Debray more than the Bible, and they seemed to be more interested in Che than in Christ; on the other hand, at least one of them was astonished to learn that I was an atheist, and started an eager discussion on what meaning there could then be in human life.

I wanted to know whether they regarded the church as a safe place for revolutionary activities, or the revolution as a way of getting the peasants to church. They quite rightly refused to accept the question. They are Catholics in an almost ethnographic way, as part of their nationality; they are revolutionaries by reflection, in opposition to the society in which they live. I think they were right to apply their critical reasoning more to their society than to their faith; particularly since this faith, in the form of Father Melo, helps and protects them in their struggle against society.

We sat talking about this in Father Melo's kitchen, eating *faroufa* and black beans. My son Aron was asleep on the sofa, covered by a towel. Father Melo himself appeared only briefly, hurrying over his meal. I asked him whether Che Guevara was a good Catholic.

'I don't know. I never received his confession.'

'Was he a good revolutionary?'

'In Cuba, yes. But not in Bolivia. He was trying to create the Cuban revolution in another country. You can't do that sort of thing, it all depends on the concrete circumstances.'

'Being a good Catholic and a good revolutionary are not the same thing then?'

'No, it's not the same thing.'

'*Then, which is the more important?*'

'Ha!' – he turned on his heel and addressed himself to the others, amused, unworried and bantering – 'Here comes a foreign Professor of Philosophy to coax me on to thin ice!'

He went on very quickly in a quite different tone, so that I thought he had changed the subject:

'Why didn't you come last night as you promised?'

I began to explain. The meeting was to start very late, at half past nine, the last bus back to town left at ten o'clock. There was no point really in ...

'Were you free to come or not?'

Still not suspecting a trap, I explained that I had been free to come in a way. But the last bus left at ten and a taxi cost five dollars, if I could have found someone willing to drive at night which was by no means ...

'*Freedom,*' he drove home his point with his umbrella against the stone floor, 'freedom and democracy, Catholic and revolutionary, all these words and phrases are all very well when it comes to setting logical traps for silly priests. But the *real* questions are always quite different. What time is the last bus? What does it cost? How much do you earn? When did the children last eat? Is your boy sleeping happily there on the sofa – or is he dead under the towel? The important thing is the *concrete circumstances*. That is what has to be changed. And that is why it is good Catholicism to work for the revolution here in Brazil.'

2

'When capitalism has driven the people to revolution, then perhaps the church can become a Church once more. Not until then.'

I remembered the words of Father Melo when I encountered, during the preparations for the episcopal meeting in Bogotá, a high dignitary of the church, who was well-informed on conditions in Cuba. What had happened there? Had the revolution given new life to the Church?

'In Cuba, everything went wrong from the beginning. The Church took up a wrong position. It did everything it could to counteract the revolution, as was natural in view of its social background and the radicalism of the reforms. The Church in Cuba was closely tied to the economic and political power in the pre-revolutionary society. The faithful belonged not to the broad masses, but to a small group which lost its every position in the revolution. Castro could have crushed the Church, and he had reason to do so. The Church's counter-revolutionary stand was well known. Going to church came to be a way of demonstrating against the government. People took Communion as a protest against Castro.

'But the revolution had no wish to crush the Church. The government had not tried to interfere in the Church's internal affairs. No one has tried to stop its life of worship. They have never requisitioned churches to make them into schools or hospitals, as has happened elsewhere. Cuba's bishops are perfectly free to attend the Church's meeting, although the government knows them to be bitter opponents of all revolutionary effort. They reject everything, even the Pope's *Populorum Progressio* encyclical, which does not totally and unreservedly condemn communism.

'One can claim that all these people were cheated by the

United States. They had been assured by the American propaganda that Castro would be overthrown. Each day they waited. When finally the Bay of Pigs [1] took place, its failure was a crushing disappointment. But the promises were continued. Jacqueline Kennedy kissed the Batista flag, promising that it would soon be raised again over Cuba. The faithful were sick with longing. Only gradually have they begun to accept that the United States will not invade Cuba.

'Instead, they are leaving the island. About 40,000 people a year leave Cuba, and many of them are believers. Many are rich people, on whom the Church was dependent. The Church, in fact, is managing in any case – since expenditures on care of the poor, schools, etc. have become unnecessary, or taken over by the state. But reckoned in people, the Church has been let of much of its blood. And the young generation growing up are either revolutionaries and thus opponents of the Church, because of its political position. Or they are counter-revolutionaries, and will leave the country.

'Those who remain? Congregations are not smaller than previously, on the contrary. Because those who remain attend church more frequently, more keenly than before. Partly because they have no other amusements, partly from a sort of loyalty that has very little to do with religion. But also because many, in the material crisis they are undergoing, have begun to live a more intense religious life.

'The Church in Cuba is anchored in a defeated population group. These ten years have created a bitterness that seems almost impossible to overcome. Their feelings prevent them from seeing clearly. Naturally, the Christian faith is incompatible with materialism as a philosophy, that is true. But it is not incompatible with Marxism as an economic system; on the contrary, the reforms carried out in Cuba have accorded in many important respects with the Church's own social teaching. Nor is the faith incompatible with Marxism as

1. The U.S.-organized invasion of Cuba in April 1961.

morality; on the contrary, when Castro preaches self-sacrifice for the good of the people, it could sometimes be the Pope speaking.

'What is there to hope for? That the revolution proves successful, and that its success breeds a more positive attitude on the part of the Cuban Church, and that it will one day be possible to be both a Christian and patriot, both a Catholic and revolutionary in Cuba.' Said the man of the Church.

'And what is the conclusion as regards Latin America? Can one hope, as certain priests do, that a continental revolution will lead to a religious revival?'

'Yes. But only if the Church, even before the revolution, works *for* it and *with* it.'

3

The position of the Catholic Church in Latin America is unique. It is the only organization that can look back on almost five centuries of unbroken history; the only organization covering all states on the continent; the only one with influence at all levels of society. One-third of the world's Catholics are Latin Americans, but only about twenty per cent of them are active believers, and these are to be found above all in the higher reaches of society.

'The Church came with the Spanish conquest,' Father Avellano explained to me in Quito, Ecuador. 'The Indians *submitted* to the Church as they submitted to a new government and a new economic system. They were beaten, and had to accept. And for the poor, we are still the Church of the rulers.'

Secularization in Latin America took a political form; anticlericalism was the core of the 'liberal' party's ideology. The Church aligned itself with its defenders, with the power and prestige of the conservatives. Thanks to this alliance, the Church has been able to preserve its status as the continent's biggest landowner and its grip on education; one-third of all education, above all for the well-to-do, is run by the Church.

'The traditional Church has locked itself into established positions', writes Professor Vallier of Berkeley University, listing the symptoms of decline. 'The laity are ignored. Rituals are carried out *pro forma*. The Sacraments are available to those who can pay the fee, and social evils are defined as implicit in the human situation.' [2]

In the Sixties, the Church has made an attempt to obliterate the landmarks of its upper-class conservative ideology. Some important measures:

• The Church has reinforced its organization by a considerable amount of national and regional collaboration. Each bishop is no longer Pope in his see.

• The Church has broadened its basis by backing the Christian trade-union movement, particularly among land workers, and among such moderate reform parties as have a Christian ideology. These movements have more bark than bite, but in particularly repressive conditions, as in Paraguay, they can serve as an axis for revolutionary forces. When in power, as in Chile until 1970, they pursue a middle-of-the-road reform policy.

• In two cases – Chile and Ecuador – the Church has gone so far as to experiment with land reforms on a small part of its own property.

• Two Papal encyclicals – *Mater et Magistra* and the *Populorum Progressio* – have promulgated a social message that gives increased play to the Church's left wing. Only in Brazil, however, does the latter as yet have any real strength.

2. Ivan Vallier: 'Religious Élites', in Lipset *et al.*: *Élites in Latin America*, Oxford University Press 1967, pp. 190 ff.

4

I went to the bishop's palace in Recife to ask for an appoint-
ment to meet Dom Helder, the revolutionary Archbishop of
north-eastern Brazil. Suddenly he himself opened the door –
small, lively and smiling – and extended a narrow old hand to
draw me inside.

'Where will the Church stand in the Seventies?'

'On the side of the people. The Church endorsed slavery
for 300 years. We have already endorsed this new slavery
long enough. Until the early Sixties, religion in this country
really was opium for the people. Now the role of the Church
has changed. We are working to make the masses conscious.'

'Does this please the authorities?'

'The Governor calls for me and tells me that the people
must not be woken up faster than he can introduce reforms.
I answer that without awareness there will be no reforms.
"You are a subversive element and a communist," he says. He
refuses to see that awareness will come in any case, without
us, but that it will then be *against* us. And then. ...' His
long sinewy hands made an expressive gesture across his
throat.

'And how do the communists react?'

'My friends the Marxists say : "So the Church has begun
at last to realize the way things are going." They say that our
policy is opportunist. But understanding has improved recently between the Catholic and the Marxist left. The
Marxists see that we in the Church are prepared to take the
consequences.'

'What consequences?'

'Repression.'

(The following day I was with the Chief of Police, a little
man with sharp eyes and a nervous tic. He asked with a thin
smile : 'How did you enjoy your visit to Dom Helder?'

'Have I been there? How do you know?' 'I'm a policeman. It's my business to know.'

Every evening during the three weeks we were in Recife, the military police stationed some 5,000 men on the streets to prevent priests and students from demonstrating. The majority of those arrested were theological students.)

'The Church, you say. But how many are prepared to defy the repression?'

'There are 250 bishops in Brazil. As yet I have only thirty. But we are making concrete proposals. The time for words is past, it is time for action.' (He gaily rolls up the sleeves of his Bishop's coat.) 'The best young people are slipping away from us, and see violence as the only answer to violence. We have to exert strong moral pressure on the government and "the great owners". Our movement has no name yet, but I should like to call it FORJA – Força do Justicia e Amor' (The Force of Justice and Love=FORJA, a forge).

'And how do you work?'

'Gandhi's birthday will be our official big day – that, surely, sets the tone clearly enough. Just now I am sending out instructions to the other bishops. The object is to build up a mass movement on the basis of what I call "the Abrahamite minority", the progressive fifteen per cent.'

'And when the military move in?'

'You can arrest *one* bishop, but you can't really arrest thirty. We have created a system of communications between us. If one of us disappears, the others will act.'

'I know that many people in the Church are already saying that Dom Helder goes too far. The military will try to isolate you, and attack you one by one.'

'It is my duty to fight. It cannot be my duty to win.'

'What the situation needs is not a man doing his moral duty in vain. It needs results.'

'But what is the alternative? Violence?'

'What would be your attitude to it?'

'Violence is impossible for two reasons. The first is the dominion of the United States here in Latin America. The United States considers this hemisphere its private property. A new Cuba is impossible, so is a new Vietnam – violence on our part would mean a continental war. I cannot lead a movement that would have consequences like these.'

'And the other reason?'

'I know the masses of Latin America. They are even less prepared than I am to take such consequences. They live in a degradation that is not conducive to courage or decisiveness. The religion of the pauper is fatalism. For centuries the Church has preached that some people are born to poverty, others to riches, according to the will of God. The poor must first realize that poverty is not God's problem but *ours*, that it is *our* business to fight it and eliminate it.'

'Without revolution?'

'Impossible.'

'Then how, ultimately, will you avoid the continental war?'

Dom Helder said nothing.

5

On 9 January 1968, two hundred workers led by Father Juan Sánchez attacked the sugar refinery of San Pablo in north-western Argentina, after a mass in the union hall. They demanded work and wages.

'What did Father Sánchez actually say in his sermon,' I asked the local vicar.

As answer he took up a worn copy of *Populorum Progressio*, which lay in the top drawer of his desk.

'Only what the Pope himself has said,' Father Sánchez simply read aloud from this book. His diction is good, he reads with warmth and power. The rest was the result of the concrete circumstances.

'The circumstances?'

'Precisely. The workers' housing is terrible. Labour is freighted in cattle trucks. We have been protesting against this sort of thing for decades. Here in San Pablo there are 400 families, whose bread-winners usually have regular work for only three months of the year. This year we have a further 100 unemployed. And those who work haven't had their pay for months.'

The union leaders, of course, were immediately arrested; and the Governor was now asking that Father Sánchez and his vicar should be reprimanded. For having read the Pope's own words to the workers? The bishop's reply stated: 'The presence of the Church is not meddling, but a holy right. Father Sánchez has interpreted the signs of the age in the light of the Gospel, and continued the work of Jesus Christ. The disturbances were provoked not by the intentions of the priest, nor by his presence, but by the injustices suffered by the people.'[3]

In its dispute with the secular authorities, the Church won. In the meantime, however, the normal guard on the refinery was expanded by sixty mounted police. Their glossy, well-polished horses contrasted strangely with the thin, hollow-eyed workers who were to be guarded. The situation of the workers never changed. Neither the bishop nor the priest tried to follow up the action triggered by the Pope's words. They were concerned only to persuade the mill-owners to 'consider the social function of capital', as they put it. And when I pressed the vicar to explain these phrases, he revealed only an old-fashioned paternalism totally incompatible with the economic realities of today's capitalist society.

3. Clarín, 17 January 1968.

6

Another recurrent phrase is 'A revolution built on love'. This was the first thing I heard from the lips of Father Henry, when we met in Chimbote, the fish-meal town of northern Peru. Father Henry came from the United States; the majority of priests in Peru are foreigners. We accompanied him for a couple of days in the slums of Chimbote to find out what he really meant. He did not want us to see only the worst parts of the town, so he took us to an attractive park with playgrounds for children and a large swimming-pool. But where were the children?

'It costs fifteen cents to get in. Unfortunately, the families with children can't afford it.'

We continued towards Villavicenzia – an area a few acres large, invaded three years ago by about two hundred families. It is here that the waste water from the swimming-pool runs out, forming a marshland which is the sewer and launderette of the slum. And here the children really do bathe, swarming and paddling about in the bubbling mud under the discharge from the pool.

'Seventy-five per cent of the population of Chimbote live like this.'

'Where has the money gone? There must have been a fortune made here when Peru became the world's biggest exporter of fish-meal in the early Sixties?'

'The banks. The corporations. Most of them started on borrowed capital, and the interest was between 30 and 45 per cent. Even so, the factory owners made quick profits. There was nothing left over for the workers.'

And he added:

'The communists want to shoot those responsible. I tell them: "Don't shoot! Just cut their balls off." '

A strange answer from a priest. But then Chimbote is not

exactly Sweden, so I was hardly surprised. Above all, however, it was impracticable advice. The following day he said:

'It's the poor who suffer in all revolutions. Look at Vietnam! Who is it that gets killed? The poor. They should shoot Johnson instead.'

'Shoot him? I thought you wanted a revolution built on love, Father. In that case, wouldn't it be sufficient to cut his balls off?'

He drove on unconcerned, delighted with the effect of his words. I began to discern a pattern, I thought. He had overcome all his verbal taboos and was outbidding his worker friends in drastic language. But the upshot was always that there was something they should *not* do.

The metal-workers' union dismissed him as a harmless clown. One of the leaders of the fishermen said:

'Father Henry is all right. He comes to our homes and eats with us, which means that people look on us with greater respect. We strike, and he says that God is on our side. The authorities call us communists, and he tells us that they said the same of Jesus Christ.'

Many of the other priests have been there longer than Father Henry. Even so, they have ended up on the defensive – jealous, confused, and suspicious. Over a glass of beer one night I asked one of them the standard question I put to priests in Latin America: 'How are the social demands of the Church reflected in the confessional?' His was the standard answer:

'The rich rarely come to a simple country priest like me. Sometimes they do, of course. Why?'

'The Church is the only power in the world that can offer remission of sins. This is an enormous responsibility. Do you really forgive economic crimes? And if so on what terms?'

'A factory owner or *hacendado* never confesses such matters.'

'He doesn't? But isn't it a mortal sin to leave out sins when confessing?'

'Well, they never confess that sort of thing.'

'If a well-known whore comes to make confession and doesn't mention her sexual lapses, do you give her absolution?'

He grinned.

'Sometimes you have to help them along a bit.'

'And if a well-known landowner comes to confess and fails to mention how he is exploiting his workers, shouldn't he too be helped along a bit ... ?'

'I never thought of it that way.'

7

The submissiveness of the great majority of priests, the empty words of most of the few radicals, these things make me very sceptical of the ability of the Church in Latin America to play any leading role in social development during the Seventies.

Those who had expected a radical breakthrough at the meeting of the Church in Bogotá, in August 1968, were disappointed. Instead of all the confessions that the Church had never dreamed of demanding, a few symbolic figures from the ruling classes came forward together with the workers to admit their imperfections, and pray for forgiveness. The representative of the Colombian government, for instance, went so far as to admit that 'our social and public institutions have not yet achieved perfection in benefiting the people.'

After this farcical performance, the Pope turned to the rural population of the continent and assured them that he could 'hear the cry arising from your suffering, and that of the greatest part of humanity'. He portrayed the Church as the champion of the oppressed.

At the same time he urged the rural population not to put their trust in violence and revolution. In a country with the continent's most conservative Church and some of its most radical priests – Father Camilo fell with the Colombian guerrilla in 1966, and his example burns as brightly as Che Guevara's before the eyes of Latin American youth – the Pope repeatedly criticized those impatiently demanding a rapid change in social conditions. The solution was to be sought rather in primary and vocational education, and in fostering the responsibilities of citizenship.

It was with the same mildly reformative attitude that the majority of the left wing of the Church started their social work. They wanted to take the wind out of the communists' sails, guide the discontent into 'constructive' paths, etc. Contact with those they were concerned to influence has changed them. The 'concrete circumstances' quoted by both Father Melo and the vicar of San Pablo have pushed them into a revolutionary approach. And the most concrete of all circumstances has been the wall of repression that meets every attempt at change.

Repression or revolution – the Pope's attitude in Bogotá offered no guidance in the most difficult choice of the Seventies. It will be impossible for the Church to play its present double role indefinitely. It cannot go on encouraging radical changes with the one hand, provided they are non-violent, and blessing with the other the arms of those who oppose with violence even the most modest of reforms. Revolution has cast a warning shadow; the repression is already there. Together they will put the Church up against the wall, and force it to choose between the rulers and the people.

The Military

Marshal X is a leading Brazilian army man in his sixties. He has the reputation in military circles of being a 'philosopher' and 'intellectual', and he is sometimes pointed out as the spokesman of an influential group of army officers. Since the military *coup* in 1964, he has been the director of a state enterprise. We met in the bar of the Chamber of Commerce. He had prepared for the interview in advance, and had with him a little hand-written lecture on Brazil, its area, length of coast and land frontiers, its history, constitution and defence – all contracted into a military summary lasting ten minutes. He read from his script slowly and clearly, after which I was allowed to ask questions. Throughout the interview he preserved an unbending paternal calm, which only deepened as my questions became more uncomfortable.

'Does Brazil today have any outside enemies?'

'No, we are a peaceful people. We have no enemies.'

'So the risk of outside attack is minimal?'

'We can say it is practically non-existent.'

'Why then does Brazil need a strong defence?'

'To maintain order.'

'So the main task of the military is to maintain order?'

'Yes, up to 95 per cent.'

'And the police?'

'The police and the military collaborate on this. The military serves as a guarantee behind the police, and intervenes when it has to.'

'A guarantee of what?'

'Order.'

'Marshal, could you develop a little what you mean by order?'

'Morality. Our customs. Our institutions.'

'What morality exactly?'

'Discipline, I mean. Honesty and hard work. We intervene when our society is threatened by chaos and corruption.'

'You could describe Chinese morality in much the same words. As a matter of fact, I lived in China for a couple of years in the early Sixties. A more disciplined society would be difficult to find. What is the difference between you and them?'

'Communist China?'

'Yes.'

'But there is a fanaticism there that even the United States had to react against. That's why the United States is at war in Vietnam. To stop China. This is why we military men in Brazil made our revolution, to stop communism in our own country from undermining our institutions.'

'What institutions are you thinking of?'

'The democratic institutions.'

'I thought it was the army that had abolished the "democratic" institutions, overthrown the President, and dissolved the Congress and the parties.'

'These were temporary measures.'

'Do you not think that democracy will be undermined in the long term if there is always a latent threat of military intervention?'

'We intervene only in a crisis, after which we return the power of government to the civilians. This is the way things have always been. Only this time the power of government is being handed back a little more gradually.'

'Even so, I feel there is some contradiction in your argument. You see it as your job to defend the democratic institutions. But isn't one of these institutions that the popularly elected President shall be left to govern without fear of being overthrown by the country's own army? That all parties and individuals should be allowed freely to promote their political views, without the military deciding when they go too far?'

'That, of course, is true. But these liberties were abused before the revolution in a manner that threatened our entire society.'

'Are you sure that it was the *entire* society that was in danger, not just a certain class of society?'

'With the inflation and corruption we had then, I am perfectly sure of it.'

'Why is it the army that is called upon to save society when it is in danger?'

'Because we are the only people with the power to do it.'

'As an intellectual, Marshal, you can see the distinction between the power and the right. Are there any other groups of society – I am thinking, for instance, of university professors or trade-union leaders, perhaps even the peasants and workers – who would have the right to make a revolution, if they considered that the society was in danger?'

'I'm a trade-union leader myself.' (He pointed to a badge in his lapel. The trade union in the state enterprise he directs had made him honorary chairman.)

'I'm sorry to harp on this point, but are there other groups of the society which would have the *right* to make a revolution?'

'No. There aren't.' (He laughs paternally.) 'But the question is an academic one, since only we are *capable* of it.'

'And why should the right to revolt be a military privilege?'

'There is no other group in Brazil with the cohesion, the hierarchy, the authority that is needed.'

'And the Church?'

'The priests' business is the cure of souls. It's never a good thing when the priests start mixing in politics. In some places recently – and this I very much regret – certain dignitaries of the Church have failed to understand this, and gone beyond what is the province of the Church.'

'In the same way, you sometimes encounter the view that the business of the army is to defend the country, and that it is exceeding its duties in trying also to preserve a given social ethos. What I wonder is who ultimately determines the boundaries of the *true* function of different occupational groups in Brazil.'

'The constitution.'

'And the constitution assigns to the military the task of overthrowing the President, when it considers that order and morality are threatened?'

'No. Not directly. We can't say it does.' (Another paternal laugh.) 'But you should have seen the chaos that existed in this country, the crisis we were in ...'

'And the military is the only group that stands above the constitution, and decides for itself the limits of its authority?'

'No, we acted in the spirit of the constitution. Brazilian democracy was lapsing into communism. Civilian politicians were helpless against subversion. It was our duty to intervene in defence of our institutions.'

'Are these institutions always given, once and for all? Is it always the duty of the army to defend the *status quo*?'

'Absolutely not. The military government was a progressive government, which was concerned to carry the country forward.'

'As a touring reporter, Marshal, I naturally meet not only military people but people from all levels of society. I am struck by how very differently they picture the proper construction of your institutions, and the measures necessary to carry the country forward. How can the military be entirely sure that *their* particular view is the right one? How do you know that you represent the good of the entire people, and not just that of a particular social class?'

'We Brazilian military men do not imagine that we are alone in being right. People of all classes think as we do, and they welcomed our revolution. Nor are we only militarists. We have specialists in everything, just as the civilian sector does. You should visit our aviation resarch institute, our engineering academy, our centre of social technology. You must realize that in a country like this we military people are everywhere, and we are masters in all fields. The military is not only military – it embraces our entire society.'

2

Spending Christmas down by Tierra del Fuego, we landed in the middle of a conflict between Chile and Argentina. The continent is very narrow down there, so we could take our morning coffee with the Argentinian officers and our evening wine with the Chileans. Both parties adopted a decisive and foreboding attitude in the bars, while sharp notes were exchanged between the capitals. What was the conflict really about? No one had actually been there, since the disputed skerry in the Antarctic is continually washed by heavy seas which prevent anyone from landing. The crisis, however, further proved the necessity of a strong defence – on both sides of the frontier.

Bolivian officers still speak of their 'right to the sea', and refuse to recognize Chile's conquest of the Bolivian Pacific coast in 1879. According to the maps in Quito, Ecuador includes also the unpopulated Amazon jungles that the country was forced to cede to Peru in 1942. The old frontier dispute between Venezuela and British Guiana has sharpened since the latter country became independent, and relatively defenceless. The military often play up imaginary or real 'external threats' for all they are worth, but it is difficult to take them seriously. The age of territorial conquests in Latin America appears to be past.

The only country with potentially dangerous foreign political ambitions is Brazil. Its Academy of War functions as a super-university, graduation from which qualifies people also for the highest civilian jobs. It is no secret that this Academy is a breeding-place of grandiose national dreams. People point to the United States–Brazil–Japan as the great power axis of the future. Some see even further: Brazil, on the edge of the field of tension between the great powers, could be the only surviving nation with nuclear weapons, once the countries of the northern hemisphere have destroyed one another. A fact is that Brazil wants to buy reactors that can produce material for nuclear weapons, and has refused to sign the Geneva agreement against the spread of such weapons.

It may have been to avoid questions like this that my Brazilian Marshal so expressly emphasized the internal functions of the war machine. My experience, however, is that Latin American officers are not shy about discussing their repressive role. They have got used to seeing their continent as one great Peterloo, in which the army always has to be called in.

3

How does it work? How do they get the soldiers to obey, the population to accept them?

Tradition is important. Ever since the wars of liberation in the mid-nineteenth century, military commanders have dominated politics in the majority of Latin American countries. Civilian resistance is paralysed by the knowledge that things have always been this way. It is the military and its ambitions that represent continuity – not the civilian governments.

In Buenos Aires I talked to the Vice-Chief of Argentina's Federal Police about the problem of subversion. Were not military *coups* themselves a form of subversion? No, he could not agree. The military, after all, was one of the powers of state.

'Do you try to see a military *coup* coming in advance, and warn the government?'

'We sometimes find out what is in the offing, but we have neither the ability nor the duty to prevent it.'

'Not the duty? Is the military above the law?'

'Our job is civilian crime. We have no heavy arms.'

The police cannot defend the government against the army. Why then bother to warn the government? Governments come and go, the army remains. It would be suicide for the police as a body, and the Chief of Police as an individual, to try to protect a civilian government against the men with the heavy arms.

The power of the military, of course, is due also to the weakness of civilian government, to the whole decline of political life. Practical politics have given way to personal connections, a network of intrigues and corruption; political programmes have been replaced by popular heroes and demagogy. Before the military takes over, these Presidents have usually been so thoroughly compromised that no one will risk anything to save them.

Apart possibly from in Chile and Uruguay, there is no cohesive civilian resistance to a military *coup*. On the contrary, the ruling classes, barricaded behind conservative constitutions, regard the military as their natural protection against any threat from below. The military are often urged by civilians to instigate a *coup*, and allow themselves 'reluctantly' to be persuaded. Their 'unwillingness' to help strengthens their position.

4

What does a Latin American military régime involve? How does it differ from a civilian government?

The ex-President leaves the country. Or if he remains, like Dr Illía in Argentina, he has only to get his feet at the dinner table, to propose a toast, for the military police to storm in and break up the meeting. The Congressional Palace becomes the seat of the National Security Council, or is left empty.

Elections are no longer held, which on the whole means only that the football clubs will get no more shirts to play in, the domino players will get no dominoes, the small prizes of the political lottery will no longer be paid out.

Selected areas of the old régime's corruption are revealed, officers take over the big posts in the administration, often drawing double pay, and the network of personal connections and intrigues is agitated a little, until everything returns to normal with the beneficiaries much the same as before. The trade unions are taken over, their leaders are appointed from above. A 'tighter economic policy' is often introduced, the main measure being wage freezes. Foreign capital is generally offered more favourable terms. In every country I visited, the foreign businessmen, Swedes and North Americans happily united, expressed their warm approval of military *coups*.

In a few cases, the new government brings very real changes. Pernambuco, in north-eastern Brazil, enjoyed in the early Sixties a governor who did not automatically put the police at the disposal of landowners. 'They stopped beating the shit out of the peasants,' as an American AID official put it. The military régime soon restored order. The trial of José López, a mill-owner accused of having shot down five workers, was discontinued. And he was appointed instead the local chief of police. Gregorio Bezerra, seventy-four years old, who had tried to organize the land workers, was dragged bloody and beaten through the streets of Recife, a rope around his neck, to be mocked by the soldiers.

On the whole, however, the difference between civilian and military government is very slight, since they both represent very similar interests. And the civilians, even when they are formally in power, always have to pay the military every consideration. The officers enjoy the right of violent veto, which seems if anything stronger when they do not have to use it. Their weapons throw a constant shadow over politics. This largely explains the botched and betrayed reforms, the cowardice, the hesitation of the civilian leaders. Which in their turn open up the road for strong men and new *coups*.

5

What then is going to happen?

In the early Sixties, many believed that the political role of the military in Latin America would soon be played out. Three reasons were quoted.

1. The military are the tool of the old upper classes. Since the power of the latter is waning, the same should be true of the military, particularly as the officers are becoming increasingly middle-class.

This has proved false. The military is not the exclusive tool of the upper classes; the new stratum of society that has come into power seems if anything still more inclined to call for the troops. And the growing demands of the masses merely increase the need for such intervention.

2. Politically ambitious army officers, it was thought, are a relic from the days of the irregulars, when local bosses kept their own armies. With the increasing professionalization of

the services, they would become like any other groups of professional men.

But what does 'professionalization' mean today? The answer can be seen, for instance, in the officers' library in Buenos Aires. This was dominated between the wars by translations from the German about the Great War; in the early post-war years by North American analyses of the Second World War; and in the Sixties by the international literature on fighting 'the inner front' – defence against subversion, riot control, anti-guerrilla techniques.

This literature, with its new definitions of 'war', 'attack' and 'defence', has given a professional alibi to the traditional task of Latin American officers – namely to control the local population. There used to be a faint air of the ridiculous about armies that devoted themselves exclusively to fighting student demonstrators, workers on strike, rebellious peasants and other unarmed opponents; today this is internationally legitimate, and they can look upon themselves with new-found respect.

3. In the early Sixties, there were some too who believed that the downfall of military rule in Latin America was imminent because the democratic United States would oppose further military *coups*.

This was an uncommonly naïve view. After a brief show of diplomatic resistance, the United States has in practice powerfully supported the military *coups* in Bolivia, Brazil and Argentina and intervened with its own troops to prevent the overthrow of the military régime in Santo Domingo. In the Sixties, the United States has become increasingly dependent on the military in maintaining its dominance in the majority of Latin American countries.

Military 'co-operation' between the United States and Latin America gained momentum during the Second World War, and has since been steadily intensified. This has markedly improved above all the repressive capacity of the military. For any defence against invasion, on the other hand, the North American advisers would be an actual drawback, since they are potential spies for their colleagues on the *enemy*'s defence staff.

I visited numerous military staffs in Latin America. They are not always situated wall to wall with the U.S. Embassy, as they are in Santo Domingo; but they have always been teamed with United States officers. These arrive in full uniform, hang up their caps and drop down behind their desks perfectly at home. They are usually listed in telephone directories as part of the local country's defence apparatus. A good friend of mine in Brazil maintained emphatically that his own country was an exception; there, if anywhere, the staff was kept free from North Americans. The other day he wrote in a letter: 'Unfortunately, I did not realize what the situation was. I would like now to correct what I told you. They really are there.'

And not only there. At airports, even in remote areas, I have frequently seen U.S.A.F. troop-transport aircraft. I have talked with Venezuelan *guerrilleros* who have repeatedly exchanged fire with North American 'advisers'. The day Che Guevara fell we were staying in a hotel in Cochabamba, Bolivia. Some twenty U.S. officers suddenly arrived, with bodyguards. They were away the whole Monday, and returned in the evening, shouting and flushed with victory.

'Is it true that Che is dead?'

'Yes, this time it's final.'

'A great victory for the U.S.A.,' I suggested.

'You bet it is. But we don't want to appear in this, the Bolivian army needs this victory. They have to believe they did it on their own.'

6

As the nearest great power, most important trading partner, greatest source of loans and owner of the main export and other key industries, the United States is in charge in Latin America. This is both clear from the statistics and observable everywhere in practice. All that is lacking for Latin America to attain full colonial status is outright military occupation. And this is willingly provided in practice by the Latin American countries' own armies.

How long will they go on doing this?

Some Latin American Marxists hope that national humiliation will one day outweigh class loyalty and fear of the masses – so that the officers or at least the sergeants can be won to the cause of the revolution. Is this not the final self-renunciation, when even the revolutionaries hope that the army will do their job for them? They answer with Lenin: 'No mass revolution can prevail without support from at least part of the army of the old régime.'

It's difficult to judge. The very few radical officers I talked to, in Guatemala and Ecuador, had little hope to offer. They believed, as I do, that the Seventies will simply underline the present trend, which can be summed up like this: 'The pressure increases. – Revolutions are put down. – The military take over.'

The Reformers

1

'Reasonable demands can always be satisfied by peaceful reform.'

The validity of this statement can be investigated, for instance, at 22 Rua Vigerio Freri in Caruarú. This is the town burial office for paupers. Over fifty people a week enjoy here the benefit of free burial. Admittedly it is only a question of six months' residence in a grave half a yard deep. But on consecrated ground. And in their own coffins. This, in fact, is a great advance. Previous to the burial reform in Caruarú a few years ago the corpses of the poor were simply thrown out on the streets, as the woman manager of the office told me with a slight shiver. They were carted away like any other refuse.

The workers did not like dying in this way. In 1955, a burial society was created on the sugar plantation of Galileo, a few miles out of Caruarú. The object was that members and their relatives should be taken to the churchyard in their own coffins. The owner of the plantation was invited to become an honorary member.

Even this modest attempt at organization on the part of the workers worried the local landowners. The plantation owner declined the offer, and threatened to evict members. One of them, João Firmino da Silva, went to Recife to obtain legal assistance. He met Francisco Julião, who accepted the case.

Step by step, the fight to obtain decent burial drove the workers into a revolutionary struggle for the land they cultivated, for power in the society that suppressed them. The burial society in Galileo became the starting-point of the 'peasant leagues', a mass movement that spread with astonishing speed over the whole of north-eastern Brazil.

The fears of the landowners were thus confirmed. They sympathized, of course, with the desire of the workers to have coffins for themselves and their children. They were no monsters. They were not even entirely negative to the workers' quite understandable hunger for land; there were various conceivable ways in which such desires could be met. 'Reasonable demands can always be satisfied by peaceful reform.' But on no account must the workers be allowed to join forces and give some weight to their claims – this would mean revolution.

In March 1964, the military struck. The peasant leagues were dissolved, or went underground. Julião fled to Mexico. João Firmino was thrown into prison. (His family, which is sometimes allowed to visit him, says he is still alive.) The landowners were once more safe in the saddle, and the upper middle class in Recife could breathe a sigh of relief.

The revolution had been put down. The reforms could start. INRA, the institute for land reform, was created to still the workers' hunger for land. This institute entertains certain plans of perhaps dividing out land some time in the future. The burial office in Caruarú was created to still the workers' fear of a pauper's death.

When I was there, they had two coffins for adults and some twenty children's coffins in stock. These were nailed together from old packing-cases, covered with black cloth. Inside the coffins you could still read: THIS SIDE UP RECIFE BRAZIL. The greater part of the premises was devoted to stacks of cardboard boxes containing FOSFATO

FERROSO, a substance that was said to speed up the process of putrefaction.

I accompanied a worker who was taking his child, embedded in *fosfato ferroso*, to a pauper's burial in the Dom Bosco cemetery. He carried the little coffin on a delivery bicycle that he had borrowed from the office. There were only the two of us. Or the three of us, if you prefer.

I might have asked him how many of his children had died. And how they had been buried. And whether he appreciated the reform. I did not. We went in silence.

Arriving at the cemetery, we first passed the better-class district. He carried his child through the marble and cast-iron mausoleums of the old aristocratic families. Their tombs were in the form of grand houses, mansions the height of a man with a cross on the roof, or miniature modern luxury villas – the class society reflected into eternity. Next came the 70-dollar graves of the less well-off, and the 30-dollar graves of the small traders. Finally, we reached the poor district.

A dozen graves stood ready.

The free burial did not include a priest. There came only a few grave-diggers and collectors of wood. A job at the cemetery is to collect the wood that is found when the coffins are dug up again after six months. These relics lay in dark little piles around the graves.

The coffin was covered with earth, and we retraced our steps. The cycle had to be returned to the office.

Now at last a poor man can get his children buried at the community's expense, I reflected as we went back past the luxury villas and mansions of the cemetery. Is this not precisely what people mean when they claim that 'reasonable demands can always be satisfied by peaceful reform'?

2

The Alliance for Progress was created in August 1961. It was launched by John Kennedy in response to the Cuban revolution, and its intention is by peaceful reform to promote the economic and social development of Latin America.

The basis of the Alliance's programme is economic growth, which is to increase the general welfare and create the resources for other reforms. It assumes an increase in Gross National Product per inhabitant of at least 2·5 per cent a year.

What is it that increases G.N.P.? Not just that factories produce more goods, and agriculture greater harvests. Ruinous state borrowing abroad also raises G.N.P. A growing bureaucracy raises it. Slum growth in the big cities also raises G.N.P.; the slum inhabitants who have moved in from the country achieve a higher level of prices and wages. They don't live any better, they don't eat any better, but they put more money in circulation – and G.N.P. increases.

The criterion chosen by the Alliance as a measure of economic growth is thus suspect. It is uncertain whether an increase of 2·5 per cent a year really would have meant very much to Latin America. It is certain, on the other hand, that this result has not been achieved.

Table 6

LATIN AMERICA: ANNUAL PERCENTAGE
INCREASE IN G.N.P. PER CAPITA 1950–68

Period	Increase	Period	Increase
1950–55	2·2	1960–65	1·7
1955–60	1·8	1965–68	1·7

Source: ECLA, *Economic Survey of Latin America 1967, 1968.*

Even these depressing figures are probably somewhat exaggerated. Latin American statistics are often faulty, and the effects of many different sources of error are summated in the G.N.P. When travelling round, for instance, in Bolivia, one sees very little trace of the rapid, even growth suggested by the official statistics.

'I'll tell you how it works,' said a Bolivian ex-Minister of Planning, now an expert with the ECLA in Santiago. 'Our first serious attempts to calculate G.N.P. were in 1962. The President needed the figure for a speech he was to make on the anniversary of the revolution. As our starting-point, we had a twelve-year-old census and other figures of similar quality. We guessed and calculated and guessed again. Finally, our conclusion was that the increase might have been something around 3 per cent. Paz Estenssoro thought this sounded a bit excessive, so in his speech he said 2·7 per cent. Even today, the ECLA statistics state that G.N.P. *per capita* increased by 2·7 per cent in Bolivia that year. Figures are calculated in the same way under General Barrientos, only I suspect he adjusts them up instead of down.'

More advanced countries than Bolivia naturally have greater opportunities to furnish correct figures. Even there, however, the statistics contain generous doses of pure guess-work, which tends to raise the figures.

Also, the expression 'G.N.P. *per capita*' is rather misleading. It means, in fact, simply that a deduction has been made for population growth. But it easily gives the impression that G.N.P. is in some way evenly divided between the inhabitants of Latin America. This, of course, is not at all the case. There are relatively rich countries in Latin America, and relatively poor, there are expanding sectors, and stagnating regions – and above all different social classes. I would recall at this point that the distribution of income is as follows:

Table 7

LATIN AMERICA: PERCENTAGE DISTRIBUTION
OF PRIVATE INCOME 1965

Income group	*Share of income*
The poor: 20 per cent	3·5%
The middle class: 60 per cent	35·9%
The rich: 20 per cent	60·6%

Source: Table 1

Of course, the entire G.N.P. does not consist of private income. And an *increase* in income, in so far as it occurs, will probably be even more unevenly distributed than total income. But the Table does give a rough picture of who is being favoured.

It is the 'modern sector' in a few progressive regions that attracts foreign investments. It is within this sector that almost all economic growth is noted. And it is not aimed at the 80 per cent of the population who can hardly afford to buy the basic necessities. It is aimed at the rich, who alone answer for more than 60 per cent of the purchasing power.

I think I can summarize economic growth in Latin America during the first decade of the Alliance for Progress as follows. In so far as the figures are correct (which is uncertain) and in so far as they truly represent a rise in standard for the population (which is even more uncertain), this rise is both small and very unevenly distributed. We cannot expect economic development by itself to solve the social problems. For the majority of the population, it will not involve any marked improvement during the Seventies. For the poorest, development will probably mean a clear deterioration.

3

The programme of the Alliance for Progress includes also a number of specific reforms. The intention is to strengthen the democratic institutions; instead, the army has dismantled them in a number of countries. It is intended to build cheap housing; in fact, the housing deficit is rising by two million units a year. It is intended to stamp out illiteracy; it is here that the greatest effort has been made, but there are still 27 million Latin American children of school age who do not attend school. It is intended to improve wages and working conditions...

It is unnecessary to recapitulate all the failures that I have already described. Let me here simply consider the two most important of the Alliance's attempts at reform, those designed directly to affect the class structure: tax reform and land reform.

A thorough tax reform would raise the state's revenues, and thus its ability to steer development along paths more favourable to the community as a whole. A thorough land reform would reduce unemployment in the rural districts, and probably also increase agricultural production. Both measures would transfer power, including purchasing power, from the few to the broad masses, thus providing a broader foundation for economic development, a less biased structure.

But what has happened?

Some sort of tax reform has been introduced in practically all Latin American countries during the Sixties. The system has been simplified, and numerous small charges have been replaced by a single tax. In many places, P.A.Y.E. has been introduced so that it is no longer possible to let inflation 'pay' the taxes. Tax collection has become more efficient.

All this should have led to increased state revenues. But

there are also a number of factors acting in a contrary direction. Improved tax-collection has often been directed at such small earners that it is doubtful whether it has paid off. Naturally an intensified control of tax evasion by the big earners would have given a greater yield. This has not been done, since it is a politically very sensitive question.

To guide the economy along the paths desired, governments have not clamped down on unproductive investments such as land speculation by introducing tougher taxes, but have tried instead to coax forth productive investments by tax exemptions. The favourable effects have not yet been forthcoming – but the tax loss occurs immediately. Finally, taxes on foreign trade (customs duty and export charges) have been cut back sharply in most countries.

These negative factors have only just been offset by increased revenues from direct and above all indirect taxes. State revenues are still very low in relation to G.N.P.: 7–10 per cent in the majority of countries and 18–19 per cent in countries like Chile and Venezuela, where the revenues from big copper and oil companies are not taxes in the usual sense but a price for the sale of irreplaceable natural resources.

One's overall impression of tax reforms in Latin America during the Sixties is thus that the improvements have been only superficial; the state's resources are still inadequate, and the tax system remains on the whole unchanged, with its strongly regressive scale. The main burden is where it has always lain, on the small people in the community.[1]

And the land reform?

Radical anti-feudal land reforms were carried out in Mexico in the Twenties and Thirties, in Bolivia in the Fifties – in both cases as the result of popular revolutions. In Cuba, a socialist land reform was introduced following the revolution in 1959.

The 'land reforms' that have been taking place during the

1. ECLA: *Economic Survey of Latin America 1967*, 1:74; pp. 212 ff.

Sixties in almost all Latin American countries have produced very little result, on the other hand. Reforms have achieved most in Venezuela, where the landowning aristocracy has never been as strong as elsewhere in Latin America, and where agriculture answers for a relatively unimportant part of G.N.P. In the majority of other countries – Paraguay, Peru, Ecuador, Colombia, Guyana, Santo Domingo, etc. – the land-reform institutes work on terms decided largely by the landowners themselves. The legislation is full of loopholes, and the economic resources provided ridiculously inadequate. At the moment (1969), the situation seems most hopeful in Chile, where President Frei will probably succeed in achieving 20,000 of the 100,000 small-holdings he promised to create during his period of government. But in such dominant countries as Argentina and Brazil, nothing whatsoever has happened.

The discrepancy between real and apparent land reforms is clearest in Guatemala, which has had experience of both. In 1953–54, President Arbenz started a radical re-allotment of the land. The big estates, which in 1950 were 2·1 per cent of all farms in the country, had their share of the land cut from 72 to 56 per cent. In 18 months 600,000 hectares of land were distributed among 70,000 families, which tripled the middle stratum in the country districts.[2]

The land reform also hit the country's largest landowner, the United Fruit Company. The United States then mobilized the native reaction, Arbenz was overthrown, and the land was returned to the landowners. A succession of governments has since had 'land reforms' on their programme. Altogether, 172,000 hectares have been divided in the thirteen years 1954–67. At this rate, which is if anything slowing down, it

2. Nathan L. Whetten: *Guatemala – The Land and the People*, Yale University Press 1961, p. 93. José Luis Paredes Moreira: *Estudios sobre reforma agraria en Guatemala*, University of San Carlos 1964, *Cuadro* No. 1.

will take almost half a century to allot the same amount of land as Arbenz did in one and a half years.

The number of landless families, of course, is increasing much more quickly. And so governments have fallen for the temptation to cut up the land into very small pieces. Of the 24,000 peasants affected by current land reforms in Guatemala, not even half have been allowed to buy sufficient land to create in time a viable family farm. The others have only small allotments of less than one hectare. This artificially raises the number of beneficiaries, without really solving any problems.

And it is precisely 'beneficiaries' that the land reforms create. When the landless have formed organizations to deal with the problem for themselves – as in the Quillabamba valley in Peru, or in north-eastern Brazil – their initiative has been rapidly put down by specially trained troops. Any organized or political struggle to acquire land has proved far too powerful a lever. With disquieting rapidity, it gives the oppressed masses of the rural districts an awareness and sense of their own power. This the middle class does not like.

The land reforms of the middle class are designed not to exploit hunger for land as a source of energy, but simply to pacify the landless.

They must not claim their rights – but by the benevolence of the authorities the elect among them can be allowed to buy a piece of land on favourable terms.

When I asked peasants who had been favoured by the reform why they in particular had been given land, they hardly ever quoted their own efforts. They felt themselves rather to have won a dubious prize in a political lottery. And the submissiveness is still there – at every reform office I saw the peasants standing up cap in hand in front of the typists and petty clerks, waiting silently for the benefits that these representatives of the middle class had the power to distribute.

I do not believe that the stagnation of the countryside can

be overcome by such methods. The difference between land in parcels of 10,000 hectares and 10 hectares is in fact not all that great. Stagnant water at a height of 10,000 metres or 10 metres is almost the same thing. But the change between these two states can develop an enormous power. The whole purpose of the middle-class land reform is to *avoid* this generation of power.

4

Why have the reforms failed?

If we analyse the reasons, we come back time and again to the concentration of power in the ruling class, the determined defence by the wealthy of their privileges. But why has this not been overcome? How has Latin American society developed this power of resistance to change?

The comparison with North America lies close to hand. There, the first immigrants were in many cases religious and social rebels. Many of them intended to create a new, egalitarian society. In the long run, they failed. But in Latin America even the intention was lacking. The Spaniards and Portuguese brought with them the feudal ideology of their native countries. They did not come in order to work and cultivate the soil they occupied. They enslaved the Indians. And where this proved unsuccessful, they imported Negro slaves. Latin America became what the United States would have been if the Southern States had dominated also the North.

Typical immigrant countries like Argentina, Uruguay, southern Brazil and Costa Rica differ from the others. But the wave of immigration from Europe came too late. The immigrants were obliged to adapt to the class structure of the established society. Hundreds of thousands of Italian workers with dreams of land became farm hands and tenants also in the new country. Many remained in the big towns.

Many still feel themselves to be guest workers, with no self-evident rights. They and their children talk not of 'my country', but 'this country'.

Nationalism is strong in Latin America. But it has never created a national solidarity which would make it possible to set the welfare of a whole people above the privileges of the few. And between Indians and mestizos, Negroes and mulattoes, coloured and immigrants, there has never arisen a class loyalty that could force the wealthy to share their possessions.

It is difficult to force those in possession. It is even more difficult if they rule from across the sea.

The Latin American economy has been dominated by foreign interests since the sixteenth century. First the Indians were plundered by *conquistadores* and treasure-hunters from Europe. When the children of the *conquistadores* remained, they became in their turn subordinate to the needs of the Spanish and Portuguese colonial powers. Trade monopolies, industrial prohibitions and a one-sided export economy hindered development until the early nineteenth century. Nor did the military war of liberation break the colonial economic structure. First the United Kingdom, then the United States assumed the hegemony. The most important sectors of the Latin American economy are still in the hands of foreigners.

This has been of great importance for the class structure. If you want cheap raw materials, it is convenient to do business with a small ruling class. I have already mentioned Presidents Gómez (1910–35) and Jiménez (1948–58), who could sell Venezuela's oil for a pittance, since they were not obliged to share the proceeds with the people. As long as Leguía (1919–30) and Odría (1948–56) retained power in Peru, the Cerro Corporation and International Petroleum did brilliant business – for the same reason. As long as the Chilean aristocracy alone enjoyed the revenues from foreign companies, the copper mines were gold mines. Etc.

Etc. But as the entire people begins to claim title to their natural resources and want something from them, it becomes increasingly difficult to do business.

As a rule, the big foreign companies have therefore used their power – which is decisive in most Latin American countries – to support and preserve the oligarchy. It is these companies' iron grip on the continent's economy that permits the ruling class successfully to resist all change.

5

All this, it may be objected, is ancient history. It is true that oil is still, totally speaking, the absolutely dominant item among foreign investments in Latin America. But in most individual countries, investments in oil, mines and plantations have been overtaken by new investments in trade and industry. These firms do not produce for export. They sell their goods in Latin America, and need expanding markets. The present class structure is directly in conflict with their interests. They support the Alliance for Progress, which is the political expression of their desire to broaden their potential basis of customers. The class dominion will be overthrown by the very forces that created and maintained it. It will succumb without revolution, as a simple consequence of changes in the structure of investments.

An attractive theory. But it is based on parallels with development in the United States and Europe. And there are major differences between our own process of industrialization and that now taking place in Latin America.

Our industrialization took place within the framework of a fairly limited supply of goods and services. The first aim of technological progress was to increase the efficiency of production within this framework – which demanded broader markets. Only thereafter did it become the aim of technology to create new goods, and new needs corresponding to them.

The industrialization of Latin America is taking place a century later, when the range of supply is incomparably broader. To a large extent, it is taking the form of import substitution; that is to say that foreign companies concerned to sell their goods in a Latin American country are forced by high tariff-barriers to enter the country and construct plants. It is in this way that the structure of investments has altered. However, these foreign firms are not interested in manufacturing simple goods which correspond to the country's real level of development. They produce their normal industrial-country products. Every year, the modern sector in Latin America thus launches increasing numbers of the new goods created by research in the world's most advanced industrial centres. And 'Latin American' industry is expanding; only not by broadened markets, but by an increasingly diversified supply to the small stratum of society with incomes at industrial-country level.

I remember a *hacienda* in the Urubamba valley, in Peru. We saw the owner's white house shining up on the hill. The road to it led us through a stately park. The villa had a built-in flower garden, enormous rooms for entertainment, a heavy magnificence – in a framework of panorama windows, central heating and other modern conveniences. Our host showed us the family's art treasures. I remember particularly a marvellous painting of the adult Jesus sucking the breast of Mary. We studied earnestly a grand collection of Inca relics, and admired the clog-like stirrups left behind by Simón Bolívar, who had spent the night there during the war of liberation in the early nineteenth century. One felt, almost, transported back to that period. But then Aron, my three-year-old son, wanted a sandwich, and we trooped out into the kitchen.

A dishwasher. A washing-machine. A dryer. An electric stove with a programmed hot-plate and separate oven. Refrigerators and freezers the height of a man. A kitchen that might have been cut from the pages of *House Beautiful* or *Woman's Own*.

Our host explained that his daughter-in-law was used to the social life of Lima; if she was to be kept here in the wilds, then at least she deserved a decent kitchen.

This seemed only fair. But round about us, the land workers lived in huts made from earth. A few miles away, we saw peasants tilling the soil with sticks – they hadn't yet reached the age of the plough.

When we Swedes plied our picks in the earth, the upper class could hardly burden the country's economy with dish-washers and programmed hot-plates. These had not been invented. There were no cars, jet aircraft, or sky-scrapers – almost nothing of what today costs money was available when Sweden was as primitive as the Urubamba valley. But now it's there, the world over. It has become possible to spend the resources of a poor nation on creating these small islands of modern technified life for the few.

The foreign companies lead the way.

They naturally do not imagine that they can sell more refrigerators and washing-machines in Urubamba, if the revenues of the *hacienda* are divided among the people in the earthen huts. On the contrary, a more just distribution of income would mean the complete disappearance of the market for most complicated industrial goods.

It therefore seems fairly improbable that changes in the structure of investment will have any major effects on the class society of Latin America. Admittedly, the captains of industry dream of future mass-markets, but in practice they are more interested in maintaining the purchasing power of their present customers. At most they aim at a careful broadening of the ruling class, but not at a pace or on a scale that would bring the 'old' and 'new' investors into conflict. Their common interests predominate; all are concerned with a 'favourable investment climate', i.e. low wages, liberal regulations, cheap state credits, tax relief for the companies, and absolute safety from disruptions. In other words, a climate that conserves the class society.⌋

6

'Reasonable demands can always be satisfied by peaceful reform.'

I do not believe it. Experience of the Sixties and prospects for the Seventies alike refute such a proposition. Its falsity, one might say, is demonstrated by the whole history of Latin America.

The Alliance for Progress is not the first attempt to re-form Latin American society. Far from it. Reforms started at much the same time as the abuses. Both have the same roots.

The Spanish colonial empire has the reputation of being one of the worst-run in history. This, perhaps, is not entirely fair. Writers have ignored the fact that the Spanish Crown also made considerable efforts to improve conditions in its colonies.[3]

The discovery of America was followed by an intense in-tellectual debate. The question was whether the Indians should be regarded as people or animals. The Spanish Crown adopted from the very beginning an enlightened attitude: the Indians were subjects of the Crown, and thus people. They were not to be treated utterly without consideration. Spain sent out a stream of inspectors and supervisors to keep the abuse of power by the colonial aristocracy within reason-able limits. Spain passed a succession of laws designed to humanize conditions, mitigate the lot of the slave labourers, and return land to the Indians. In essential respects, the tax and land reforms initiated by the Spanish Crown were more

3. John Edwin Fagg: *Latin America, A General History*, New York 1963, pp. 94 ff., 207 ff.

far-reaching than those of the Sixties. And they were equally ineffective.

The United States today, like Spain yesterday, adopts what is in many ways an enlightened position by comparison with the ruling classes of Latin America. The United States works within the framework of the Alliance for a succession of important improvements – roads, schools, water, training, cheap housing, etc. It is the United States that is pressuring the current structural reforms – the tax and land reforms.

But the United States, like Spain, is ultimately dependent on those who are on the spot and have the local power. *For their own continued dominion,* both Spain and the United States have had to go on supporting the ruling classes of Latin America. The continent's colonial and semi-colonial status under these two powers has thus helped to maintain a class rule which nullifies reform.

And the United States, like Spain, is ultimately bound by its own economic interests. Neither Spain nor the United States has been concerned or able to carry through reforms which would reduce their profit from Latin America. This sets very narrow limits for possible change.

This political and economic dependence on the promoter of reform, Spain yesterday, today the United States, is thus the most important obstacle to meaningful reform in Latin America. Liberation from this dependence must not and cannot be simply a remote goal, glimpsed somewhere in the final phase of development. Such liberation is a necessary condition for progress.

The Revolution

Bolivia, October 1967

I saw Che Guevara in Vallegrande the night before he was buried. In the dusk, we walked up the steep, narrow cobbled streets towards Señor de Malta, the cottage hospital. The town is built of clay bricks with whitewashed walls, the only display window in the small shops is the door. There is electricity, but the cables are overgrown with lichen-like parasites, as if prehistory were crawling back even over this modern innovation.

The rumour of Che Guevara's death had brought the peasants in from the surrounding countryside. They came on horseback and by mule, in dark garments and black hats. They came on foot, and their women wore long black shawls. It was impossible to get any proper answer as to whether this was the natural habit of the district or whether they were in mourning.

What were they thinking of as they came in dense groups up towards the hill over the cottage hospital? 'The peasants are impenetrable as stones,' wrote Che Guevara in his diary.

A helicopter thunders in from the combat zone. All stop and peer up towards the long bundles lashed fast under the body of the helicopter.

'How many?'

'Two more!'

Then silence. Victory music and triumphal reports flow

from radio sets. But in the faces in Vallegrande I see only solemnity, sadness, almost loss.

The primitive mortuary has only three walls. Che Guevara lies on a military stretcher, his torso bare and his slim shoulders pushed forward. He seems tired out but happy, as if he were dreaming not of battle but of love.

The naked feet display not a scratch. The soft hands look as if they have never touched a tool or weapon. Seven heavy-calibre bullet-holes, of which one in the heart, have been spirited away; only faint bruises remain. The Bolivian army has granted its enemy a beautiful death.

Beside the head stands a soldier on guard. A sturdy peasant lad who stands there sweating, although dusk is falling and there is quite a nip in the air. And while the sweat runs from his own heavy, tanned face, he slowly, almost tenderly wipes the forehead of the dead man with a white handkerchief.

The face is easily recognized. Two months ago, it flared towards me from giant posters with the device 'Create two, three, many Vietnams'.

This was at the OLAS conference in Havana, where a representative body of revolutionaries from the whole of Latin America agreed that armed combat is the continent's only way out from poverty and oppression. The conference endorsed a third type of revolution, unlike both the Russian and Chinese; a Latin American revolution, with Cuba as its pattern, to be fought by the outlaws in the hills. They do not have to be workers. They do not have to be peasants. They do not even have to be communists. All that is demanded is that they should be willing to fight.

Such was the programme, born of a desperation that, at least, is easy to share. Delegates from more than twenty countries decided to follow the line of the guerrilla in Guatemala, in Colombia, and in Venezuela.

But it was Bolivia that was the centre of interest. Experienced experts on Latin America who followed the conference explained to me that in Bolivia this policy of the OLAS could be expected to give rapid, concrete results. It was a poor, easily inflamed country, which had already once – in 1952 – come close to achieving a radical revolution. The government, dominated by the military, lacked a political substratum. The guerrilla action was well prepared, the organization outstanding, the terrain favourable. And probably Che Guevara himself was there.

Che Guevara was there. And now he lay dead in Vallegrande, together with four of his men. Some forty others were dead, captured or had deserted. Only a dozen remained, and these were in flight.

We put up at the Hotel Teresita, where the beds were made of old car tyres. Down in the courtyard sat Colonel Joaquín Zenteno Anaya, Officer Commanding VIII Division, plying his fellow officers with whisky while waiting for his promotion to General. The Bolivian journalists were drinking beer. How had Che Guevara died?

He had been captured, badly wounded, at 1 p.m. on Sunday.

He died, according to a medical examination on Monday morning, from a bullet in the heart, causing instantaneous death. So he had been executed, not killed in battle.

With this, of course, the Colonel could not agree. We moved on to the disputed subject of Che's last words. According to one version, he had spoken of immortality – not that of the soul, but of the revolution. The Colonel claimed that he said: 'I am Che. I have failed.'

But why had he failed?

'Over half of Che's men were foreigners. None of them was from this district. It's the army that has the peasants on its side.'

Foreigners! A journalist remarked in passing:

'Here in Vallegrande tonight there is only one man who knows that we are all Latin Americans, And he is dead.'

But there was more than one. New bodies were still

arriving. I went with the driver in the jeep to pick up the prisoner called 'León', who was to identify the latest bodies. He came and sat in the back seat beside me, without a guard. Why should he escape now, when everything was over? Fourteen days ago they had been fighting together in the woods. Now he bent over their bodies, which looked as if they had been dug up from the soil. He said simply 'Willy', and – rather more hesitantly, as half the head was blown away – 'El Chino'.

'*Perfecto*,' said the officer. '*Vamos!*'

A Bolivian miner and a Peruvian Chinese, who lay on the planks behind the mortuary with their heads thrown back in the ultimate helplessness of death. Together with three Cubans and another Bolivian. Six Latin Americans. In death, they all looked remarkably alike.

In the light of the officer's torch, I saw Che Guevara for the last time. The following morning they had all been taken away and buried.

'In a secret place, without ceremony, at 04.00 hours,' said Colonel Joaquín Zenteno Anaya.

2

Why did Che Guevara fail?

The answer is to be sought in Bolivia's tin-mines. The workers there constitute the most important power factor in the country, after the army. They comprise 1 per cent of the population, but answer for 80 per cent of the country's exports. They are politically conscious, determined, and well organized.

It was the miners who marched into La Paz with dynamite in their pockets and created the 1952 revolution, one of the three genuine revolutions to occur in Latin America during the twentieth century. The three largest mining companies were then nationalized, the land of the *haciendas* was parcelled out to the peasants, and the army was reduced to reasonable proportions, many of its functions being taken over by a workers' and peasants' militia armed with rifles and sub-machine guns.

In November 1964, General Barrientos overthrew the lawful President. The army now took its revenge. One of its first measures was to disarm the miners, an action that cost many human lives. In Siglo XX, South America's largest tin-mine, 7,700 workers were dismissed, and 4,900 reinstated. Wages were cut by 38 per cent. This created an explosive situation, which Che Guevara is known to have counted on.

But 1967 was not 1952. It was no longer possible to complete a revolution in three days, with a pocketful of dynamite. There existed by now specially trained rangers, instructed by American officers with experience from Vietnam, who could deal with situations like this.

In June 1967, the army took command of the mines. According to official reports, this cost seven dead and twenty-four injured among the civilian population; if you ask the priests and consult the cemetery, the figure was twenty dead and some sixty wounded in Siglo XX alone.

Today, the mines are still in a state of siege. The transport police, the company police, and the secret police (the DIC) watch over every movement. The army has put an iron ring around the entire district, and no one can get in or out without special permission.

The trade unions are crushed, their leaders in prison or exile, their premises transformed into cinemas. In Siglo XX they were showing 'Double Love'.

The soldiers walk the streets of Huanuni with sub-machine guns under their arms, and an armed detail is always kept on stand-by at the entrance to the mine. And in Siglo XX, Colonel Villapando is the real man in charge.

'We were forced to move in,' he says. 'There was a radio station here in the mine, the "*Voz del minero*", which openly demanded revolution. The unions were collecting clothes and money for the guerrilla, which had succeeded in recruiting about a hundred workers. There was a training-centre with arms and "uniforms", and on Sundays they practised firing in an abandoned gallery inside the mountain.'

I asked Colonel Villapando, who seemed a gifted and humane officer, what real difference there was between overthrowing the legal government if you were a general, or if you were a worker. The answer was enlightening in its ambiguity: 'What the army does is the will of the people.'

He explained that the presence of the troops in the mines would probably be permanent. 'Most people are satisfied with the security and order that now prevail.'

But in the darkness of the mines, the impression was quite different. I have never felt so unsure of myself as when I walked round inside the San José together with the security officer, Colonel Montenegro, who was installed by the military régime in 1965. The workers stood round us with bitter, contemptuous, turned-away faces, and I asked him if he was not afraid they might throw themselves over us.

'I'm not a Colonel in the Salvation Army,' he answered.

In Huanuni and Siglo XX, I was accompanied instead by a Bolivian journalist whom the workers knew. They flocked around us, describing with supreme bitterness the heavy, dangerous work they performed for a dollar a day. They showed us the flasks of tea and pieces of bread they had with them in the mines, and the coca leaves they all chew while at work to forget the cold and fatigue. And they openly expressed their sympathy for Che Guevara.

We saw their homes, most of them dilapidated dwellings of mud brick, in which the beds occupied the whole floorspace. Ten people are crowded into two rooms, twelve into three. We talked with teachers who told us that the workers beat their children if they are unsuccessful at school. 'They only have one aim in life, to get their children out of here.'

And yet the miners are a sort of aristocracy in Bolivia. Three dollars a day is a not unusual wage for a skilful team boss, and there are miners who earn 200 dollars a month – which is a lot of money at Bolivian prices. Only it does not last long. The first degree of silicosis occurs as a rule after three years, and only in exceptional cases can a man go on working in the mines for more than ten years.

The real proletariat are the 'independents', who have permission to operate on the company's ground, but who enjoy neither wages nor social benefits. Six hundred women, mainly the widows of dead workers, pick ore in the giant piles of stones spewed out by Siglo XX. Four thousand eight hundred men – more than the regular strength – wash and dig away on the side of the mountain. They let themselves down into wells that can be over 30 metres deep, they crawl along seams that can penetrate 250 metres into the rock and are so narrow that a man can't turn round. Naturally there are no safety arrangements whatsoever, and the ore is hacked by hand with the most primitive of methods.

At six in the morning, when I was out scraping the ice off my windscreen, they had already started; when I returned at dusk, they were still at it.

And what is the alternative?

Many say that with the present world market prices for tin, which are set by England and the United States, the only answer is gradually to close down the Bolivian mines. COMIBOL, the state mining company, was expected to make a loss of two million dollars in 1967. A further 3,000 workers will have to be laid off in the immediate future. The optimistic say that Bolivia's future lies in the tropical jungles east of Santa Cruz. Here those who are fired will be moved to work as oil prospectors or land workers.

But in Santa Cruz they tell a different story. Bolivian Gulf's representatives there explain that petroleum is an industry which requires a minimum of labour. Gulf, which produces 75 per cent of Bolivia's oil, has only 650 employees, none of them ex-miners.

Which leaves agriculture. We visited Puerto Fernando, sixty miles outside Santa Cruz, a colony of Indians migrating from the highlands. Among 1,500 families we found only a couple of miners. There had been more, the colony's technician explained, but they were dead now.

'The miners can't stand it here. They have got silicosis and tuberculosis. They can't survive the jungle climate.'

In this trap, Bolivia's 40,000 miners are caught. They created a revolution, and nationalized the mines. But they could not nationalize the world market price of tin, which is set with no thought of reasonable living conditions for the men who produce it. They could not nationalize the world distribution of capital, which is made regardless of the needs of humanity.

3

The road to Camiri is more interesting than the trial of Régis Debray.

The trial was a staged spectacle. A spectacle for the ladies of Camiri, who with gently-fluttering fans spread a heavy fragrance of perfume over the courtroom as they tried to attract a glance from the romantic revolutionary. A spectacle for the world press, which could see day by day Bolivian justice at work on the Frenchman and his five fellow-accused – while ten times as many Bolivian union leaders sat forgotten in the prison in La Paz, most of them neither tried nor sentenced. Debray himself told me as I stood outside his cell door in the Casino Militar that the charge brought against him was in a way correct, 'although not as formulated'.

I asked what he thought of the evidence produced.

'So far there have only been two false witnesses. It is fewer than one might expect. Naturally it is true that I carried arms, and did sentry duty.'

'How do you think the case will go?'

'It doesn't interest me any longer. At first I was fighting to be freed, since I hoped to be able to do something for this cause. Now that Che Guevara is dead, I know it is impossible. What does it matter whether I get 20 or 30 years?' (He got 30 years imprisonment, but was released Christmas 1970.)

'If you had stayed, you would probably be dead now. Why did you leave the guerrilla?'

'I fell ill. Che didn't think I was suitable. And there is a guerrilla without arms. He sent me on a journalistic commission, he thought I could do more good that way. It proved to be a mistake, one of the many mistakes that were committed.'

Many mistakes? I thought I knew something about these mistakes having driven along the road to Camiri.

It starts in Sucre, Bolivia's legal capital, which stands white and decorative in a mountain landscape populated almost entirely by Indians. The latter are clad in felt helmets fringed with pearls, and look like medieval soldiers. Spanish is practically unknown. The peasant farms lie in groups in villages, closed and distinctive collectives which live for their market days and *chicha* feasts. This part of Bolivia is steeped in tradition, and extremely inaccessible to any outside revolutionary. Otherwise the landscape is so bare and barren that a fly could be picked out and shot from an aircraft.

After Padilla, the road passes over the eastern Cordillera, plunging suddenly 3,000 metres straight down into dense impenetrable tropical jungle. Here it is easy to avoid discovery, but almost impossible to get about. The landscape is broken up and traversed by ravines like no other place I have seen, not even in southern China. Nowhere can you find fifty yards of flat ground, it is all overgrown slopes and chasms.

And the peasants around the guerrilla camp in Nanchahuazú? They are mestizos related on the Indian side to the

Guarani in Paraguay – a different people from the highland Indians. They are people who have left the community, pioneers on small isolated farms, incurable individualists, new settlers who practise a primitive form of burnt earth farming. They rarely see another human being, pay no taxes and have as much land as they can preserve from the jungle. In a word, the last people in the world to join the guerrilla.

There are a couple of small communities: Muyupampa, where Debray was captured, and Monteagudo, where the guerrilla went sometimes for supplies. It would not have occurred to anyone to report them, as long as they paid twice and ten times the price for foodstuffs; on the other hand, they seem to have excited no more than economic sympathy. There is only one road, a road for jeeps and trucks with difficult fords and deep loose sand in which 90 miles is a good day's journey. Finally it arrives at Camiri, which consists simply of a few buildings around an oil refinery.

When we arrived, the army showed a pronounced interest in my beard, and in the contents of this car that had managed, in some miraculous manner, to find its way from Sucre to Camiri, straight through the guerrilla zone. They had us spread our entire luggage for inspection in the courtyard behind the Casino Militar.

While I stood there trying to explain to the soldiers how one uses a packet of cellulose diaper wadding, Debray came walking over the sandy square with his guards. He seemed unbroken, lively and accessible. A few hours later, I stood outside his cell door with an officer who carried the H.Q. tape-recorder. Why had Che Guevara failed?

He leaned forward to answer. His pale, sensitive face, which falls so easily into a contemptuous pose, was just visible behind the wire netting in the door. Dusk fell, and there was a smell of crushed cockroaches, as everywhere in hot, damp Camiri.

'That's a difficult question, and one that cannot yet be answered. Certain groups had promised to take part, but they failed to keep their promises. They were found to be disloyal.'

'What groups?'

'No details for the tape-recorder. But I am naturally thinking of those whose primary duty it was to create a revolution in Bolivia, the communist parties.'

But had not Debray himself written that one can never rely on the participation of the communist parties? One of the main theses of his book *Revolution in the Revolution* is that the guerrilla must take matters into its own hands, and not wait for the leftist parties. So it was somewhat illogical to blame the defeat on precisely these parties.

In accordance with Debray's thesis that the political parties should be ignored, the guerrilla in Bolivia had failed even to inform its supporters of what was to take place. The leaders of the POR, the smallest but most militant of the Bolivian left-wing parties, told me that they read of the guerrilla action in the newspapers.

And yet the guerrilla had enjoyed support in the town. When I arrived in Bolivia at the end of September 1963, the oil workers were on strike. Student riots were taking place throughout the country, and in Oruro a student was killed when the army dispersed the demonstrations; that same afternoon, the students counter-attacked with sticks and stones. In the evening, primary-school teachers who were striking held a meeting in La Paz; the police broke it up with dogs and tear-gas. All this was presented by the government, not without reason, as action in support of the guerrilla.

No, the reasons for failure had to be sought elsewhere, mainly in the guerrilla zone itself. I said to Debray that I had driven through it by car, and told him something of my impressions.

'Yes,' he said, 'the area was badly chosen. It is too sparsely populated, the terrain is enormously difficult, the climate almost unbearable. When the guerrilla fell victim to the army, it was already exhausted by hunger and disease.'

'What was your relationship like with the peasants?'

'Never very much. There were too few people, quite simply. The first contacts were cautious. Not hostile, nor the opposite, just cautious. This is only natural. Che had expected it. He knew, of course, that the peasants had their land here, that it's not like Peru, for instance. The peasants are satisfied. He knew this.'

'And why was this particular area chosen, in spite of everything?'

'It was largely an accident. And, of course, this area is very tempting for a strategist. Che Guevara was a strategist.'

There our conversation ended. But I thought I had been given some sort of answer. 'Che Guevara was a strategist.' That was his downfall.

Local revolutions are no longer possible. They are drawn at once into the international field of tension, and engage the interest of the great powers. Che Guevara had realized this, and was concerned to make a revolution that aimed at such a target from the very beginning.

Even if a local revolution should succeed, as the Bolivian miners succeeded in 1952, it is doomed to ebb out into nothing, since independence is an impossibility for small nations in the world today. This applies particularly to a country like Bolivia, which is completely dependent on the world market price for tin. A local revolution may perhaps overthrow the government in La Paz, but not the centres of power that determine the terms of life and death in poor countries like Bolivia.

I therefore do not believe that Che Guevara expected for a moment that the revolution would 'succeed'. If he had wanted to create the second socialist state in Latin America he would never have chosen Bolivia. Soviet ships can provide

Cuba with everything the American blockade shuts out. But Bolivia has no coast. A determined trade-blockade could choke the country in the space of a few weeks. What would Che Guevara have done with a successful revolution on his hands?

Che Guevara entertained no hope of creating a socialist Bolivia. He was concerned to create 'two, three, many Vietnams'. And for this purpose Bolivia, situated as it is in the heart of the continent, is extremely suitable.

But the Vietnamese leaders who led their peoples against the French, the Japanese and the Americans, were concerned to create a 'Vietnam' in an entirely different sense. They had tyrants to overthrow, a country to liberate. It was entirely against their will that their revolution became international.

Che Guevara, on the other hand, was concerned to use the guerrilla war as a strategic weapon, his aims being not local but continental and intercontinental. He wanted to exploit the opportunity created by Vietnam. At the same time, he wanted to help the Vietnamese in the only way that could prove truly effective – by opening a second front.

But even a strategic revolutionary is bound, if he chooses guerrilla warfare as his weapon, to put his life in the hands of the peasants. The last entry in Che's diary describes how he offers a peasant woman money not to betray him and his friends. 'Little hope that she will keep her promises,' he adds.

He tried to buy a collaboration that he had not prepared, not won. And how could he win such collaboration in this place? He could not parcel out land; the peasants already had it. He could not nationalize the mines; this had already been done, without result. He knew that he had nothing to offer the people to whom he turned – at least not this side of a major war.

This, of course, he could not say to the peasants between Vallegrande and Camiri. He had to say something else. And he recorded in his diary that in the depths of their eyes they disbelieved him.

This is why he failed.[1]

4

The forecasts I have made in this book are based on the assumption that Latin America will preserve its present political and economic system for another ten years. Is this reasonable? Will there not be a revolution?

Throughout the Sixties, Latin America has been described as being 'on the brink of revolution'. It is easy to see how this idea has emerged. Revolution would seem to be the logical way out of the blind alley the continent has entered. 'You can't keep a whole people down for ever,' an honest Swedish foreman told me in Brazil. Perhaps not for ever. But it has worked for 400 years, and the ruling classes reckon it will work for a while yet.

They are probably quite right. The Sixties has been a decade of reaction. The revolutionary forces have suffered a succession of severe defeats. Seats of revolt like Tequendama and Marquetalia in Colombia and the tin-mines in Bolivia have been neutralized. The main line of revolutionary thought which considered that an armed struggle should be developed from a political mass movement has suffered defeat with Francisco Julião in Brazil and Hugo Blanco in Peru. The other main line of thought, which wants to start with armed resistance and develop a mass political movement from it, has suffered defeat with Héctor Béjar in Peru and Che Guevara in Bolivia. Not a single major success has been noted. I asked Hugo Blanco on the prison island of El Frontón why he had failed.

'We had a mass movement. It was dominated entirely by

1. The above analysis is based on the information available in Bolivia, October 1967.

the peasants – only two of its leaders were intellectuals. It had strong popular support, even in the lower middle class. What we lacked was a revolutionary party. There was no one to channel the sea of sympathy that surrounded us. Then the military struck.'

I put the same question to Héctor Béjar at the prison of the Prefecture in Lima.

'We lost because we were outsiders, and without military experience. The army is well trained. It has more of a peasant background than we do, who are mostly students and intellectuals. It was difficult for us to gain trust, to be accepted.'

'Does this mean that the peasants must create their own revolution?'

'No, this is impossible, they are kept too much under. Nor will the workers lead them. There's a dangerous gap between the workers and peasants; the workers are second-generation emigrants to the town. They have no interest in the problems of the rural districts. This leaves the students and intellectuals as the organizers of revolt. And we – to the peasants we are *gringos*, white gentlemen from the city.'

Béjar's and Blanco's answers bring us to some of the main problems of Latin American revolution.

1. If you start, like Hugo Blanco, by organizing a mass movement, then there will be a very vulnerable period before the transition to armed resistance – a period in which the movement is at once menacing and defenceless.

If you start, like Héctor Béjar, directly with armed resistance in the hope that it will collect a mass movement, then the fight is purely military right from the start – and the army has the better training and weapons.

Everyone agrees that the solution lies in a combination of these two strategies. Only how? How can the secrecy necessary in any attempt at armed revolt be combined with the building-up of a mass organization? Each little group has its own opinion.

2. Fragmentation. Brazil has five different parties that call themselves the National Communist Party. Colombia has three active guerrilla movements, with no internal co-ordination. In Peru I established contact with a dozen different organizations that said they were preparing armed resistance. Almost every country has the entire standard assortment: Moscow communists, Maoists, Trotskyists and Castroists. Many countries also have national variations on these themes, like the '*febreristas*' in Paraguay. Then there are revolutionary breakaway groups from the middle-class parties, like the revolutionary Peronists in Argentina. Plus a whole flora of combinations like the '*Vanguardia Revolucionaria*' in Peru. And a succession of attempted coalitions and fronts, frequently under the title 'Unity of the Left'.

Some consider that this fragmentation is a good thing, since it has liberated revolutionary initiative that would otherwise have been smothered in a uniform organization. Others take it as further confirmation of the Latin American left's traditional incapacity for unity and action.

3. The differences between town and country. Most of these groups are composed of town people. They have one thing in common, namely a belief that any mass revolt in the cities is doomed to fail, since the military will have it clearly located. The revolution must thus take place in the country. There, however, the town dweller is a 'gringo', a 'señor', almost a foreigner. Differences in race and language further emphasize his status as an outsider.

Also, the proportion of the population living in rural districts is declining year by year. When Mao's peasant armies took power in China in 1949, the rural areas represented 90 per cent of all Chinese. It was on this basis that they reversed the classical Marxist doctrine of the industrial workers as the *avant-garde* of the revolution. Can Mao's method ever lead to success in countries where the rural population is a backward *minority*? This question has not been sufficiently discussed by Latin American revolutionaries.[2]

5

'Up until 1955, we had established "guerrilla fronts",' the Venezuelan guerrilla leader Francisco Prada told me. 'This meant that our units moved within certain delimited areas' (above all in the provinces of Falcón and Lara). 'The enemy, however, got to know these areas almost as well as we did. They had practically an X-ray picture of the social structure, and knew exactly where to strike. We have therefore gone over to "group tactics". Small units are continually on the march within very wide areas. We never stop long enough for it to be worth while trying to win over the peasants by hospitals or irrigation. The government troops, which no longer know our base, have gone over to mass repression. Hundreds of peasants have now been tortured, mutilated and executed.'

While revolutionary techniques are based mainly on the examples of China and Cuba, the techniques of repression have quickly drawn on American experience in Vietnam. In practically all countries, the previous musical-comedy armies of Latin America now have special anti-guerrilla units, deeply feared for their merciless efficiency.

They are trained at the U.S. anti-guerrilla school in Panama, or at one of its 'branches' – we visited one of these in Colombia, which took trainees from five other Latin American countries. The physical results were impressive. We saw the final test, in which a patrol that had spent a week in the jungle was forced to throw itself fifteen yards down

2. The activities of the urban guerrilla have intensified since 1969 in a number of Latin American countries.

into a fast-running river, and swim ashore. Their ideological education was provided by a chaplain who preached on such subjects as 'The duty of the Christian to his country' and 'Jesus as Supreme Commander' (I quote from the training schedule). During tests, the soldiers unceasingly moaned words like 'God', 'War' and 'Courage'.

The officers are kept up to date on guerrilla tactics by fresh, detailed, richly-illustrated reports on the more important engagements. These are often based on diaries. 'In the guerrilla, almost every corpse has a diary hidden in his uniform,' the officers told me. 'They think they are making history, they are part of an adventure they want to remember. These diaries are our best source of information.'

Strategy is based on a North American model, the gist of which is to co-ordinate civilian and military measures in any area where the guerrilla stay long enough to make an impression on the local population.

A quick sociological study is made to chart the local community, with particular attention to shortcomings and complaints that could be exploited by the guerrilla and suspect persons who might be willing to join it. This is the 'X-ray' that Prada mentioned. All state bodies (often including the Church) are then co-ordinated under the military command for an intensive local campaign – schools, roads, hospitals and wells, to convince the local population that the government has the resources, while the guerrilla can so far only make promises. At the same time, the military deploys its toughest troops to track down and eliminate the guerrilla, who will have been isolated by the civilian campaign from their underlying basis of population.

<u>That is how the model looks</u>. How does it function in practice?

In Guatemala there operate two guerrilla movements, which are now co-ordinated. In the mid-Sixties they comprised several hundred men and had the military initiative within their sphere of operations. The asphalted arterial roads between the town of Zacapa and the banana port of Puerto Barrios could be used by the military only in strong units. In 1966–67 the army started a counter-offensive, planned by the United States. Its civilian part was called 'Plan Piloto'. I saw it in action together with Major Fred Warnes of the ever-present American military mission and some Guatemalan officers.

We travelled into the little, white, hot town of Zapaca. Machine-guns at the street corners, patrolling military jeeps. The local radio station sends out U.S.-manufactured anti-communist propaganda from 6 in the morning to 10 at night. A ghostly voice was in the middle of a description which concluded : 'This inferno has a name – C-U-B-A.' The music then became light and caressing, while mild seductive voices spoke of 'your own home', 'your own little piece of land', which the state had taken from the Cubans. The programme concluded with a hymn of praise to 'private property – the precious foundation of our human personality'.

'Doesn't that make you want to cry?' said Major Warnes appreciatively.

'The point,' I said, 'seems to be that Castro took away the house and land of the Cuban small farmer. Do you actually believe that?'

'How do you mean?'

'Do you believe that is what Castro did?'

'What difference does it make? True or not, what does it matter?'

We went on to see an irrigation project, which was to cover 4,500 hectares.

'Who owns the land?'

'The poor people here in Zacapa.'

'According to the latest census, ten per cent of landowners own ninety per cent of the land here in this department. Won't it be they who mostly benefit?'

A colonel now started to reckon up big estates that owned land in the area to be irrigated. He thought that about two thirds of the land was in big units.

'In that case, shouldn't you combine the irrigation project with an action by the Institute of Land Reform to get a greater political effect?'

The ethical side of the matter suddenly became relevant to Major Warnes:

'It would be *wrong* to take the land from its owners,' he decided.

We were also going to see the new road built under 'Plan Piloto' to Jones, previously a base of the guerrilla up in the hills. We travelled for a couple of hundred yards along an excellent newly-laid gravel road. A captain suggested that we should leave it at this. When I insisted on continuing, it emerged that neither the captain nor the major, who had been working on 'Plan Piloto' for more than two years, had ever been to Jones. They had often shown people the road, but it was customary to stop at this point.

'You see, it used to be very dangerous up here. People turned their backs on us, we met a wall of silence. Now look how friendly they are!'

This I did not notice. After a further few hundred yards the new road came to an end, and we jeeped our way over logs and stones, one wheel at a time. After more than one hour's driving in the terrain we reached Jones. The peasants complained that they did not dare work on their outlying fields in the forest. They had not, however, seen the guerrilla. It was impossible to decide whose side they were on. We hurriedly returned to town, Major Warnes with his hand on the revolver in his back pocket.

I cannot say I was impressed by the assistance offered to the civilian population by the military. Guatemala's contribution to the development of repressive techniques consists rather of engaging civilians for purely military duties. The officers do not rely on their own soldiers, and employ private bodyguards; landowners and factory owners keep their own 'armies'. 'Plan Piloto' has been accompanied by an unusually merciless campaign of terror on the part of right-wing extremists armed and protected by the military. I asked Major Warnes what these *'confidenciales'* had meant to the operation, and he acknowledged that they were a decisive factor.

'But if you ask me about their political attitude, I will have to refuse to answer,' he added.

These groups are the major point in the reactionary M.N.L. party programme of August 1967, which states: 'See to it that the secret groups working under official control or in semi-official form become better organized, increase in number and quality, and act on a larger scale and with greater exactitude.' [3]

There are dozens of such organizations. The best known is MANO – the Movimiento Acción Nacionalista Organizado. Some idea of their activities can be obtained by questioning Jaime Monge Donis, Secretary-General of Guatemala's leading trade-union movement. A study submitted to the U.N. Commission for Human Rights lists 4,000 persons killed in the space of two years, he says. 3,000 of these were peasants. [4]

'In Zacapa we had only one union, the bakery workers. This was dissolved in November 1967 under the threat of death.'

'Do you know anyone I could talk to there?'

'No ...' (hesitates, searching his memory). 'I have had many friends in Zacapa. They are all dead.'

He has just received his twenty-third threatening letter. He always goes armed, of course. He is most afraid for his wife and children. The police 'protect' his house, but no one knows whose side they will be on when something happens.

'Have you been to Cuba?' he wonders. 'Yes, I know, there

3. *Primera conferencia de solidaridad de los pueblos de América Latina*, Guatemala City 1967.
4. cf. Henry Giniger in the *New York Times*, 16 June 1968.

are things there one does not like, but compared with the desperate situation we live in . . .'

6

Vague preparations for guerrilla warfare are being made in almost every country. Defeated guerrilla movements are having difficulty in reorganizing themselves in Peru and Bolivia (Beni). An urban guerrilla has begun to operate in Uruguay and Brazil. Fighting guerrilla movements exist in three countries: Guatemala, Venezuela and Colombia.

In none of these countries does the guerrilla comprise more than a couple of hundred men. It is growing very slowly or not at all – the loss in dead and deserted roughly keeps pace with recruitment. Its leaders are middle-class intellectuals or military men. The guerrilla consists almost exclusively of white men and mestizos – the Indian population remains entirely unaffected. The only exception is the FARC in Colombia, which has a more popular leadership and recruitment.

The guerrilla started in Guatemala in 1961, in Venezuela in 1962 and in Colombia (in its present form) in 1964. During 1967 and 1968 it has been very hard pressed by the military. The pressure of government troops is forcing it to operate in very small groups and with an extreme mobility that complicates contacts with the population.

This, roughly, is what we know with some certainty about the Latin American guerrilla. Visits by journalists have been impossible for several years. I did have an agreement with Francisco Prada to meet him in the jungles of Venezuela in the spring of 1968, but the contacts we had agreed on failed to function. I learned a few months later from FALN of Cuba that their contact with Venezuela was broken at about the same time, probably because the guerrilla there were very much under pressure.

Che Guevara notes in his diary with a smile the tales told in the press about the size of the guerrilla; the proclamations of a small troop of hunted men had succeeded in portraying them as a victorious popular army. When the struggle has been continuing for many years, as in Venezuela or Guatemala, it is naturally more difficult to maintain this sort of illusion. But the motive for exaggeration is still there. Nor are the military and civilian authorities any more reliable. They play up their own victories, and underestimate the real strength of the guerrilla.

If only it were this simple, the truth could perhaps be sought somewhere between the figures quoted by both sides.

Unfortunately, the picture is complicated by the fact that service in the guerrilla areas is counted as front-line service and carries higher pay, twice the seniority in years of service, and other benefits. The military therefore have a clear financial interest in keeping the threat of the guerrilla alive.

While we were in Colombia there was only one engagement between the military and the guerrilla. This was in an area of the '*llanos*', which has long been considered peaceful. According to the first communiqué a military patrol had been fired upon and had killed a guerrilla soldier in self-defence. In Bogotá they laughed, and said that 'attacks' of this kind were customary when the state of emergency was about to expire – the military had now ensured its benefits for at least another year.

The following day, a fresh communiqué gave a different version of the event. The military had now neutralized an individual who was a danger to the community by a broadly-conceived operation against his stronghold. No explanation was given of the discrepancy between the two communiqués. Photographs of the 'stronghold' showed a modest farm-house, badly shot up. A wise government does not look too closely at such pictures. It is willing enough to pay the front-line bonus to keep its officers busy, and dispersed at small outposts far from the capital. It makes for a quieter life.

The guerrilla can also be used to motivate a number of practical acts and measures which facilitate government. It is an open secret that political opponents are arrested, dressed in rags, freighted up to the hills and shot. In this way you not only note a new brilliant 'victory' over the guerrilla, but also silence difficult opponents.

In Venezuela we tried on two occasions to check press reports of such 'victories' by appearing on the scene without warning. The officers had strict orders not to talk to the press. They refused even to confirm the communiqué put out by the Ministry of War. Naturally it was unthinkable that we should be allowed to inspect any corpses or prisoners, or talk to any soldiers who had taken part in the 'fighting'. The local population had plenty of rumours to offer but no concrete information, since the 'fighting' had taken place in uninhabited districts to which entry was forbidden.

It was thus impossible to find out about events alleged just to have occurred in two places – El Tocayo and Aroa – where we were at the time. Not surprisingly, many therefore claim that most reports of engagements between the guerrilla and military are mere fabrications and that both parties have agreed to exaggerate the threat of the guerrilla out of all proportion. While others believe that the real engagements are far more than reported, and the power of the guerrilla greater than the authorities will admit.

It is thus very difficult to judge the future prospects of the guerrilla. My own conclusion is that none of the fighting guerrilla movements have any chance at present of developing in a way that would permit them to take power.

More important than this, perhaps, is to try to establish what circumstances might alter the picture. An alliance between revolutionaries and nationalist officers; an acute economic or political crisis that also really hit the middle class; a decisive revolutionary victory in some Latin American country; or a major conflict totally engaging the United States in other parts of the world – each and every one of these factors would be sufficient to transform sporadic guerrilla action into open warfare during the Seventies.

7

We sat in the guardroom outside the cells. He was in pyjamas, bare-footed, with badly scarred feet. We talked more or less undisturbed, interrupted only by his five-year-old daughter on her Sunday visit to the prison. She was playing with some tame chickens that peasants from the *sierra* had brought with them as a present.

'How do you see the future?'

'The first criterion of a revolutionary in Latin America today is that he should think in continental terms. One country alone cannot be liberated. An isolated revolution is bound to sell out to the United States, or be destroyed.'

The chickens strutted along her outstretched arm on to his knee. He smiled at her, took them carefully in his cupped hands and went on.

'The second criterion is that he should take the long-term view. Anyone who believes that things will happen quickly is a dreamer, or a simple *coup*-maker. Latin America can expect to pay ten to fifteen years of war for its freedom. Probably, we will only overcome in connection with some larger war elsewhere, which ties the hands of the United States.'

This, I thought, is what Latin American revolutionaries have to offer. Death or torture and imprisonment if you fail. Ten to fifteen years of war if you succeed. The victory probably dependent on an even larger conflict, with unforeseeable consequences. Héctor Béjar was convinced even so that this was the only road to a future for his people.

A frightening price. But who sets the price? Who profits from it? Whose safety is it intended to protect?

Revolution in Latin America would deprive the United States of an automatic majority in the United Nations. Revolution in Latin America would deprive the United States of sources of raw materials and markets of incalculable value. Revolution in Latin America would put the United States in the same situation as the Soviet, or the big European powers, all of which have a military threat close to their own frontiers. In other words, it is inconceivable that the United States would let itself be defeated in Latin America.

This is why a bare-footed man, who could still smile upon his daughter and carefully take tame birds into his cupped hands, sat talking so naturally of a future which involved ten to fifteen years of war.

Cuba

1

'To hell with green fodder,' said Marina and sat down in the shade.

I could understand her. Marina was supposed to show us Cuba, and she was happy enough to do the job. But as for crawling around on your hands and knees, tearing up grass to see the depth of the roots, well, you need a special interest to keep you going. And who cares? If someone had suggested in 1959 that in ten years' time I would be asking to go out in the pasture-lands of Cuba in 90 degrees of heat looking for weeds and ant-hills, I would have told him he was out of his mind. This was Marina's diagnosis. So 100 cows, for heaven's sake, can graze for three days all year round on 1·2 hectares, what's the fuss?

I tried to explain.

We had driven through central Chile, I said, just before Christmas, and got honey all over the windscreen. It was almost midsummer, and we drove through wonderful leafy glades that had never been put to the plough. Natural pasture is a wonderful thing. But it means using only a fraction of what the soil has to offer. Which is why Chile spends one quarter of its foreign currency on buying food, including large quantities of meat and dairy produce.

It was the same in Cuba, I added, before the revolution. You used one-fifth of your currency to buy food from the United States. And almost half the land in Cuba was natural pasture.

We had been to Colombia and seen how the land is culti-vated in small plots up on the hillsides, while the fertile, well irrigated valleys are used as natural pasture. Colombia could be one of the world's great meat producers, if ill-managed natural pasture did not take up seventeen-eighteenths of the land, much of it the best land available. Because only the rich can afford to own the best land, and they have so much else on their minds. Extensive cattle-farming is thus the most convenient solution. The profit comes from the rising value of the land, not from production.

We had visited the giant *estancias* of Argentina. The owners are interested only in breeding, in aristocratic pedi-grees. Green fodder is not posh enough.

'Here we feed five head per hectare by cultivating fodder,' said Onelio Marengo, manager of La Danesa, one of the world's biggest bull-breeding farms. 'With natural pasture we could only keep one or two head per hectare.'

'Why don't the others do the same?'

'To spend a peso in order to make three? That would be undignified, it might look as if the owner were short of money or something.'

Paraguay is in a class of its own. The world record in meat production is reputed to be over 1,000 kilos per hectare. There is no difficulty in producing 500. The average in Uruguay is 72 kilos. Paraguay notes seven kilos of meat per hectare.

It still pays, as the *estancias* are pretty big; 200,000 to 400,000 hectares is no unusual figure. The production value in cattle-farming is higher than in industry, 1,400 dollars per worker in 1966.[1] The workers are paid in kind, and the plan-ning secretariat says that 100 dollars a year is a very generous estimate of their pay. The capital factor thus claimed 1,300 dollars, or more than 90 per cent of the pro-duction value per worker. Nor is any capital required, apart

1. *Plan nacional de desarrollo económico y social*, 1967–68, Asunción 1966, p. 33.

from the land, which the owners were given more or less free, and the animals, which are left to breed on their own.

The most interesting situation, though, is that in Uruguay, the world's first welfare state. An eight-hour working day, paid holidays, unemployment insurance, health insurance, national retirement pensions, all before other countries had even thought about it. Uruguay has enjoyed for decades all the benefits the Cubans have derived from the revolution – and Uruguay never had a revolution.

They only forgot one thing: the economic basis on which all these things must rest. Uruguay lives from selling its cattle. But four per cent of the landowners own almost 60 per cent of the land, which consists mainly of badly-managed natural pasture. At the Instituto Alberto Boerger in Uruguay a well-managed natural pasture gives one ton of dry substance per hectare. By adding 60 kilos of phosphate they have raised production to three tons. By ploughing and sowing the same field they got 5 to 15 tons, depending on the rain. And by artificial irrigation they raised production to 18 tons. An increase of 1,700 per cent!

Large areas of the country would not stand intensive management of this kind. Cautious estimates, however, show that Uruguay could increase its production of meat – its second largest export – by 500 per cent. The big landowners have done nothing – except turn out their cows to pasture.

This is why the number of livestock in Uruguay today is no greater than at the beginning of the century. The population, on the other hand, has grown. There used to be eight head of cattle per inhabitant, now there are three. There used to be 25 sheep per inhabitant, now there are eight. This is not enough. Rich Uruguay has become a poor country, plagued by inflation and devaluations that have rendered all its social benefits valueless.

The conclusion is obvious. There is no point in trying to paste social reforms on to an unprogressive economic structure. Here, in Cuba, you have chosen the path of revolution. The structure of the economy has been radically altered. And what I want to know is how the pasture is developing.]

Before the revolution, Cuba with 1·5 head of cattle per hectare lay slightly above the average for Latin America.[2] Since the revolution, the statistics say that you have cultivated 800,000 hectares of pasture. I have been keeping a look-out for it; I noticed the other day some twenty large cattle-farms surrounded by cultivated pasture. I began to believe the statistics. At Los Naranjos yesterday, the previous owner had kept 200 animals on 120 hectares of natural pasture. Now fodder plants are grown on 90 of these hectares, and 500 animals are maintained. Here, on this farm, 100 cows can graze three days a month throughout the year on 1·2 hectares. Don't you understand, Marina, that this is a remarkable thing? Over eight animals per hectare!

2

What has the revolution achieved? What will happen? To facilitate comparison with the rest of Latin America I should like to consider point by point the same problems as I have discussed in previous chapters.

The balance between town and country

Before the revolution, half of Cuba's capital was invested in Havana, the majority of the country's 300,000 cars were used in the town's expensive traffic-apparatus, and its shop windows were full of imported goods. Eighty thousand families lived in the slums.

2. Cuban Economic Research Project: *Cuba, Agriculture and Planning*, University of Miami 1965, p. 59, p. 61.

Today the countryside is moving forward, while the towns are decaying. Cuba has nine tractors per thousand hectares, which is a Latin American record. An armada of harvesters and trucks has succeeded the private cars, which have been left worn-out and petrol-less to rust on the streets of Havana.

Cuba has one doctor to every thousand inhabitants, and the majority of them work in the rural districts. 2·1 million pupils are studying in schools throughout the country.[4] But in Havana the façades are flaking off, the shop windows are empty, and the food queues wind round the blocks.

Before the revolution, the housing shortage was estimated at 650,000 dwellings. It is still enormous, but luxury villas are no longer given priority to the inadequate resources available. Priority is given to schools, hospitals and productive facilities.

Immediately after the revolution, slum dwellers were given building materials and wages to set their dwellings in order. In this way, more than 100,000 homes in the country were given cement floors and hygienic sewerage, and large slum areas in the towns were cleaned up. Building at present consists mostly of small prefabricated houses and flats.

The basic issue, however, is not residential construction. The important thing is that the unemployment and illiteracy inherent in the slums have been abolished. The result has been the disappearance of slum life, even when the old slum buildings remain.

The class society

The upper class fled at the time of the revolution, the middle class began to emigrate when the revolution became socialistic. About 40,000 people a year leave Cuba, predominantly for the United States.

4. The Cuban delegation to the UNESCO conference in Geneva, July 1968.

It is impossible to make any comparison with the rest of Latin America on this point, since the social classes that there have reason to emigrate would not be allowed to enter the United States.

For Cuba, this emigration means a terrible brain-drain. Of 3,700 Latin American doctors practising in the United States in the mid-Sixties, 1,300 came from Cuba.[5] Almost all the technicians, experts and teachers you meet in Cuba today are young and newly trained. The result, in many cases, is disorganization and inefficiency.

Was this really necessary?

I am convinced that it was. The revolution was concerned to get medical and dental care quickly out to the people, and the doctors' incomes suffered as a result. The revolution wanted to cut rents – and so a property owner could not make more than 600 dollars a year. The revolution cut the prices on utility goods, and the businessmen suddenly found themselves in nationalized shops with the pay of an ordinary employee.

At point after point, the necessary reforms of the revolution conflicted with the interests of the middle class. This applies in particular to the break with the United States, and this was inevitable if the revolution was to achieve its aims.

Will a new privileged class emerge? It is conceivable that Cuba, like the Soviet Union today, will need a second revolution. So far, equality is the very basis on which everything in Cuba is growing.

Two million mouths

Population growth in Cuba is probably slightly smaller than elsewhere in Latin America. It is true that Cuba has

5. Oficina Sanitaria Panamericana, quoted from *America Latina – principales indicadores de salud*, Havana 1967, p. 65.

the lowest infant-mortality rate, less than four per cent. On the other hand, half a per cent of the population emigrates every year, and information on birth control is more effective than in most other places in Latin America.

By 1980 the population will probably reach ten million, which is an increase by two million.[6] This will mean a particularly great strain, in so far as Cuba is the only Latin American country that really assumes responsibility for offering education, work and food to all its citizens.

In the case of education and work, a Cuban has better prospects than anyone in Latin America. The food shortage is difficult to compare with that in other countries, since the social structure is so different. Those who feel it most today are probably those who used to see others go hungry. But, obviously, the shortage of food is a heavy burden to bear, particularly in the towns.

Rice and meat are strictly rationed. Bread, eggs and beans are not rationed, but you have to know exactly when they will arrive and get in the queue early. And apart from food, there is hardly anything to buy for personal use. A visitor finds the shortage of goods in Havana frightening. This shortage is painful to all Cubans, not just to the upper classes. Many reports from Cuba try to conceal this obvious fact. But I think it very important that we should realize that this is the price of the development and equality. This is what it will cost, even in other Latin American countries.

How do people get by? I asked this question frequently, and obtained both firm attitudes and hesitant confessions in response. Here are some examples:

'No, things aren't so bad. If I haven't got my plate of rice I eat some sugar or drink some good mineral water, and get by like that.' (67-year-old foreman in the sugar industry. Sugar has since been rationed.)

'I'm old, sir, and I'll tell you the truth. I sympathize with

6. ECLA, quoted from Véliz, op. cit., p. 253.

my Fidel, he's pure gold is young Fidel. But they're not all like him, and he can't know how things are with us. The revolution has bad people too, and to tell you the truth we're always a bit hungry.' (Mother of land worker. A dozen or so eggs stood in a basket on the kitchen table.)

'No, I eat better now.'

'How often do you eat meat?'

'Every week, like everyone else. Now everyone eats alike.'

'Milk for the children?'

'Every day.'

'Eggs?'

'Every week. I buy what comes. There's nothing to buy that I can't buy.' (40-year-old wife of a sugar worker.)

This last I think is important. 'There's nothing to buy that I can't buy.' What sugar-worker's wife can say that, outside Cuba?

Fifty million people in Latin America live at or below starvation level. Of them, only the Cubans do so with a certain security, and for a reasonable purpose.

How long will the food shortage last? Meat and rice are the main ingredients of the Cuban diet. In the first years of the revolution, poor management and an over-consumption of meat reduced the stock of cattle; the area devoted to rice was cut down, in the hope that it would be possible to exchange sugar for rice with China. In recent years, both cattle-farming and the cultivation of rice have greatly expanded. If this continues, the acute food crisis will be over by the mid-Seventies. However, the population growth and investment requirements will limit the consumption of most goods for many years to come.

Debts

Cuba has large debts to the Soviet Union and other socialist countries. How large we do not know, since Cuba, unlike all other Latin American countries, does not publish statistics on this. We know, however, that unsuccessful attempts at industrialization in the early Sixties left large bills unpaid; we know also that the investments necessary to deal with agricultural harvests will mean a growing debt during the Seventies.

In one respect, Cuba's situation is worse than that of other Latin American countries – the blockade forces them to trade above all with the socialist world. Cuban technicians are not always happy about the quality of equipment supplied. They would like to see an increase in trade with Western Europe.

In three respects, Cuba is in a better situation than the rest of Latin America.

1. Cuba has nationalized the American companies that dominated its economy before the revolution. This has rid the country of the heaviest burden on its balance of payments.

2. Also, Cuba has borrowed for productive purposes – agricultural machinery, cement and fertilizer factories, freezing plant, etc. – and not, as the rest of Latin America does to a great extent, in order to maintain the luxury consumption of the upper class, and clearly anti-social methods of production.

3. Finally, it is sometimes said that Cuba 'costs' the Soviet Union one million dollars a day. This is a meaningless simplification based on many unknown factors. It is certain, however, that Cuba has had an import surplus in its trade with the Soviet Union during the Sixties. Cuba has thus received

goods in return for its debt. While Latin America, as I have previously shown, has increased its debts without getting an opportunity to import more than it exports.

Violence

If you come from Latin America, Cuba seems very peaceful. No machine-guns at the street corners, no armed road checkpoints, no steel-helmeted police, no military forces around the universities.

This is partly because the press's right to criticize has been pruned down even more in Cuba than in the rest of Latin America; and because the invisible control, exercised particularly through the Committees for the Defence of the Revolution, is more effective.

But the calmer atmosphere of Cuba is due above all to Cuba's already having had the revolution that the violence in Latin America is intended to prevent. The weapons are in the hands of the majority.

This is particularly noticeable at places of work. I have seldom seen such natural relationships between foremen and workers as in Cuba. When I mentioned this, a land worker said :

'Why do you think we had a revolution? Not to get new bosses shooting their mouths off !'

Two categories of people are frightened.

Those who entertain plans of leaving the country. These are not only the profiteers, who smell better profits elsewhere, but many who would stay and form an opposition if this were permitted in Cuba.

The other group are the homosexuals and 'psychopaths'. They feel vulnerable and watched, they speak of their difficulties only in whispers.

The most marked reflection of violence in Cuba is the

25,000 political prisoners. Castro admitted a figure of 20,000 in the mid-Sixties,[7] and even this figure is the highest in Latin America. He described the prisoners as old Batista men, and people who had been sentenced for corruption and sabotage after the revolution. Many, however, have been given very long sentences for very minor collaboration with the counter-revolutionaries. And no legal opposition, after all, is permitted.

Race

The original population of Cuba was exterminated without trace centuries ago. Of today's Cubans, almost three-quarters are white, the rest Negroes and mulattoes. The previous discrimination was essentially economic and social. Economic and social restructurization has radically improved the position of the coloured population. All reports agree that this is one of the most important gains made by the revolution.

The Church

The Catholic Church in Cuba is anchored in a defeated middle class. It has not been put down. No one has tried to interfere in its internal affairs. The 22 churches in Havana hold one or more masses every Sunday. The one I visited had collected a fair congregation. The bishops of Cuba were able to travel freely to the meeting in Bogotá, although the government knows them to be bitter opponents of the revolution. They reject everything, including the Pope's *De Populorum Progressio* encyclical, which does not totally and

7. Lee Lockwood: *Castro's Cuba, Cuba's Fidel*, New York 1967, p. 210.

unreservedly condemn communism. By taking this position, the Church has lost all opportunity of influencing the present development of Cuban society.

The military

Cuba is the only country in Latin America in which the primary task of the armed forces is to defend the country. Following the attempted invasion by the United States in 1961, Cuba built up the strongest defence on the continent, with material provided free by the Soviet Union. This has naturally created political dependency, and an increased influence on the part of the military. A military take-over, however, seems inconceivable, at least while Castro is alive.

The reformers

Cuba publishes no figures on G.N.P. growth. The Cuban Communist Party obviously has no intention of 'strengthening the democratic institutions' in our sense of the term.

With these two exceptions, we can say that Cuba, which is outside the Alliance for Progress, is the only Latin American country to have taken the Alliance's programme seriously. But it would be more proper to put the matter the other way round. The Alliance's programme was written because such reforms had already been initiated in Cuba.

In decisive respects, the Cubans have gone far beyond the aims of the Alliance for Progress. This applies particularly to land reform, which has not been restricted to a programme of pacification. Cuba's tenant-farmers have become owner-farmers, and the country today has 100,000 small-holdings. The big agricultural firms have been nationalized, and are now conducting a drive towards expansion and mechanization that has no parallel in Latin America.

The Cubans intend during the Seventies to strengthen their position as the world's biggest sugar producer, to expand strongly as coffee producers, and harvest seven times as much fruit as the world's largest fruit company to date – the American firm of Sunkist.

The real content of reforms, and the opportunities for further reform, will depend essentially on the success or failure of this venture. Twelve years after the revolution, there is no more to be gained from a more just distribution within the framework of the old community's productive resources. Further advances presuppose an actual increase in resources. It seems to be sound enough policy to invest predominantly in agriculture; to build this sector up with a mass input of human labour, at the same time mechanizing as rapidly as possible; and then, in the mid-Seventies, to move on and start constructing a manufacturing industry on the basis of raw materials from agriculture.

It is uncertain, however, how far such plans can be realized. The utmost priority was given to the 1970 sugar harvest, and this caused serious reverses in other sections of the economy. In spite of this, sugar production reached only 8.5 million tons, as compared with a target of 10 million tons. And in 1971 production fell back to a pre-revolutionary level of 5.9 million tons.

The choice of products is also problematical. Sugar and coffee are typical low-price goods, with strongly-fluctuating markets. The processing and marketing of fruit demand advanced techniques. The uncertain export prospects make Cuba's investments something of a speculation. If they prove successful, Castro will be able to keep all his promises. If they fail, fifteen years of hard work will lie buried under millions of tons of unsaleable coffee and putrefying fruit.

The revolution

For Cuba, the Latin American revolution is one and indivisible. Since the death of Che Guevara, however, even the Cubans put the revolution more in the future. The change in attitude between my two visits, in the summer of 1967 and 1968, was very marked. Cuba seemed to have accustomed itself to the idea of socialism's surviving 'on one island' for another decade.

Will it survive?

Cuba has gained a great deal of strength from its isolation and exposed position. But these same factors have also put Cuba in the hands of the Soviet Union. This has led to a shortage of goods which threatens to replace revolutionary enthusiasm with a black market mentality or apathetic queues. It has created an atmosphere of siege which is incompatible with free criticism and the keeping of a watchful eye on the government by its citizens. In a disturbing way, it has concentrated the revolution around a single person. Seldom has a country been so dependent on the force and judgement of one man as Castro's Cuba.

3

I came home from India in 1964 with a feeling of hopelessness and despair. I did not believe that any economic or political system had the answer to India's problems.

Returning from Latin America, my mood was entirely different.

The misery there is great, but not so deep and all-embracing as that of India. Latin America is not sunk in religious lethargy; in places, religion is actually a spur to social reform. The injustices are frightful – but not so institutionalized as in India. The corruption and waste of resources is striking, but in Latin America a change seems at least possible.

This possibility of change is indicated above all by the progress made in Cuba during the Sixties.

This does not mean that I saw only positive things in Cuba. But the institutional obstacles to progress have been removed. The revolution has liberated forces that have made it possible for Cuba to defy the blockade and the isolation, overcome the emigration of the middle class, and make large investments in the future.

What has been done, and is still being done, in Cuba shows that Latin America is not a 'hopeless' continent. Its present paralysis is artificial, as artificial as the debt and unemployment. The resources are there. A minimum of common sense would get them to flourish.

But this minimum of common sense is conspicuously far away. It seems to lie on the other side of a revolution, which lies in its turn on the other side of a major war.

Why?

Some of the answers are obvious.

1. Because only the present system allows the ruling class, 5 per cent of the population, to claim 30 per cent of private consumption. While 50 per cent of the population share 14 per cent of consumption.

2. Because Latin America, throughout its history, has been in colonial or semi-colonial dependence on more powerful parts of the world, first Europe and now the United States. And the United States, out of concern for its security and its capital, continues to guarantee the power of the ruling classes.

The present Latin America is firmly bolted and shuttered. This is a continent full of opportunities, which its people are denied. The great exception is Cuba. Today, however, certain other doors to the future seem to be opening.

Peru - a Check-up

Peru - a Check-up

As the nearest great power, most important trading partner, greatest source of loans and owner of the main export and other key industries, the United States is in charge in Latin America. This is both clear from the statistics and observable everywhere in practice. All that is lacking for Latin America to attain full colonial status is outright military occupation. And this is willingly provided in practice by the Latin American countries' own armies.

How long will they go on doing this?

Some Latin American Marxists hope that national humiliation will one day outweigh class loyalty and fear of the masses – so that the officers or at least the sergeants can be won to the cause of the revolution. Is this not the final self-renunciation, when even the revolutionaries hope that the army will do their job for them? They answer with Lenin: 'No mass revolution can prevail without support from at least part of the army of the old régime.'

It's difficult to judge. The very few radical officers I talked to, in Guatemala and Ecuador, had little hope to offer. They believed, as I do, that the Seventies will simply underline the present trend, which can be summed up like this. 'The pressure increases. – Revolutions are put down. – The military take over.'

So ends my chapter on the role of the military in Latin America. Even while I was writing it, events were taking a new and more interesting turn.

On 3 October 1968, General Velasco assumed power in

Peru at the head of a military junta. He was not acting on behalf of American big business; this at least became clear on 9 October, when he ordered Peruvian troops to occupy I.P.C.'s refinery in Talara. I.P.C. is the International Petroleum Company, a subsidiary of the world's most powerful oil group – Standard Oil of New Jersey (ESSO).

Six months later, Peru was faced with the threat of immediate economic sanctions by the United States. The prospect of a settlement had come no closer; on the contrary, after a succession of moves and counter-moves the I.P.C. had ceased to exist as a company in Peru, and its assets had been taken over *in toto* by the state.

Other news-items followed in rapid succession. 'Peru opens diplomatic relations with the Soviet Union.' 'Peruvian Navy fires on American fishing-boats.' 'Peru expropriates 270,000 hectares of pasture from American mining-company.'

Something was happening in Peru. Once more the old questions came up. Is a Nasserist development possible in Latin America? Will the military take over where bourgeois reform policies fail? Might an alliance actually be conceivable, in the name of nationalism, between the continent's two mortal enemies – revolutionaries and officers? Velasco's government could be the first step in this direction.

In March 1969, I returned to Peru to investigate.

THE GOVERNMENT OF GENERALS

'Every Peruvian government has been concerned to solve the I.P.C. problem. Every government has promised to solve it. But none of them has dared. They were frightened of *precisely the moment* that has now arrived. The revolutionary government has solved the problem, and does not fear the consequences.'

But of course he was afraid, this tense, determined little

General Velasco. Time and again he turned in appeal to the American journalists who were present at the press conference:

'You don't think, surely, that the United States will resort to sanctions? You can't believe that, surely?'

And when he got no reply, he went on:

'I *don't* believe it. Who would the sanctions hit? They would hit this miserable people – yes, I say "miserable", since they live in misery. Six million Peruvians have neither food, nor clothing, nor a roof over their heads. It is they who would be hurt by sanctions.'

'That's not going to worry the Americans,' commented a Latin American journalist.

'It should worry them, sir. Because what will be the consequence? If the United States takes an economic stranglehold on our country – what will happen? They will have opened the doors to anarchy, to armed combat. The army will be overwhelmed by the masses. And you know when the masses are in motion, when the masses cannot be controlled, then ... *another sort of people* can take over.'

It was interesting to study the shifts in his voice and facial expression. As long as General Velasco speaks of the misery of the Peruvian people, of six million people without food and clothing, his expression is one of paternal pity. But at the next moment this same Peruvian people has become the 'masses' who are set 'in motion' – and it sounds as if he is speaking of an invasion of cockroaches.

General Juan Velasco Alvarado was Supreme Commander in Peru before he became President of the junta. He is a provincial boy, born in Piura in northernmost Peru, the son of a lower echelon official in the Ministry of Finance. One of his brothers is a primary-school teacher. He is married to the daughter of an APRA politician from the anti-imperialist period of this party in the Thirties. He began as a private soldier, and travelled the long road to his General's stars. But by that time he had become a conservative officer. This is evident enough from his way of speaking about the people.

Several of this government's most startling measures prove fairly harmless on closer inspection.

Peru has opened diplomatic relations with the Soviet Union and several other Eastern-bloc states. This, however, is no sudden gambit in a game of chess with the United States, but part of a movement common to all Latin America. Governments as disparate as those of Argentina, Chile, Ecuador and Colombia have diplomatic relations with the Soviet. Negotiations started under Belaúnde's government, and would have given results early in 1969 more or less regardless of who was in power.

American fishing-boats have been fired upon. Yes, like Chile, Ecuador, and many other countries, Peru asserts territorial rights over 200 miles of its coastal waters. In the past ten years, 80 boats have been arrested and forced to pay a total of 534,000 dollars in fines for illegal fishing. The *San Juan*, the boat fired upon in February 1969, had previously dodged its fines in November 1968, and now succeeded in escaping again until it was finally caught and fined in March. The fine was paid automatically by the U.S. government, which equally automatically deducts a corresponding sum from its military aid to Peru.

On point after point, the military government has simply followed existing policy, although perhaps with the somewhat greater energy of the beginner. But what view of Peruvian society does the military hold? Where is it trying to lead the country?

The first communiqués after the *coup* spoke fairly generally of moral and economic chaos, and promised 'structural reforms'.

Then everything was quiet until the end of November 1968.

At that point, government members suddenly began to

make long speeches, larded with figures and opinions, brand-
ing with criticism a succession of abuses in Peruvian society.

What had happened? The trail leads back to the ECLA, the
U.N.'s Economic Commission for Latin America. The motive
force behind the government is a group of young officers who
were trained at the Centro de Altos Estudios Militares in
Lima, where great emphasis is given to social and economic
studies. The lecturers in these subjects come from the ECLA,
which has thus acquired an influence on the young generation of officers. These officers are permeated by the reform
and planning ideology of the ECLA.

These young men are as yet only colonels and majors. It is
their conservative superior officers who are in government.
But they do have a certain influence.

More or less simultaneously with the military *coup*, a group
of U.N. economists and sociologists arrived in Peru to analyse
the situation. A confidential report was presented to the
government at the end of November 1968. Studying subsequent government statements, we find that the material is
taken almost 100 per cent from this report. It is the U.N.
experts in Santiago, supported by the younger officers, who
speak from the mouths of the generals.

THE REAL POWER

The ECLA report states that Peru has noted a high, even
growth-rate during the Fifties and Sixties, by comparison
with other Latin American countries. G.N.P. *per capita* has
risen on the average by 2·5 per cent.

Growth, however, has been mainly in the export sectors,
which are all foreign-owned – for this reason, the progress
made has not benefited the Peruvian economy to any great
extent.

Also, an assembly industry has been artificially nurtured,

with a view to meeting demands in 'the modern sector', i.e. a small group of consumers who have so much money and such advanced tastes that they even buy more imported goods today than at the beginning of the decade. The companies have been given a free hand to repeat all the mistakes previously made in other Latin American countries.

To an increasing extent, operations by the state have been financed by loans abroad; at the same time, the tax burden has been increasingly shouldered off on to the small earners. Taxes on companies and capital, which answered in 1960 for 24 per cent of state revenues, now comprise 11 per cent. During the same period, the proportion of indirect taxes has risen from 20 to 48 per cent.

Agriculture has stagnated in underemployment and idle land: the supply of foodstuffs from the rural districts rose during the period 1950–65 by only 2.7 per cent per annum, while the demand for food in the towns increased by 5 per cent p.a. Peru is therefore forced to use 150 million dollars a year to import foodstuffs.

Analysing the power structure in Peru, the ECLA report points out that 1.2 per cent of farms claim 75 per cent of the land, while 82 per cent answer for only 6 per cent. The strong concentration of property produces a corresponding inequality in income distribution: 0.3 per cent of the active population in the rural districts enjoy 20 per cent of the income, while 2 per cent have 40 per cent. The great majority of the active population, 65 per cent, has to content itself with 28 per cent of the income-cake.

Locally, the power of the landowning oligarchy is still practically absolute, and its political influence on the national scene disproportionately great. But the economic power has shifted towards the coast and the towns.

There, the middle class represents a newly-achieved vertical mobility on the social scale. But opportunities for advancement function within a patron–client system, which makes an independent attitude more or less impossible. 'In other words, the middle class has grown without being able to consolidate its power.'

And the patrons of the middle class – the modern oligarchy of bankers, importers and industrialists – are in turn the clients of powerful foreign interests. The report quotes Jorge Bravo Bressani's analysis: the ruling class of Peru is a body of middle-men, an intermediate link between the people and the true holders of power – 'mere deputies and agents in the service of the foreign companies'.[1]

The report speaks – and here the military officers must be particularly susceptible to persuasion – of the 'illegitimacy' of the democratic processes in a country like Peru. Over half of all adult Peruvians lack the vote. And it makes very little difference what policies the voters approve, since political power in Peru is subject to the economic power. All the state can do is maintain a hazardous balance between various powerful pressure-groups; it lacks the resources actually to steer development.

But perhaps a group of determined military officers, who were not bound by political considerations, could give the state apparatus a new role?

Peru has experienced thirty-three attempted *coups* and seven military assumptions of power since the Great War. The Peruvians have in time become fairly sceptical.

'Some officers wanted to take power purely in order to expropriate the I.P.C.; for others, the I.P.C. question was merely a brilliant occasion to take power without opposition,' argued a leading journalist in Lima. Ambitious military officers are always to be found. Some of them want to initiate expensive reforms, others are concerned to put the country's chaotic economy in order by a strict financial policy. Some are concerned to prevent Haya de la Torre from

1. Jorge Bravo Bressani: *Mito y realidad de la oligarquía peruana*, Instituto de Estudios Peruanos, Lima 1966.

becoming President in this year's election, others want free hands against the country's 'subversive elements'. Others, again, simply want better pay and status.

The left viewed the 'progressive' features of the military government with great suspicion. I again met Héctor Béjar, who had been moved to the Lurigancho prison in the desert outside Lima, a giant penitentiary for 2,400 prisoners, fourteen to a cell.

'Repression has if anything increased,' he told me. 'This autumn the military twice fired on landworkers to stop invasions of the land. In both cases, lives were lost. This sort of thing goes unpunished. At the same time, some 60 landworkers have been charged in court for relationships with the guerrilla in 1965. One of the judges is the landowner on whose land they work.'

He could have mentioned several cases. While I was in Lima, military police forced their way into the University of San Marcos to stop a demonstration against the new Universities Act passed by the junta. The Act forbids political activities by students, and gives the police new authority within the University gates.

In Mala, on the following day, 400 workers went on strike at the 'Raúl' mine, which belongs to the Miolosisch – Marcionelli – Hanza group, and the brothers de Osma Gildemeister. The workers who went on strike were surrounded by special units from the Guardia Civil, and about a hundred of them arrested, including those who were in need of hospital treatment. Work in the mine was resumed the following day.

'It is by measures like these that the United States recognizes its allies,' Héctor Béjar claimed. 'When Velasco threatens to "unleash the masses", it is only a trick to blackmail the United States. He knows perfectly well that no revolutionary situation exists in Peru today. And the United States knows that *if* it existed, the General would be the last to want to exploit it. There are no short-cuts to the revolution.'

The American analysis of the situation proved very similar to that of the extreme left. 'The masses haven't woken up yet,' said an American official in Lima. 'They will, of course. But it's not going to happen today. Or tomorrow.'

The big American companies naturally took their precautions. The ITT, which is responsible for the awful telephone service in Lima and its surroundings, twice flew over groups of Swedish auditors to evaluate and re-evaluate its assets in Peru – against the possibility of expropriation. (One of them told me: 'It's terrible really – here we sit guessing, while half a per cent one way or the other can mean millions in the way of claims on Peru.') Most people, however, believed the military would sooner or later give in. A Cuban or Nasserist development was considered extremely unlikely. 'The officers, with a few exceptions, are highly conservative.'

The expropriation of the I.P.C. shows what even highly conservative officers can resort to, when pushed to the limit. Expropriation, however, is not revolution. President Velasco talks as if Peru had recovered its national independence, simply by the I.P.C.'s being out of the country. This, of course, is not the case. The I.P.C. is only a symbol, the most hated of all the foreign companies that dominate the Peruvian economy. The symbol had been overthrown, but the realities of power remained.

THE FUMES OF LA OROYA

Largest of the old American companies in Peru, and oldest of the larger ones, is the Cerro de Pasco Corporation. The company's history goes back to the nineteenth century, when railroad constructor and adventurer Henry Meiggs acquired mining rights in the Cerro de Pasco, a massif of the Andes above Lima. Rich finds of copper were made in 1897, and the Cerro de Pasco Investment Company in New York was formed in 1902. One of the major holders was Casa Grace, the most powerful foreign company in Peru at the time. Today, the Cerro corporation is a world-wide group, whose Peruvian subsidiary (registered in Delaware, U.S.A.) has a turnover of 123 million dollars and employs 14,000 Peruvians. The company's ancient managerial palace lies just across from the 'Círculo Militar' on the Plaza San Martín in the heart of Lima.

And now, the army had apparently marched over the square and expropriated 270,000 hectares of the company's land. It seemed almost incredible.

The directors of the company, however, confirmed what was said in the newspapers. They did not even seem particularly upset. The measure had been prepared for a number of years, they said, and the agreement was now ready to be signed. It was in accordance with the Peruvian Land Reform Act, which does not deprive the landowner of all rights and benefits. Compensation was considered adequate.

'We were forced originally to buy these properties, and are not sorry to see them go.'

Forced?

No explanation was forthcoming at the time, but I found one a few weeks later in *Peru – Tenencia de la tierra y dessarrollo socio-económico del sector agrícola*, Washington 1966. This is a study performed by CIDA – a joint organization for collaboration between two U.N. agencies, the OAS, the Inter-American Development Bank, and the Inter-American Institute of Agricultural Sciences. The chapter discussing the concentration of property in the countryside of Peru contains a couple of passages of interest:

A remarkable and perhaps unique feature of this process of concentration is the acquisition by the Cerro de Pasco Copper Corporation of land in the Peruvian *sierra*. Cerro is a powerful North American mining company that operates in Central Peru.

In 1922, Cerro installed a foundry in La Oroya, in the department of Junín. The location was poorly chosen, a deep ravine in which the exhaust gases from the plant could find outlet only in the pass leading out into the agricultural areas in the valley of the Mantaro River. These fumes contained arsenic, lead, zinc, sulphur, and other poisonous substances, which seriously affected the health of the population and caused severe damage to agriculture and cattle farming in the surrounding *haciendas* and Indian communities.

These poisonous substances had terrible consequences among the population of La Oroya. Numerous fatal cases of poisoning were noted.

The main crops damaged by the gases were potatoes, barley, fodder plants, and natural pasture. The lead and arsenic were deposited on the pasture-land, causing death or serious diseases among livestock. During the worst period, it was estimated that the poisons caused an average mortality of 18 per cent among sheep and 14 per cent among cattle. A marked decline in productivity was observed among the surviving animals.

According to official studies, damage was caused over an area of 700,000 hectares in one of the best agricultural and cattle regions in the country. All provinces in the department of Junín and the province of Yauyos in the department of Lima were threatened. By January 1924 the nearest Indian communities (Huaynacancha, Huay-Huay, and Huari) and the Quiulla *hacienda* had been completely ruined.

Understandably enough, these serious events provoked energetic protests among the local inhabitants. The latter filed a succession of complaints, which were not always treated with due consideration and speed. Intervention by the government was delayed, but in 1925 a decree was passed requiring the Cerro de Pasco Copper Corporation to install a Cotrel cleaning-plant to eliminate dangerous substances from their waste gases. Part of this equipment was installed in the same year, 1925. But not until 1942 – twenty years after the damage had started – was the foundry equipped with a complete purification plant.

Meanwhile, however, the company had solved the problem in a peculiar way, namely by buying the greater part of the land ruined by discharges. By June 1924 the company had acquired the greater part of properties within a radius of 30 kilometres around the foundry – 320,000 hectares, or almost half the area affected.

A year later, Cerro also purchased the extensive domains of the Sociedad Ganadera de Junín. The purchasing price of 342,000 Peruvian pounds was reported to be below the true value of the property. However, since the interested parties included powerful members of the Peruvian landowning class, the price was probably closer to the real value than with the defenceless Indian communities.

Also, the company has been forced to pay compensation to various individuals and local authorities, following a succession of complaints to authorities and courts. All in all, the total costs of damages, purification plant, and land purchase seem to have reached several million dollars.

How could it happen? A leader in the reputable farming periodical *La Vida Agrícola* maintained in January 1924 that Cerro had certainly foreseen the consequences of the foundry's location; already similar problems had seriously disturbed public opinion in the United States. Even in Peru, similar effects had been experienced with the Smelter and Huaranoca foundries, although on a much smaller scale.

If it really was possible to foresee the effects of the foundry's location, the question of the company's motives arises. Numerous hypotheses have been suggested. It is conceivable that Cerro intended from the very beginning to acquire the neighbouring land in order to create a large-scale agricultural enterprise – which is what happened in fact. In this way, the company became almost completely self-supporting as regards food. It is conceivable, also, that the company was interested in the proletarization of the local population, which has ensured the company an ample supply of labour.

At any rate, the result was that this zone, previously owned by Indian communities and *haciendas*, is now concentrated into a single giant *latifundo*, owned by the Cerro de Pasco Corporation.

Thus far the CIDA study.

It was 270,000 hectares of this *latifundo* that the military government had expropriated, within the framework of a Land Reform Act that guaranteed the landowner compensation at market prices. One can understand why Cerro didn't complain. The Peruvians might easily start remembering how the land once came into the company's ownership.

Also:

Cerro itself may not be entirely without blame for the military *coup* in Peru.

The *coup* would hardly have occurred if the Peruvian currency had not been devalued.

Devaluation was on 4 September 1967. The following day, Congress opened its long-postponed autumn session. I was in the office of one of Cerro's directors to ask for permission to visit the mines. While he was dissuading me, the telephone rang. I waited, looking around the room, which was clad in legal literature bound in red leather. I heard him say:

'Hallo, Mike, how's our little revolution going ...'

'Well, I only hope nothing comes out in Congress ...'

'Right, once they start out spitting and screaming in Congress you never know what they'll say. They're just not reliable ...'

The conversation continued. They were obviously talking about the devaluation. I knew, of course, that this would favour the speculators and exporters, among whom Cerro de Pasco occupy a dominant position. I knew also that Cerro had had a decisive influence on Peruvian politics for half a century. But to sit there hearing that ghastly little industrialist (when he spoke, it sounded as if he had his mouth full of broken teeth, and was chewing them with a sharp chomping sound) talking about 'our little revolution' and the risk of its being discovered when the Peruvian Congress started 'spitting and screaming' – it was a bit too much.

As I came out on to the plaza outside the company's palace, it was already filled with military police preparing to crush the expected storm of popular opinion. The equipment and technique were imported direct from the United States. Soon, the tear-gas lay thick as the fumes of La Oroya over the square of San Martín, the Liberator.

IT ALL DEPENDS ON HOW YOU COUNT [2]

The Southern Peru Copper Corporation is the largest American company in Peru. It exploits the Toquepala mine in the southern part of the country, with an option on the neighbouring finds at Quellaveco and Cuajone – over 1,000 million tons of copper ore.

The ore was found by a Peruvian named Juan Oviedo, who sold his rights to Cerro. Cerro, however, failed to start extracting the copper within the time stipulated; Oviedo therefore considered himself free to offer his rights to the Northern Peru Copper Corporation, a subsidiary of the American Smelting and Refining Company. After a prolonged legal dispute, American Smelting and Cerro jointly founded the Southern Peru Copper Corporation. The structure of its ownership was as follows:

American Smelting 51·5 per cent
Cerro 22·25 per cent
Phelps Dodge 16 per cent
Newmont Mining 10·25 per cent

Drilling started in the early Fifties, and the mine began to produce in 1960. It's a fantastic sight. Modern mining is not galleries inside the rock. Machines simply move away the entire mountain, and then hew into the bared body of ore. In Toquepala some 200,000 tons of rock a day are moved, of which 40,000 tons are copper. Half a million tons of explosive

2. The calculations in this and the following section have been checked by a certified accountant, Mr Carl Aspegren, Stockholm.

are used every month. The giant crater descends in steps 300 metres down into the mountain.

Such figures are made generously available. But if you start talking money, it is more difficult to get an answer. I was there in November 1967, a few months after devaluation; I was interested to know how much the company had made on the revised exchange-rate.

'Oh my goodness,' said Mr Keath, the Public Relations Officer. 'We've lost on it.'

'But isn't your income in dollars, and a large part of your expenditure in the local currency, in *soles*? Surely you must win by the devaluation?'

'You'd better talk to Mr Bears,' said Mr Keath.

Mr Bears is the company's economic manager. We went to him. He explained. Expenditures on material answer for 70 per cent of all expenses, almost all in dollars. The company has 240 employees who are paid in dollars, and they make together almost as much as the employees who are paid in *soles*.

'In other words our expenditure in *soles* is very low. So we haven't made on the devaluation.'

With this, Mr Bears had unintentionally given a clear picture of how little these giant mining-companies affect the nation's economy at large. A low expenditure in *soles* means that very little of the company's revenues remains in the country. They import 80 per cent of all material. They export 100 per cent of the copper. The mine is in the middle of the desert, where there is not a single small industry, not a single small enterprise of the kind that otherwise tends to grow up around a major investment.

A Parliamentary Commission created in 1967 to study La Southern's dealings made the same reflection, and gave it more precise shape than I could manage on the basis of my interview with Mr Bears.

Table 8

SOUTHERN PERU COPPER CORPORATION:
EXPENDITURE IN SOLES AND DOLLARS 1960–65.
U.S. DOLLARS MILL.

Expenditure in soles		*Expenditure in dollars*	
Wages	23·4		
Salaries	7·2	Salaries	15·8
Local purchases	21·4	Imported material	85·6
Total	52·0	Total	101·4

Source : *Dictamen de la Comisión Bicameral Multipartidaria encargada de revisar el Convenio entre el Gobierno y la Southern Peru Copper Corporation*, quoted from Malpica: *Los Dueños del Perú*, third edition, Lima 1968, p. 183.

During the first six years of operation, the company's expenditure in *soles* thus amounted to only 52 million dollars. During the same period, it paid 30 million dollars in tax. And sold copper abroad for 450 million. Altogether, 82 million out of 450 stayed in the country. This is 18·2 per cent.

But the company's expenses in *soles* are not so small that they cannot be reduced still further. Even if wages paid in *soles* answer for only 20 per cent of direct operating expenditures, a 30-per-cent devaluation still means a saving in the wage bill that can be counted in millions of dollars. A saving that is taken directly from the pocket of the Peruvian employees.

'Yes, well,' I said to Mr Bears. 'You don't consider the company to have *made* anything on devaluation. But how on earth can you have *lost* on it?'

'We've lost because the value of our investment has fallen.'

'Fallen?'

'Yes, devaluation has reduced our investment value at a single stroke from 242 million to 166.'

This, admittedly, must have been a blow. Losing 76

million dollars just like that. We dwelt on this for a while, and Mr Keath seemed pleased that I should realize the gravity of their situation. It is certainly a risk to place your capital in countries where such things can occur. But most people refuse to realize just how real these risks are etc., etc.

Suddenly, I recalled something that one of the company's accountants had told me the previous evening. The accounts had been kept in dollars until one year ago, when a new Act had been passed requiring also foreign companies to keep their accounts in local currency.

'Yes, but wait a minute,' I said. 'If your book-keeping had still been in dollars as it was two years ago, then there would have been no loss from devaluation. And the stuff is all here, isn't it? The mine is here, the machinery, the whole lot. So where have you lost your 76 million? It must be a loss purely on paper, not a real loss.'

They looked at each other.

'Let's take it another way,' said Mr Bears. 'You understand, the loss is real enough. We have the right to deduct for depreciation to the full value of our investment. Now that this investment is worth less in *soles*, our openings for writing-off are that much smaller. What we have lost is the right not to pay tax on 76 million dollars.'

That, of course, was a bit different.

This detail, too, was cleared up a few months later, by a regulation which permitted foreign countries to write up the value of their investments in *soles* to a par with the new dollar exchange-rate.

'You mentioned tax,' I said. 'How much tax do you pay?'

'So far, 30 per cent of taxable income.'

'And what proportion of your income is taxable?'

'To be honest, I would prefer not to say. The figure might be abused. There are different ways of calculating profit. Quite honestly, I could give you almost any figure for profit you care to name – it all depends how you calculate.'

The discrepancy between different ways of calculating profit is admirably illustrated by the following Table, taken from the report of the Parliamentary Commission. La Southern has reported for the U.S. authorities a net profit almost twice as great as that declared for the Peruvians.

Table 9

SOUTHERN PERU COPPER CORPORATION:
RECEIPTS AND EXPENDITURES 1960–65 ACCORDING
TO STATEMENTS MADE TO THE PERUVIAN TAX
AUTHORITY, AND TO THE SECURITIES AND EXCHANGE
COMMISSION. U.S. DOLLARS MILL.

	To Peru	To U.S.	Difference
Total receipts	448·9	449·9	1·0
Direct costs	129·1	129·5	0·4
Indirect costs	43·9	44·9	1·0
Depreciation	91·4	73·9	17·5
Amortization	14·8	10·3	4·5
Depletion allowance	45·9	1·5	44·4
Tax	29·6	30·0	0·4
[...]	[...]	[...]	[...]
Net profit	69·1	135·1	66·0

Source: *Dictamen* etc., op. cit. p. 103 and Appendix 23, quoted from Malpica, op. cit. p. 178. '...' denotes a residual of 25·1 and 24·7 million lacking in the accounts.

Mr Bears warned me during our conversation not to draw any far-reaching conclusions from this Table, which 'simply reflects the difference between tax legislation in the United States and Peru'.

As clear from the Table, the Peruvian legislation – in this case the Mines Act, introduced by the dictator Manuel Odría in 1950 – allows for considerably faster write-offs than the North American. The greatest difference, however, is in the 'depletion allowance'. This allowance means that tax is to be paid only on 66·7 per cent of the profit; 33·3 per cent can be deducted, and counted as expenditure rather than profit.

Apart from the generally favourable terms of Odría's Mines Act, the founders of the company were accorded certain special tax benefits by a special agreement with Odría in 1954. By the terms of the Mines Act, these benefits can be enjoyed only in the case of 'marginal' ore finds. In Toquepala, the ore contained during the first year an average of 1·7 per cent copper, during the first six years 1·3 per cent; the entire ore-body is calculated to hold on average 1 per cent copper. As the Parliamentary Commission points out, an ore find like this can hardly be called 'marginal' in the meaning of the Act.

The Commission was doubtful also about the true scale of investments. 205 million seemed an exaggerated figure, particularly as indirect expenditures (administration, etc.) answered for 55·2 per cent of direct costs. Since the company, in 1965, had already taken out 221 million in the form of depreciation, amortization, depletion allowance, and net profit, the Commission considered that the special tax-relief should be discontinued, as in fact it was from and including 1968.

'It all depends how you calculate,' Mr Bears said. 'In our internal calculations, we have to count on making at least 30 per cent. Otherwise, we've made a bad deal. Anyone who works in mining knows that. Remember, this is a question of large, high-risk investment.'

'Yes,' I said, 'the original investment was 205 million, half of which was a loan from Eximbank, wasn't it? Has it been possible to pay back that loan?'

'Yes, we paid it off in seven years. There's only a few million left.'

'And the rest of the capital amounted to 70 per cent of loans from share-holders?'

'Yes, we decided to capitalize the corporation at a very low level, 32·6 million, and borrow the rest. The loan from share-holders is also practically repaid. In the meanwhile, we have made new investments amounting to about 37 million. About 70 million remains to be paid off.'

'Amortizing 140 million in seven years, that's not bad at all. And in the meanwhile you've paid 30 million in tax to Peru?'

'No, 51 million. Last year alone we paid over 21 million in tax.'

'And how much profit did you transfer to New York in the same year?'

'You can easily work it out, you might as well get the figure from me – 49 million. It was a good year.'

49 million. In spite of everything, that is only 20·2 per cent profit on a total investment of 242 million dollars.

But on top of this comes the 'depletion allowance', which appears to have amounted in 1966 to 35 million. The true profit was thus 49 plus 35 million, or 84 million.

And 84 million in profit on a total investment of 242 million is 34·7 per cent.

Also, 209·4 million of the 242 million invested consisted of loans that had already been largely repaid. The company's own capital was only 32·6 million. And 84 million in profit on 32·6 million is 257·7 per cent.

So Mr Bears was quite right when he told me that he could honestly quote any figure he liked for profit. It all depends how you calculate. But a reasonable approach, surely, is to put the profit in relation to the capital really invested by the company's owners in 1966, in the form either of paid-up capital, 32·6 million, or loans, 70 million. *In toto*, then, rightly 100 million. To make 84 million in profit is then at any rate 84 per cent, and not bad going.

RISKS AND RISK PREMIUMS

You own a company that deals in copper products. You want
to buy copper from yourself in accordance with the prices on
a market that you can help control. So you invest 100 million
in a mine like the Toquepala. You have to have 100 million,
and be able to borrow as much again. Of course, you want a
normal interest on your money. This interest is written off
as an overhead. Naturally, also, you want your money back
in reasonable time. Most of it you get back in seven years, the
rest in another three. All right and proper.

But then, when these all very right and proper demands
have been met, the ore body is still there, and good for
another 30, perhaps 50 years. The buildings are still there.
Much of the equipment is still there. You own all this. Nor
is that all. This property that, having got your money back,
you own, continues not only to produce copper for you but
also produces a surplus, a surplus on the capital you have
already had back, a surplus that in 1966 amounted to 84
million dollars.

It is at this point that ordinary people begin to think they
are dreaming.

When you talk about these problems with gentlemen like
Mr Bears, they say that all profit over and above normal rates
of interest and amortization represents a risk premium. And
this is reasonable, as long as the capital is outstanding, as
long as you haven't yet got it back with interest. But this
risk premium then continues to pay off year after year, and
for what risk is it then supposed to compensate? Mr Bears
could never explain this so that I understood.

All this talk of 'risks' must also be seen in a historical
perspective. The Cerro and other big companies have
operated very profitably indeed in Peru since the turn of the
century. They have always seemed to operate on the brink of

revolution and civil war, but somehow these dangers have never materialized. It is the same in Chile. The largest copper-mine in Chile, one of the largest in the world, is the Chuqui-camata, which makes even the Toquepala look small. It was discovered just after the turn of the century by an American amateur geologist who bought it 'for peanuts', as Mr Fahm, the present head of the mine, put it. This was on our first evening in Chuqui. The directors had a little party for one another and were very outspoken.

Anyway, when this geologist realized that there was a for-tune here which he couldn't exploit himself, he went up to Guggenheim and said 'Look, Harry', etc. and sold it for 100 times what he had paid. He then retired to a little place in New Jersey, and lived happily ever afterwards. What risk did he take?

Guggenheim admittedly knew that the find was worth many times what he had paid for it, but he didn't really know *how* many times more – so he sold it to Anaconda for 60 million dollars, and made 50 on the deal. In this, he actually took a risk – a risk of selling a gold-mine at a give-away price. And this risk, according to Mr Fahm, Guggen-heim should never have taken. 'He's turned in his grave since then every time Anaconda publish their balance sheet.'

Anaconda knew what they were buying. Since it was opened on the outbreak of the Great War, the Chuqui has steadily remained one of the most productive coppermines in the world.

'It's fantastic working here,' Mr Fahm told me that even-ing. 'Expenditures are just no worry at all, there's that much to draw on. Young engineers can come over here, get the mistakes out of their system, waste a few million here and there, it doesn't make any difference. The mine can take it.'

Worst of all, this feeling of inexhaustible wealth had spread to the workers. Could I imagine what those idle bastards had thought up now? They wanted fur linings to their leather jackets. The bastards had one leather jacket a year free from the company, and since it was only cold for a few months of the year the jackets lasted for ten. The other nine jackets they sold. Anyway, when they came up with their demand for a fur lining, a compromise was suggested – fur in the jacket, but only a jacket every other year. They wouldn't buy that one, oh no. So now they are refusing to work overtime, and we're having a hell of a time ...

'But on this one, at least, we haven't given in. Too many concessions have already been made to the workers in this corporation. What those goddam Indians really want is an honest-to-god German – a real German officer-type who'll scream AttenSHUN!!! And march them up and down until they faint from exhaustion. Then, you bet' (he gave a credible imitation of a fainting man who gets to his feet and salutes, a rapturous expression on his face), 'after that they'd die for that German. They love it, every time ... My blood!'

It suddenly occurred to him that this might sound a bit odd, that it wasn't an entirely modern attitude to labour. He added:

'I don't mean you've got to stand over them with a whip, exactly. That's not what I mean, right? But the corporation has to be firm, show a strong hand.'

All the executives agreed that the Chilean workers were lazy, ungrateful animals; one of them, however, gave a rather more scientific explanation:

'This place is like a government department. All the workers want is in. Once they are signed on, they don't have to work. All they have to do is make sure they are sober on the job, and not arrive late too often. Then they've got it made for the rest of their lives.'

'Right,' agreed Fahm. 'We're far too paternalistic here. The corporation holds the workers' hands from womb to tomb. They have no initiative.'

'Isn't that how they usually describe the People's Communes in China?' I wondered.

'Sure. It's pure communism. Except that with a communist régime they'd know how to beat the idleness out of these bastards.'

'Know how we keep them at work?' said the other. 'Hire-purchase contracts. It's the only way. Radios, bicycles, sewing-machines. ... Most of them are up over their ears in debt. There's nothing like hire purchase to keep things quiet. These guys just can't afford to strike.'

They went on complaining like this for a bit. But they loved their mine.

'Would you believe it? We extract two tons of ore for every ton of rock we throw away!'

'Would you believe it? Our total costs are 16 cents a pound!'

Copper was then at 60 cents.

The following morning, at the office, I reminded Mr Fahm of these figures. By now, he had had second thoughts about discussing them. But we managed to agree that the average selling price in 1966 was 45 cents a pound. The profit 29 cents a pound, or almost 200 per cent of the cost of extraction. Production 668 million pounds. Which meant a profit before taxation of 193 million dollars. No 'depletion allowance'. But a 'deduction for amortization' of 2·5 cents a pound or 16·7 million dollars. On the rest of its profit Anaconda paid tax, which in Chile in 1966 was around 60 per cent. Tax paid: 97·8 million. Take-home profit: 78·5 million. Profit plus tax-free deduction for amortization: 95·2 million dollars.

In 1966 the tax-rate for Anaconda in Chile was twice as high as for La Southern in Peru. Three years later the difference had been evened out, in that La Southern had lost its tax privileges while company tax in Chile had been reduced. Both companies then paid about 52 per cent. It was in the calculation of taxable profit that the two countries differed – control by the Peruvian state was less effective, the rules on depreciation were more liberal, and the 'depletion allowance' permitted the mines to deduct one-third of their profit before taxation.

The Chilean state, under President Frei's government, purchased part-ownership in certain mines. That was probably a step forward, But would it not, in spite of everything, have been more to Chile's advantage to nationalize the mines? I put this question to the Chief Accountant in Chuqui, a dry and gloomy Englishman.

'Well, yes, in the sense that it's always "to the advantage" of a thief to grab someone else's property, at least until the police catch up with him.'

'But Chile could easily pay you the full book-value of the mine, 400 million.'

'We would have to be paid for the risks we have taken, on top of that.'

'Hasn't the company already received such payment in the form of the risk premiums included in the profit each year?'

No reply.

'Anyway, what risk do you mean? This must be one of the least risky mines in the world – with a large, stable ore-body in a stable and fairly democratic country that, historically, has always enjoyed the best relations with foreign capital.'

'Mining is always a lottery. To begin with, you never know if the ore is really there ...'

'With modern methods it's practically impossible not to know. Only an idiot invests today in a mine where there's no ore. Right? And here in Chuqui there's never been any doubt, there was enough ore lying visible to the naked eye to warrant any investment you care to name ...'

'Copper prices can fall ...'

'Yes, but not *that* much. They may not stay as high as

they are now, at 60 cents.[3] But since your costs are only 16 cents you do have a certain margin ...'

'That's the margin we have to keep to protect ourselves against risk.'

'What risk?'

'Let me take a concrete example. I won't go into the technical details, but you may know that we have two sorts of copper ore here at the mine. Anyway, in a year or two's time, one sort will be finished. If we hadn't, by sheer accident, found a big new ore-body next to the first – then our entire equipment handling this sort of ore would have run out of material. You can imagine what a loss that would have meant.'

'Wouldn't it be more adequate to say absence of profit? I mean, the company would never have installed the plant if there hadn't – when it was installed – been enough ore to make it pay. Surely?'

'Well, of course, that's true enough ...'

'And now that the ore which originally warranted the investment has run out, and you've had the fabulous good luck to find new ore, which unexpectedly makes it possible to go on coining money from the same plant, you actually talk of the *loss* you would have made if you hadn't had such a staggering bit of luck, you talk about the *risks* you have taken. I still want to know *what* risks.'[4]

INVASION IN THE DESERT

The Panamericana, on its way south from Lima, follows the beach down on the threshold of the continent, just out of reach of the giant breakers. You travel along a narrow rim between mountain and sea. Never before had I had such a

3. By 27 June 1969, the price had risen to 64·265 cents.
4. See postscript to this Chapter.

strong feeling of being on the back of things, the other side, at the world's end.

Brazil is the hanging belly, the Andes are the backbone – all Latin America lay there like a toppled body. Outside the towns there was hardly a single dwelling fit for human use. The best are of sun-dried brick, but they are the exceptions. Most of them are huts put together of reeds or maize tops, often smeared over with a thin layer of clay. Sometimes well enough constructed, but for the most part very dilapidated, and naturally without any facilities for water, electricity or drainage. They could hardly have been any worse during the Stone Age. And the nights are desert-cold.

The road leads through an Icelandic lunar landscape. Climbing over dunes several hundred yards high that are continuously trying to reclaim the asphalt, and often succeeding. Through rocky cactus deserts, where the ground suddenly displays corrosive sores of poisonous colours, ill-smelling as vomit. The material is often taken directly from the spot – a red road leads through a red desert, a road of ash-grey through ash-grey. When Aron got out to pee, he thought the stones were all made of iron – and all equally rusty.

Some sixty miles south of Nasca a road takes off to the right towards San Juan. And what has happened in San Juan? The Utah Construction Company's annual report for 1953 states:

In January last year, San Juan on the south coast of Peru was a sleepy little bay on a deserted shore. Inhabited by a few fisher-Indians who practised their profession much as their forefathers had done in the days of the Incas.

But their quiet, peaceful life was soon to be disturbed by an invasion, organized by Utah. Today, less than ten months later, San Juan is a lively port, with one of the busiest harbours on the South American West Coast. A town of almost 3,000 inhabitants has grown up in the desert.

At the beginning of 1953, the Utah Construction Company joined with the Cyprus Mining Company, a well-known name in mining, to form a new corporation, the Marcona Mining Company. The intention is to develop the extensive iron-ore finds of the Marcona plateau. The new subsidiary engaged Utah of the Americas, a fully-owned subsidiary of the Utah Construction Company, to build the plant and get the mine working.

The first task was to transport thousands of tons of material and equipment to this isolated area. Careful planning was necessary. Material flowed from factories and warehouses by road and rail to ports in the United States. Ships were loaded in Portland, San Francisco, San Pedro, Mobile and New York – all carefully co-ordinated to arrive at the remote bay of San Juan exactly when needed, during the first months of the year.

An efficient team of technicians from the United States, backed by a growing army of local Peruvians, were working rapidly towards their common goal – ore shipments had to start in May. The result was a record in rapid development. Nothing like it had ever been seen in those parts. The twenty-mile road from mine to harbour was rebuilt to withstand specially designed 60-ton ore trucks. An ore-crusher was installed at the mine to reduce the ore to a suitable size for smelting works in the United States. This facility is one of the largest of its kind in the world.

On 1 May, three months after the first technicians had arrived from the United States, the first iron ore was put on board the first ship, the M.S. Libertad. By 8 May, loading had been completed. Followed by the cheers of tired but happy workers, the ship slowly left the road on its long voyage through the Panama Canal to the United States.

Now the ore is already flowing in a steady stream from the mines to growing depots on the quayside. The ships load in eight hours, and 20 shiploads a week leave the harbour.

The construction feat performed by the Utah Company of the Americas at San Juan will long be remembered throughout Latin America. It was a truly remarkable performance, etc. . . . And as a result of this feat the Marcona Mining Company is today involved in profitable, large-scale ore extraction. The Marcona

Mining Company has rapidly assumed a position as a major permanent factor in the economy of the United States and of Peru.

Fifteen years later, one September day in 1967, I arrived in San Juan to view the miracle. The Marcona Mining Company did not receive me. They referred to the lack of accommodation. And since everything in San Juan is owned by the company and it was too cold to spend the night in the car, we were forced to return to Nasca.

'This isn't my job,' I thought furiously, as we left. 'This is a job the economists and contemporary historians should have done for me. I'm a writer.'

The mist came rolling in from the sea, over the desert. The yellow sand sifted over the road, dry as in an hour-glass. The wall of mist approached, and we didn't know if what was coming was sand or sea – until the rainbow suddenly rose shimmering in the fog.

Every minor poet these days qualifies for a biography. But who will write a biography of the Marcona Mining Company? Who is currently studying the influence of the Southern Peru Copper Corporation? Who is researching the history of the Cerro de Pasco Corporation? These giant companies that move mountains, create towns and level them once more to the ground, that intervene in the lives of millions, and whose influence extends over centuries and continents – what makes them so uninteresting from the scientific point of view?

At most they have been the subject of a commissioned work to commemorate some anniversary, or a romanticized brochure from the company's public relations department.

There must be something radically wrong with research, when it turns its back like this on the great questions in economics and contemporary history – leaving it to the writers to dig for the most elementary facts about the world we live in.

THE POETRY OF FIGURES

The iron ore of the Marcona plateau was discovered as early as 1905 by a Peruvian mining engineer named Federico Fuchs.

In 1929 'La Comisión Carbonera y Siderúrgica Nacional' was formed to prepare its exploitation.

In the Thirties Peruvian engineers completed large-scale investigations, together with the consulting firm of C. C. Morfitt.

In the late Forties the finds were further documented by drillings performed by Peruvian engineers, who demonstrated conclusively that profitable extraction was possible.

The 'Corporación del Santa' had a road built from the Panamericana to the fishing harbour of San Juan. Workers' accommodation and offices were put up. They started building a shipping port, and procured the first mining trucks and excavators.

Two million dollars had already been invested. Six, perhaps eight, million more were needed to start operations.

The Corporación del Santa didn't have the money. The Utah Construction Company did. So exploitation of the ore was transferred to a Utah subsidiary, the Marcona Mining Company.

Everyone knows that it's expensive to be poor. But just *how* expensive is it? In March 1968 we were back in Lima, and I looked up the Marcona Mining Company's head office, Camana 780, to try to get an answer. It was Dr Enrique East, Vice President and the company's legal adviser, who received me. I had with me John Gerassi's book *The Great Fear*, and used it as a provocative opening to the conversation.

'From 1954 to 1960, in the space of only six years, Marcona made over 30 million dollars net (after tax) on an investment of half a million,' writes Gerassi. 'This is a yield of no less than 6,000 per cent.'

'Gerassi's figure is surprising,' I began. 'And one error in his text is easy to see. 1954 to 60 isn't six years as he says, it's seven. But even in seven years . . .'

'The whole thing's crazy,' said Dr East. 'What kind of book is that?'

'It was published in 1963 by Macmillan's in New York, a reputable publisher. The author has been the Latin American correspondent for both *Time* magazine and the *New York Times*.'

'Well, it's all wrong anyway,' said Dr East. 'To begin with it wasn't 1954 we started up. It was 1953. Also, the original investment wasn't half a million, it was eight million. And since then this investment has been increased by a large amount every year. Let's have a look . . .'

The quotation from Gerassi had fulfilled its purpose. He started looking in his desk, pulled out some papers, and began reading out figures. (See Table 10 below.)

'Well, this is an entirely different set of figures,' I said. 'It seems a bit odd, in fact, that you have kept the mine in operation, with the profit in recent years often below 2 per cent.'

He referred to the duty of private capital to promote the development of Latin America, even if it wasn't exactly a profitable business in the short term. His address assumed tones almost of pathos as he complained how frightful it was to see suspicion cast upon these honest endeavours, something which was unfortunately becoming increasingly common, even in the American press, etc., etc.

Finally, I managed to get a word in.

'To get back to the figures for a moment – has the "depletion allowance" been included in the profit?'

'No, that's in the expenditure column, which is the usual practice.'

'And the total investment given here, 121 million, is that before or after depreciation?'

'The depreciation isn't included, no.'

'How much has been written off?'

'About nine per cent of the investment, on average.'

'What can that make since 1954?'

'Between 50 and 60 million.'

His answers became increasingly terse. He obviously didn't like the turn the conversation had taken. I took my leave, asking if I could come back when I had studied the Table a bit more closely. I would be very welcome.

I went round the corner and sat down in a café to go through the figures.

Table 10

MARCONA MINING COMPANY: FINANCIAL
STATISTICS 1953–66. U.S. DOLLARS MILL.

Year	A. Receipts	B. Expenditures	C. Profit	D. Investment	E. C. in % of D.
1953	6·2	4·4	1·8	9·9	18·6
54	12·8	10·8	2·0	13·4	15·1
55	8·4	7·9	0·5	13·7	3·8
56	15·6	13·4	2·2	15·7	14·3
57	24·6	19·3	5·3	17·7	30·0
58	17·2	14·7	2·5	23·0	10·0
59	17·9	16·1	1·8	25·6	7·1
1960	24·8	21·3	3·5	32·0	10·9
61	28·0	23·8	4·2	49·6	8·4
62	27·8	25·8	2·0	70·3	2·9
63	31·5	30·0	1·5	80·1	1·9
64	38·0	36·9	1·2	83·1	1·4
65	44·8	42·8	2·0	103·7	2·0
66	51·2	49·3	1·9	121·0	1·6
Total	349·0	316·4	32·4	121·0	
				Average	9·1

Source: Marcona Mining Company, *Financial Statistics* 13 April 1967. Figures rounded off to one decimal point.

The first task was to calculate the 'depletion allowance'. According to the legislation (Act 11357, Article 54) this is to comprise 15 per cent of the gross value of sales, but must not exceed 50 per cent of net profit. In practice, the allowance comprises one-third of gross profit before the allowance and taxation. I knew the tax figure (A) and net profit (B). A+B is two-thirds of the gross profit. The depletion allowance (C) is thus half of A+B. The results can be seen in the following Table.

Table 11

MARCONA MINING COMPANY: DEPLETION
ALLOWANCE 1953–66. U.S. DOLLARS MILL.

Year	A. Tax	B. Reported profit	C. Depletion allowance	D. True profit
1953	0·8	1·8	1·3	3·1
54	1·5	2·0	1·8	3·8
55	1·0	0·5	0·8	1·3
56	1·6	2·2	1·9	4·1
57	3·1	5·3	4·2	9·5
58	1·7	2·5	2·1	4·6
59	1·7	1·8	1·8	3·6
1960	2·4	3·5	2·9	6·4
61	2·7	4·2	3·5	7·7
62	2·3	2·0	2·1	4·1
63	2·5	1·5	2·0	3·5
64	3·3	1·2	2·3	3·5
65	3·7	2·0	2·9	4·9
1966	4·2	1·9	3·1	5·0
Total	32·5	32·4	32·7	65·1

Source: A and B: Marcona Mining Company, *Financial Statistics* 13 April 1967 to 3 October 1967. C=½ (A+B). D=B+C.

In all, during these fourteen years, the 'depletion allowance' thus amounted to 32·7 million dollars – something more than the profit as reported. Which means that the

Marcona Mining Company, in the financial statistics it
provides for the general public, has 'forgotten' over half its
profit.

It can be objected that the Peruvians, by various laws
passed during the Sixties, have tried to restrict the free dis-
position by companies of this 'depletion allowance', and
channel this share of the profit into new investments within
the country. So it is perhaps a matter of taste whether you
prefer to have the 'depletion allowance' increase the profit
or deduct it from the investment figures – but in one of these
two places the allowance must be accounted for. I have
assigned it to the profit – which thus increases from the
reported 32·4 million to 65·1 million dollars.

I then got to work on the investments (column D, Table
11). One observes that investments are the only item Marcona reports cumulatively – which naturally makes them
appear extra large. Also, they fail to take into account the
depreciation, which Dr East had said averaged 9 per cent.
These are deductions the company make for wear and loss in
value on its assets in Peru. But since new procurements are
booked either as expenditures (column B) or as new investments (column D), depreciation must be booked as a reduction in investments (column D). See Table 12.

The depreciation thus brings down the invested capital
from 121 million to 61·7 million dollars. Obviously, the latter
figure isn't as exact as it sounds, since it is calculated on the
basis of 9 per cent, which is a rough average. Probably,
depreciation was somewhat greater than shown by the Table
at the beginning of the period, and somewhat smaller towards
the end. But the final sum, 59·3, is within the limit given by
Dr East when he said that total depreciation had been 'between 50 and 60 million'.

A further peculiarity remains. According to Marcona's
figures, reported in column A, the original investment was
9·9 million dollars. Dr East said 8 million dollars. It is the

latter figure that agrees with the contemporary newspaper accounts – Marcona apparently started with 0·5 million in paid-up capital and 7·5 million as a loan from the parent company.

Then where does the figure 9·9 million come from? The

Table 12

MARCONA MINING COMPANY: INVESTMENTS
AND DEPRECIATION 1953–66. U.S. DOLLARS
MILL.

Year	A. Total investment	B. Annual investment	C. Annual depreciation	D. Total investment minus depreciation	E. D minus 1·9
1953	9·9	9·9	0·9	9·0	7·1
54	13·4	3·5	1·2	11·3	9·4
55	13·7	0·3	1·2	10·4	8·5
56	15·7	2·0	1·4	11·0	9·1
57	17·7	2·0	1·6	11·4	9·5
58	23·0	5·3	2·1	14·6	12·7
59	25·6	2·6	2·3	14·9	13·0
1960	32·0	6·4	2·9	18·4	16·5
61	49·6	17·6	4·5	31·5	29·6
62	70·3	20·7	6·3	45·9	44·0
63	80·1	9·8	7·2	48·5	46·6
64	83·1	3·0	7·5	44·0	42·1
65	103·7	20·6	9·3	55·3	53·4
1966	121·0	17·3	10·9	61·7	59·8
Total	121·0	121·0	59·3	61·7	59·8

Source: A: Table 10, column D. C: 9% of figures in column A. D: Total investment minus cumulative depreciation. E: See commentary in text.

Peruvian state is known to have spent about 2 million dollars
on investigations and development of the find before Marcona
took over its exploitation. It is common for a mine to be
capitalized at the sum spent on investigation and development. This can be correct enough from the standpoint of
depreciation, but when it comes to assessing Marcona's
return on invested capital it is more proper to reckon only
with the capital Marcona themselves contributed. In column
E I have therefore reduced Marcona's investment after depreciation by 1·9 million dollars.

The end result is that the Marcona Mining Company, in
the financial statistics provided for the general public, put
their own investment at twice the true figure.

On the basis of the calculations in Tables 11 and 12, I could
now make the following reconstruction of the figures I had
received from the company.

Table 13

MARCONA MINING COMPANY: FIRST
RECONSTRUCTION OF INVESTMENTS AND PROFITS
1953–66. U.S. DOLLARS MILL.

Year	A. Annual net invest- ment	B. Annual profit	C. Total net invest- ment	D. Total profit	E. Annual profit in % of total net invest- ment
1953	7·1	3·1	7·1	3·1	43·7
54	2·3	3·8	9·4	6·9	40·4
55	—0·9	1·3	8·5	8·2	15·3
56	0·6	4·1	9·1	12·3	45·1
57	0·4	9·5	9·5	21·8	100·0
58	3·2	4·6	12·7	26·4	36·2
59	0·3	3·6	13·0	30·0	27·7
1960	3·5	6·4	16·5	36·4	38·8

Year	A. Annual net investment	B. Annual profit	C. Total net investment	D. Total profit	E. Annual profit in % of total net investment
1961	13·1	7·7	29·6	44·1	26·0
62	14·4	4·1	44·0	48·2	9·3
63	2·6	3·5	46·6	51·7	7·5
64	−4·5	3·5	42·1	55·2	8·3
65	11·3	4·9	53·4	60·1	9·2
1966	6·4	5·0	59·8	65·1	8·4
Total	59·8	65·1	59·8	65·1	415·9
				Average	29·7%

Source: A and C: Table 12, column E. B and D: Table 11, column D.

This Table seemed to give a more realistic picture of the company's return on its capital than that Dr East was trying to give me. For safety's sake I thought I would check it with Dr East himself, so I went back to the Marcona office. The secretary went in to announce my arrival, but came back and inquired as to my business. I explained that I had spent the day on the statistics I had been given that morning, and that I should like to have Dr East's opinions on my calculations. After a while the secretary came back and said that it was rather late in the afternoon, and Dr East had no opportunity to see me before the office closed. I was welcome back some other time.

I believed that my results followed inevitably from Marcona's own figures and the Peruvian legislation. But there are numerous loopholes. According to a commission appointed by the Corporación del Santa on 14 January 1964 to study contacts between the Corporación and Marcona, the company's investments, depreciation and profits were instead as follows:

Table 14

MARCONA MINING COMPANY: INVESTMENTS AND
PROFITS 1953–62 ACCORDING TO THE CORPORACIÓN
DEL SANTA'S COMMISSION OF INQUIRY. U.S. DOLLARS
MILL.

Year	Total investment	Total depreciation	Total profit
1953	8·5	...	...
54	11·0	2·5	5·0
55	11·5	4·5	6·5
56	13·0	7·5	12·0
57	14·5	10·0	23·5
58	20·0	12·5	29·5
59	22·0	15·0	34·5
1960	27·0	17·0	42·5
61	43·5	19·0	53·0
1962	64·0	22·5	58·0

Source: *Informe de la Comisión nombrada por el Directorio de la Corporación del Santa el 14 de Enero 1964*, folio XIX, quoted from Malpica, op. cit., p. 195. Total profit includes 'depletion allowance'. '. .'=no information available.

The commission's report is not available to the general public, and Malpica's presentation of its results leaves many question's unanswered. But the figures in the Table agree very well with those that Gerassi, without quoting his sources, gives in *The Great Fear*, 1963. It looks as if Marcona's profits were much higher than those I had reached. Here is a Table which permits a comparison.

Table 15

MARCONA MINING COMPANY: INVESTMENTS AND
PROFITS 1953–62 ACCORDING TO THE CORPORACIÓN
DEL SANTA'S COMMISSION OF INQUIRY. PROCESSED.
U.S. DOLLARS MILL.

Year	Total investment after depreciation	Annual profit including depletion allowance	Annual profit in % of total investment after depreciation
1953	8·5	...	...
54	8·5	5·0	58·8
55	7·0	1·5	21·4
56	5·5	5·5	100·0
57	4·5	11·5	255·6
58	7·5	6·0	80·0
59	7·0	5·5	78·6
1960	10·0	8·0	80·0
61	24·5	10·5	42·9
1962	41·5	5·0	12·0
Total	41·5	58·5	729·3
			Average 81%

Source: Table 14

The commission also draws attention to Marcona's policy
on prices. Marcona sell the ore to an affiliated company, the
Cía San Juan, registered in Panama, which sells it in turn –
often to another affiliated company. The booked value of
sales has averaged 6·1 dollars a ton, FOB. A consultant employed by the commission, engineer Lloyd M. Scofield,
estimated that the value of 60-per-cent iron ore of the type
exported by Marcona in the years concerned should have
been instead between 7·5 and 8 dollars per ton, FOB.

A couple of days after my visit to Marcona I tried to discuss this problem with the Corporación del Santa, which has
its premises in the Cerro del Pasco's great building, a stone's

throw from Marcona Mining. The answers I got were very evasive. Nothing could be proved. Royalties from Marcona constituted the corporation's main source of income – they were unwilling to say anything that could disrupt the good relationship existing between themselves and the company.

However, if you look at the contract reached in 1966 as a result of the commission's activities, you find a series of very detailed specifications of how the ore is to be valued for the calculation of royalties. Such specifications were lacking in previous contracts, and this, it is remarked, gave rise to 'controversies'.

Table 16

MARCONA MINING COMPANY: HYPOTHETICAL
RECONSTRUCTION OF INVESTMENTS AND PROFITS
1953–62. U.S. DOLLARS MILL.

Year	Total investment after depreciation	Estimated profit	Estimated profit in % of total investment after depreciation
1953	8·5	...	...
54	8·5	7·9	92·9
55	7·0	3·4	48·6
56	5·5	9·1	165·5
57	4·5	17·2	382·2
58	7·5	10·0	133·3
59	7·0	9·6	137·1
1960	10·0	13·7	137·0
61	24·5	16·9	69·0
1962	41·5	11·4	27·5
Total	41·5	99·2	1,193·1
			Average 132·6%

Source: Table 15: 'Estimated profit'=profit+depletion allowance +23% of the receipts given in Table 10, column A.

On the grounds cited, I find it extremely probable that Marcona under-debited the ore during the period preceding the 1966 contract. If the discrepancy was as great as suggested by the commission's consultant, Marcona's receipts during the years 1953–66 should be written up by between 23 and 31 per cent to arrive at the true sales value. On the income reported in Table 10, 349·0 million dollars, this would have given between 80 and 108 million in concealed profit, taken out in Panama, where the tax is very low.

If one accepts (a) the commission's account of Marcona's investments and profits, and (b) the lower limit quoted by the consultant for Marcona's undervaluation of their exports – two hypothetical but by no means unreasonable assumptions – we can reconstruct Marcona's investments as in Table 16.

Just as a multi-national company can adjust its income downwards so it can adjust its expenditure upwards. One can over-debit equipment that a subsidiary buys from or via the parent company. One can take a good price for the services rendered to the subsidiary by the parent company, or by one allied to it. When new investments are made, one can have an affiliated company handle the construction work – the opportunities to salt the accounts are obvious. It is the Utah Company of the Americas, a fully-owned subsidiary of the Utah Construction Company, that has done the construction work for the Marcona Mining Company.

Another popular way of placing income on the expenditure side is to bring in the bulk of the capital in the form of a loan from the parent company. The interest can then be booked as an expenditure, although it is a part of the yield on the investment that goes back to the parent company. In this respect, Marcona have gone even further than the Southern Peru Copper Corporation – of the original investment, 7·5 million was a loan from the Utah Construction

Company. According to the investigating commission, this debt has developed as in Table 17.

Table 17

MARCONA MINING CORPORATION:
INVESTMENTS AND LIABILITIES 1953–66 ACCORDING
TO THE CORPORACIÓN DEL SANTA'S COMMISSION
OF INQUIRY. U.S. DOLLARS MILL.

Year	Total investment after depreciation	Debt to parent company
1953	8·5	7·5
54	8·5	7·5
55	7·0	7·0
56	5·5	4·0
57	4·5	0·0
58	7·5	3·5
59	7·0	3·0
1960	10·0	1·5
61	24·5	12·5
1962	41·5	10·5

Source: *Informe de la Comisión nombrada por el Directorio de la Corporación del Santa el 14 de Enero 1964*, folio XIX, quoted from Malpica, op cit., p. 196.

It is impossible to posit an even fairly reasonable hypothesis as to how far Marcona's expenditures and investments as booked have been increased by over-debiting, and how these two factors plus rates of interest have affected the company's true yield. I therefore refrained from making any further tables.

I thought, however, that I had sufficient material to continue my discussion with Dr East. I therefore took advantage of his kind promise to see me again. It proved, however, impossible to get a time to see Dr East or any other management representative while I was in Lima.

I therefore asked to see the annual reports to shareholders. The answer was that these reports were available only in the United States, since Marcona were an American company. I wrote to an agent in the United States, who went to the Utah Construction Company, the parent company, and asked to see Marcona's annual reports. The answer was that these were available only in Lima, since Marcona were a company operating in Peru. When I returned to Peru in March 1969, I again had someone ask about these annual reports, quoting the parent company's answer. Without result.

With which I pass the case on with pleasure to the next interested party who visits Lima.

WHAT THE FIGHT IS ABOUT

I have discussed four American companies that are – or in Anaconda's case hoped to become – major enterprises in Peru. But they are far from being the only ones. In 1968, when the military took over, the economic power of the United States permeated the entire Peruvian economy.

Eighty-five per cent of the country's mining production was owned by foreign firms.

The same applied to 88 per cent of oil extraction.

Fourteen of the 20 largest fishing enterprises were dominated by foreign capital.

Six of the largest sugar-mills belonged to foreigners.

Exports of cotton, wool, and coffee were all in the hands of foreigners, who to a large extent also financed production.

Three of the most important banks were controlled from outside, as of course were the branches of foreign banks established in Peru.

Telecommunications, a large part of the railways, and the production of electric power were handled by foreign firms.

Eighty per cent of the total advertising volume was handled by seven foreign advertising agencies.

Industry consisted predominantly of subsidiaries which answered for the final processing of imported foreign-brand goods.

The import trade was dominated by foreign companies, as were the leading department and multiple stores.

All in all, predominantly U.S.-owned firms answered for 35 to 40 per cent of Peru's national product.

Add to this a national debt that had grown by 400 per cent in six years and consisted largely of short loans at high interest, loans which had to be re-financed in the near future – and you have a picture of total economic dependence.

Mr Fahm told me how the founder of his company came upon its registered name in a newspaper report from the time of the American Civil War. 'General Grant's armies will surround and crush the armies of General Lee like a giant anaconda.' This excited his imagination. He called his company the Anaconda.

Peru is caught in a deadly embrace. Peruvian opinion has been forced to accept this fact, and its indignation is stifled by its helplessness.

But even helpless fury must find an outlet somewhere. Peru has turned upon the International Petroleum Company.

Why just the I.P.C.?

I visited the company in the autumn of 1967 and the spring of 1968. On both occasions they refused me an interview, quoting the sensitive negotiating situation. When I went back in the spring of 1969 there was no longer any company to interview.

Yet so far as I can understand, the I.P.C.'s business methods differ very little from those of other American companies. If anything, the big export companies have been in a better position to take out concealed profits – precisely because they sell on the export market. But the I.P.C., which in the past few decades has produced mainly for the home market, has become more directly involved in the country's internal politics. The ordinary Peruvian consumer has felt the I.P.C.'s power more directly than he has that of Cerro, Southern, or Marcona. So the I.P.C. was made the scapegoat, and the whole fury of Peru's helplessness has descended upon its head.

It is not entirely fair.

On the other hand, the I.P.C. has trailed its coat very blatantly. The big mining-companies at least recognize Peru's titular ownership to the ore they extract. From the legal point of view, they simply have concessions to exploit it. But the I.P.C. claims to *own* its oilfields in Peru.

This is what stirred up all the emotion. To the Peruvians, the I.P.C.'s claim to ownership is a national insult. The arguments are as follows.

Peru maintains:

The I.P.C. has by fraudulent means obtained title to Peruvian oilfields that by law can belong only to the state. Since 1924, the I.P.C. has there extracted ore to the value of 690 million dollars. To compensate for the loss thus caused to the country, the government has now expropriated the I.P.C.'s facilities in Peru.

The U.S. answers:

Contrary to agreements contracted, the military junta in Peru has expropriated property to a value of 120 million dollars from the largest tax-payer in the country. The pretext is an ancient dispute concerning title. This dispute is nothing to do with the I.P.C., since it was finally decided by arbitration in 1922. And the I.P.C. did not buy the oil find until 1924.

Who is in the right?

As usual, the figures quoted by both parties are suspect. The Peruvians have never been able satisfactorily to explain how they have reached a figure of just 690 million dollars for the oil extracted.

The I.P.C. has been equally unable to explain why its facilities in Peru should be worth just 120 million. Sometimes a figure of 200 million has actually been mentioned. The Peruvian government has valued these facilities at 54 million. And in 1965 the U.S. Department of Commerce valued *total* North American oil investments in Peru at 60 million dollars.[6]

Since then the I.P.C. has borrowed a total of 40 million dollars from American banks. Following expropriation, however, the Peruvians claim to have discovered that the I.P.C. never actually bought the equipment these loans were supposed to pay for, and to some extent used the amortization as a way of getting capital illegally out of the country. It seems probable that the I.P.C. management had long foreseen the inevitable, and got its capital to safety in good time.

And the I.P.C. as a tax-payer? Here the Americans are right. At the beginning of the Fifties, legislation was introduced requiring foreign countries to file their accounts in Peru. The I.P.C. then became the country's largest tax-payer. Its high taxes indicated even greater profits, and many people wondered why these profits had previously been allowed to leave the country practically untaxed. This criticism was silenced, since the I.P.C. was not only a big tax-payer but also a major contributor to bought unions, compliant political parties, and journalists willing to do a service.

In 1957, however, the I.P.C. bought a majority interest in an oilfield belonging to its largest competitor, Lobitos, thus further strengthening its position on the Peruvian market. In the following year a major price-increase was announced, which in practice passed on the tax burden to the Peruvian consumer. This roused popular opinion. People began to ask themselves how the I.P.C. had acquired the oil the price of

6. U.S. Department of Commerce, *Survey of Current Business*, September 1966, pp. 34–35. The same source gives, for 1965, 21 million dollars in interest and dividends on this 60 million.

which it was trying to raise. And there began a debate which has now – ten years later – resulted in expropriation and international conflict.

WHO OWNS THE OIL?

The news agencies and journalists have usually taken their answer to this question from the U.S. Embassy's *Background information on the I.P.C. question in Peru*, dated 14 February 1969. A more detailed and slightly less slanted version of the I.P.C.'s position is given by an article that is regularly re-printed in the *Peruvian Times* every time the I.P.C. question comes up. In the paper's archives in Lima, this picture can be filled out with the I.P.C.'s own contributions to the debate in the Fifties, printed as paid advertisements. These offer some aspects to the problem that have since been forgotten.

The Peruvian position is formulated in *Petroleum in Peru*, Lima 1969, a poorly-translated rush job, anonymously written at the government's request by the Chief Editor of *El Comercio*, Augusto Zimmerman Zavala. Better documented and more detailed is the same author's *La Historia Secreta del Petróleo*, Lima 1968. This reprints Alfonso Montesino's famous speech to the Senate on 27 August 1959. The position of the army is also described in initiated detail. The best historical presentation, however, is still E. Ramírez Novoa's *Recuperación de la Brea y Pariñas*, Lima 1964, which has become very difficult to obtain. A later version by the same writer, dated 5 March 1969, is called *El Problema del Petróleo en el Perú*.

The difficulty is thus not lack of material. What is difficult is to pick out the decisive arguments, which the combatants have buried beneath a mountain of accusations and counter-accusations. Time and again one is enticed on to paths leading absolutely nowhere. Particularly the Peruvians have excelled in legal quibbles; they make great play, for instance, with a suggestion that the president of the Federal Court in Switzerland was not president of the Federal Court in Switzerland when he signed the so-called 'Paris award', and that this judgement is nowhere to be found in the original. Arguments like this seem important and take a long time to study, but they are ultimately – as far as I can see – all irrelevant. The Americans find it easier to stick to the essentials – although unfortunately not always to the truth.

The main points, in my own view, are as follows.

The history of the dispute dates back to the 1870s. In the same year as John D. Rockefeller founded Standard Oil, a Jewish pedlar, wandering through the northernmost coastal deserts of Peru, happened to find oil. A British consortium became interested, and test drillings revealed an enormous lagoon of oil beneath an *hacienda* called La Brea y Pariñas.

The British entered negotiations with the owner of the *hacienda*, Genaro Helguera, and discovered that there existed on his land a little mine, the *Amotape*. The black substance extracted from it was used to caulk boats. The interesting thing was that the state had once, fifty years previously, and under special legislation for regulation of the national debt following the War of Independence, sold this mine for 5,000 *soles*. Helguera *owned* the mine and its contents. And the boundaries of the mine were not clearly indicated in the old documents. This opened up fantastic possibilities – if only it could be claimed that the Amotape mine, a couple of hectares in circumference, really covered the entire La Brea y Pariñas *hacienda*, of 1,664 square kilometres.[7]

7. The I.P.C. has opposed practically every detail of this argument, quoting the *Legal report on the case of La Brea y Pariñas* and other legal pleas for the defence that the company had written in 1960. One basic point is how large the Amotape mine sold by the Peruvian state in 1826 actually was. The Peruvians maintain that it covered only a few hectares, the I.P.C. that it extended over the entire La Brea

Under the tutelage of the British, Helguera began to assert vis-à-vis the Peruvian authorities a title not only to the *content* of the mine and the *ground* of the *hacienda,* but also to the entire vast lagoon of oil *beneath* his property. In this he failed. Peruvian law, which on this point has remained identical throughout the Inca, Colonial and Republican periods, is very explicit: all finds under the ground belong to the nation. But Helguera obtained registered title to the land, and sole right to exploit the oil on his property. And in accordance with the Mines Act, Judge Hernández from the petty court in Paita arrived one day in January 1888 to establish the number of 'claims' constituted by the property. The mining law stated that a 'claim' must not exceed 40,000 square metres.

No one knows any more what happened that day. Possibly Judge Hernández was tired and sweaty after a long ride in the hot January sun. He probably had no idea what petroleum was. Perhaps he was bribed. Perhaps he was simply tricked. But the official protocol records: 'Owing to the irregularity of the finds and the difficulty of exploiting them – it frequently happens that costly works are performed without result – the Judge ordered that the land should be registered as 10 claims, with a tax obligation of 300 *soles* a year.'

That was enough for the British. Nine days after the Judge's order had acquired legal force, they bought the property of Genaro Helguera for £18,000 sterling. In the following year they formed the London & Pacific Petroleum Company, which in its very first year extracted 1,133 tons of crude oil, and by 1891 was up in a production figure of 12,000 tons. In a few years, Peru became South America's

---

y Pariñas *hacienda.* In other words, according to the company, the state had sold a mine that covered 1,664 square kilometres and was worked on the surface – although this same surface already belonged to another landowner. The Peruvian claim seems to me the more probable.

biggest exploiter of petroleum, a position it retained for more than thirty years.

And the Peruvians didn't even notice.

Until 1911. At that time a young Peruvian engineer named Ricardo Deustua made the sensational discovery that the London & Pacific had for the past twenty years been operating in a desolate coastal district in northern Peru, pumping out oil to a value of three million *soles* a year – and paying only 300 *soles* in tax. A hundredth of a per cent of the product value.

Deustua sounded the alarm. The government had the property remeasured. It proved to contain not ten but 41,614 claims. The London & Pacific was presented with a tax increase of 1·2 million *soles*.

The company fell back on the claim to ownership that Helguera had failed to assert. The state, it was claimed, had sold the oil under La Brea y Pariñas in 1826, when it sold the Amotape mine. The company had bought the property in good faith, including the oil, and with a legally-confirmed tax obligation of only 300 *soles* a year. It refused to pay more.

The government maintained its view. The oil in La Brea y Pariñas, like all other oil in Peru, belonged to the nation – whoever owned the land. If the London & Pacific wished to retain its oil-rights on all 41,614 claims then it must also pay the tax. Otherwise it could keep the claims that were actually under exploitation, plus a suitable reserve, and convey the rest to other concessionaries.

The London & Pacific refused. The company paid its shareholders 20 per cent in 1912, 22 per cent in 1913, and (after quadrupling its share capital) 10 per cent in 1914. It founded a subsidiary, Lagunitos, which paid 37·5 per cent in 1914 and 20 per cent in 1915.

In the spring of 1915, Great Britain went into diplomatic action, seconded by the United States. In a haughty communication to the Peruvian government, the British Ambassador demanded that the tax increase be revoked. With this, an internal Peruvian tax dispute was raised to the international level, and became a conflict between the country and the mightiest empire of the time.

But what has all this to do with the I.P.C.? The I.P.C. cannot fairly be held to account for the shady dealings of the London & Pacific, and its diplomatic pressures. It was ten years later, in 1924, by which time the conflict had already been settled, that the I.P.C. in good faith purchased La Brea y Pariñas.

This is the American account and the Peruvians have accepted it.

To make absolutely sure, however, I stopped off in London and went up to the British Museum. There I asked for the 1924 edition of Skinner's standard work, the *Oil and Petroleum Manual*.

Odd!

There was nothing about the I.P.C. buying any oilfield that year. The London & Pacific wasn't even mentioned in the book.

I started going back through the manuals from previous years. It emerged that the London & Pacific and its subsidiary, Lagunitos, both flourishing concerns, had dissolved themselves in 1916! So *in 1924 when the I.P.C. was said to have bought La Brea y Pariñas in good faith from the London & Pacific, the latter had been non-existent for the past eight years.* And why? The 1914 manual gave me the answer: in that year, the I.P.C. acquired a majority of shares in the London & Pacific. It was thus, in reality, the I.P.C. itself which was behind the diplomatic pressures brought to bear on Peru in 1915.

All right. But even if the I.P.C. did not buy the oilfields in good faith but was itself a party to the conflict, this conflict was still settled in the I.P.C.'s favour in 1922, by an international court of law.

This is what the Americans claim. *In actual fact, no international arbitration ever came about.*

THE 'PARIS AWARD'

This is what happened.

In the spring of 1919 a Peruvian businessman and politician by the name of Leguía was on his way home to take part in the presidential elections. He had spent the war years in London where he had good contacts, and *en route* for Peru he visited New York and Washington to seek support also among American financial interests. He spoke to the press of his plans for 'closer commercial and political relationships between the United States and Peru' and his desire to 'encourage the investment of North American capital in the exploitation of the innumerable and inexhaustible riches of Peru ...'

It is still uncertain who attracted most votes in the presidential elections. What is certain is that on 4 July 1919 Leguía assumed power in a successful *coup d'état*, supported by the military and by foreign financial interests. This was the introduction to an eleven-year dictatorship that afforded brilliant terms for the conduct of foreign enterprise in Peru.

In 1927, J. M. Durrell, Vice-President of the First National City Bank, summed up the result as follows:

'Peru's principal sources of wealth, the mines and oil-wells, are nearly all foreign-owned, and excepting for wages and taxes, no part of the value of their production remains in the country.... As a whole, I have no great faith in any material betterment of Peru's economic condition in the near future.'

In 1929, another senior executive of the same bank wrote:

'Metals, minerals and oils bring into the country only a part of their real value, for the reason that the production of these articles is largely in the hands of foreign companies which sell exchange sufficient only to cover their operating costs.'

In return for the services he had rendered American capital, Leguía was bolstered up throughout his period of government by bond loans launched by American bankers in the United States. The nominal value of these loans grew to 130 million dollars – at that time a staggering sum. The banks knew that Peru was not creditworthy, but they could not resist the fabulous prospects of profit involved in their having to pay Peru only 85 to 90 per cent of the nominal value of the loans. A great deal of the money went into the President's own pocket – at a senatorial inquiry in 1933 it emerged that one of the loans had involved a total of 416,000 dollars in bribes.

In James Carey's book *Peru and the United States 1900–1962* (University of Notre Dame Press), which deals with these transactions in detail, the Leguía loans emerge as one of the darkest chapters in the history of international banking.

It was this same Leguía, intimately allied with foreign financial interests, who a couple of months after taking power entered into negotiations with the British envoy in Peru. Meanwhile the oil continued to gush and the taxes failed to appear. In 1921 the parties agreed that the conflict over La Brea y Pariñas be submitted to a three-man tribunal of arbitration under the Chairmanship of the President of the Federal Court of Switzerland. A codicil stipulated that if the two governments arrived at a mutual agreement, then this should be regarded as the decision of the tribunal.

It was this codicil that decided the issue. Before the tribunal had had time to meet, Leguía made an agreement with the British government. He gave the London & Pacific title of ownership to the oil under the entire La Brea y Pariñas *hacienda*. The company was to adjust its tax debt by a payment of 1 million dollars. Subsequent tax was fixed for

the *next fifty years* at thirty *soles* per claim where drilling
was taking place, and one *sol* per claim held in reserve. The
company was also exempted from export charges for a period
of twenty years.

Thus, when the tribunal met in Paris on 24 February 1922,
there was no longer any dispute to settle. No legal consideration of the two parties' cases ever came about. The codicil
automatically fulfilled its function. The tribunal met only
to raise I.P.C.'s uniquely favourable deal with a bought Peruvian President to the dignity of an international award.

It is on the basis of this 'award' that the United States was
now threatening Peru with economic sanctions for its expropriation of an honest American company.

FROM LEGUÍA TO BELAÚNDE

Peru has been forced to accept this 'award' for forty-six years,
always under protest. As long as Leguía was dictator, nothing
could be done. But he fell with his American financiers
shortly after the Wall Street crash in 1929. The new government immediately stopped payment on his loans, and the
agreement on La Brea y Pariñas came in for sharp criticism.
In 1932 the government was authorized to request a review
of the 'Paris award'. Owing to internal political disputes, this
could not be done until ten years later. The application was
rejected on formal grounds by the International Court in The
Hague.

The United States pressed Peru for twenty years to resume
payment on Leguía's loans. An agreement was reached in
1953 with another Peruvian dictator, Odría. Even as late as
1969, 80 million dollars still remained to be paid.

The I.P.C. went on pumping out the oil. First for twenty
years paying only the minimal taxes laid down by the 'Paris
award'. Then for a further ten years with certain minor

export-charges. Since 1951, finally, with the company tax, which the I.P.C. succeeded in 1958 in unburdening on to the Peruvian consumers. At this, criticism began to grow. El *Comercio*, the largest morning paper in Peru, took up the petroleum question as a main aspect of its editorial policy. In 1960 even the army joined the critics – at a secret meeting between the chiefs of services it was decided to work for expropriation as the only reasonable solution.

Belaúnde, when he became President in 1963, promised to solve the I.P.C. problem within 90 days. Later that year Peru solemnly declared the 'Paris award' invalid. The United States and England protested, and negotiations started between the Peruvian government and the I.P.C. The latter had nothing against negotiation. The fifty-year period of the 'Paris award' was coming to an end. The I.P.C. needed a new basis for its operations in Peru, and the prospects of arriving at a result favourable to the company seemed bright.

This was because Belaúnde resembled Leguía, in so far as he very rapidly came to depend on foreign financiers. During his six years in power, Peru's foreign debt increased from 188 million (of which half comprised Leguía's loans) to 742 million, an increase by almost 400 per cent. A large part of the debt consisted of short bank-loans at high rates of interest. Belaúnde found himself with less and less room to manoeuvre, and in 1967 when speculators and exporters forced a devaluation of Peru's currency Belaúnde was ripe for a deal with the I.P.C.

The deal was made public on 13 August 1968. The I.P.C. was to stay in Peru. The little state oil-company of E.P.F. was to assume the role of supplier of crude oil to the I.P.C. refinery in Talara, and to I.P.C.'s widely-extended distribution network in Peru. The country was to get back the now almost exhausted oilfields of La Brea y Pariñas – but without any compensation for the oil extracted there over the space of eighty years.

Peru seethed. This was a fresh act of treachery, a new sellout, a new 'Paris award'. The Generals met to deliberate. Of the 36 present, 29 were for intervention, 2 against, and 5 did not vote. On 9 October the military struck.

GENERAL VELASCO

So there stood General Velasco, frightened but determined, a conservative Peruvian officer who throughout his life had fought communism and defended the U.S. hegemony, who shivered at the very idea of the 'masses' being unleashed – and who had expropriated what the United States regarded as 120 million dollars' worth of American property.

There was a single sheet of white paper under the glass leaf over his desk. What was this document that he always wanted to keep in front of him? I leaned over and read it. It was a list of the investments that Cerro, Southern, Anaconda, Marcona, and other American mining- and oil-companies were prepared to make in Peru during the Seventies – if Peru gave in to the demands of the United States in the matter of I.P.C.'s expropriation.

There lay the real threat.

U.S. foreign aid to Peru is fairly negligible. Its military aid is greater, but still only 7 million dollars. The sugar quota is the most important factor – here it was a question of 25 to 30 million dollars which Peru was to lose during 1969. But the United States' strongest card was the investments, a thousand million dollars, which could be delayed year after year if Peru did not cave in.

Paradoxically enough, then, the decisive threat to Peru was the loss of American investments, which if they came about could further increase the dominance of the United States in Peru. It was necessary to give the Americans still more power – otherwise where would the money come from, now that they already owned practically the whole economy? The country's dependence had apparently reached a point at which every step forward, in fact even its continued existence, could be purchased only at the price of further dependence.

Peru's economy has always dictated its politics, and the United States dictated its economy. There was very little free play for Nasserist efforts in the direction of independence – unless the officers were prepared to climb right out of the economic system to which they belonged.

That was still a long way off.

But they were toying with the idea. I asked General Velasco:

'What is the government's ideology?'

'Nationalism. We are quite simply Peruvians. We have nothing in common with any other revolution.'

'Not even the Cuban?'

He started.

'Least of all with that. Although, obviously...'

An aide leaned forward and whispered.

'He's got the tape-recorder on, Mr President.'

'We have nothing to hide. Our revolution is further removed from the Cuban than any other. But if the United States resorts to sanctions to force us to our knees – then I cannot be responsible for what happens.'

POSTSCRIPT, AUGUST 1971

It was at the end of March 1969 that I met General Velasco. The count-down to 9 April – the date on which sanctions were to begin – had entered the critical final stage. Day by day, the tension increased. The Americans were expecting Velasco to give way.

But he stood his ground, and it turned out that Nixon, who had been subjected to violent demonstrations during his Latin American tour in 1958, was unwilling to make a comeback with an unpopular sanction. Perhaps he also realized that the I.P.C.'s case was too weak to provide a suitable cause of hostilities. And he hesitated to employ a weapon that had proved counter-productive in Cuba ten years previously. So the sanctions were postponed, first until 6 August, then indefinitely.

'The threat of sanctions has shown itself a meaningless bluff, an unsuccessful attempt at political blackmail,' wrote the *Peruvian Times*, the special voice of Peru's foreign colony, not without disappointment. The paper's political commentaries are no longer politely insulting, they breathe a new respect for the government of the Generals.

His prestige in all camps greatly enhanced, Velasco continued his programme of reform. He started with a new Water Act which nationalized all Peru's water resources, and a new Land Reform Act which looked as if it could be the most effective in all South America.

The most important points in this new Act are as follows. Estates of over 150 hectares on the coast and 15 hectares in the mountain areas are to be expropriated at their taxation value and paid for in government bonds, to be amortized in twenty to thirty years. Large estates that are functioning will not be broken up, but run as co-operatives. Minifundios of under three hectares will be merged to make larger units.

The Land Reform Institute immediately took over the country's six largest sugar-plantations, totalling 66,000 hectares, which hit above all the American sugar interests. In the space of a year and a half, over three million hectares of land were then expropriated within the framework of the reform.

A currency reform introduced in May 1970 makes it more

difficult to take capital out of the country. The state has bought up several private commercial banks, and put an end to foreign dominance in banking.

In July 1970 an Industries Act was passed, which divides industrial firms into four different priority classes. The base industries – iron and steel, the chemical industry, cement – are to be run by the state. In the other priority classes, foreign-owned firms are gradually to be forced to incorporate Peruvian capital until at least two-thirds of their shares are owned by Peruvian citizens.

Also, 10 per cent of the company's net profit for the year is to be divided up among its employees. A further 15 per cent of profit is to be used for the purchase of shares, which will accrue collectively to the company's workers. After a transitional period of a maximum 15 years, the company's workers will collectively own half the shares, and hold half the posts on the Board of the company.

This Act has naturally provoked violent opposition among the previous shareholders, and it is possible that some of these more radical enactments will remain on paper. A sign that this may be the case is provided by the Fisheries and Mining Acts, passed in 1971, which make considerably greater provision for the interests of the shareholders.

The state, however, has assumed control of fish-meal exports, and revoked a number of unutilized mining concessions previously granted to Cerro and other American-owned companies.

The mining companies, naturally, are deeply disturbed by the turn events have taken in Peru.

In his speech to Cerro's shareholders at the 1969 general meeting, Chairman of the Board Robert P. Koenig maintained that the mining companies were often burdened by restrictions that hindered rather than encouraged economic progress. In his view, a static and improper attitude had gained ground in many developing countries; they had come to regard their oil finds as a 'national treasure-chamber', to be defended as the property of the people.

Why then bother to extract the ore in countries with such a misguided approach? The trouble was that other, more easily accessible finds were already exhausted. It was estimated, Koenig said, that the United States alone had in the past thirty years consumed more metal than all mankind throughout its previous history. The world's consumption of its natural resources had expanded very rapidly, and the supplies that could maintain expansion were to be found only in the developing countries.

Since Robert P. Koenig gave his speech, this 'static attitude' has emerged in other countries also – in Zambia, which nationalized its copper mines in 1969, and in Chile, where development was directly influenced by events in Peru.

It was Velasco's victory in the I.P.C. affair that decided the outcome of negotiations between President Frei and the Anaconda copper-company. A deal was reached as soon as it became obvious that the United States was not going to open economic hostilities in Peru.

Under the threat of expropriation, Anaconda were forced to sell 51 per cent of shares in their two Chilean mines, Chuqui and Los Andes, at the book value of 197 million dollars. (The *Wall Street Journal* on 30 June put the reprocurement value of plant and equipment at something between 700 million and 1,000 million dollars. These mines also contain established ore-finds to a current value of at least 18,000 million dollars.) The contract gave Chile the option of buying the remaining 49 per cent of the shares as early as in 1973, but then at roughly twice the book value. The total purchasing sum would then be around 600 million dollars.

According to the professional press, it would be difficult for Anaconda to find an equally profitable investment for this money. Since Salvador Allende, a socialist, won the 1970

elections in Chile, the Congress of that country has unani-
mously decided for the direct expropriation of the American
mining-companies. At the time of writing, the question of
compensation has still not been settled.

It is clear enough, anyway, that the risks for which the
American mining-companies have year after year been exacting their 'risk premiums' have at last materialized, in Anaconda's case after half a century. A wave of measures to
promote economic independence is sweeping Latin America.
The majority of American companies mentioned in this book
are operating today on very different terms from those of
1968. In Guyana, DEMBA has been nationalized. In Venezuela, a new Petroleum Act has nationalized all finds of
natural gas, and radically tightened up the terms on which
foreign companies can operate. The 'Andean Pact' – i.e.
Colombia, Ecuador, Peru, Bolivia and Chile – has adopted
very strict joint regulations on the treatment of foreign
capital. Within a space of ten to twenty years, 51 per cent
of the share capital must be transferred to native shareholders. Only 14 per cent of profit can be taken out of the
country. Etc., etc.

The American government, its hands full in Vietnam and
on the home front, has taken only the lamest of action –
verbal warnings, and in some cases a freeze on loans. However, the openings for foreign financial interests to bring
pressure to bear are by no means exhausted. In April 1971,
56 North American companies announced their decision to
discontinue a total of 84 investment projects in the Andean
Pact's five member-countries. And of all the investment
projects listed on the white paper under the glass leaf over
President Velasco's desk, only the Southern Peru Copper
Corporation's investment in Cuajone has so far been carried
to its conclusion.

In the majority of these countries, the striving towards
economic independence has no counterpart in a radical policy

at home. The main exception is Chile, where Salvador Allende's government has consciously striven, by parliamentary means, to make Chile a socialist state. At the time of writing, Bolivia still hangs indecisively on the brink of civil war. And in Peru the government of the Generals continues to speak of their measures as if they were politically sterile surgical operations, as if the operation of the Peruvian body-politic required no support other than from the experts of the U.N. Economic Commission for Latin America. The reforms are to be imposed from above, and popular initiative is either met half-heartedly, or rejected out of hand.

The left in Peru is even more fragmented than it was. Héctor Béjar and Hugo Blanco, both of whom have been given amnesty, have gone their separate ways. Béjar is collaborating with the government, Blanco has come out against it. And the Generals continue their work of reform, brooking interference from no one.

Some countries, then, have taken important steps towards creating a new and independent Latin America. Even in these countries, however, it is uncertain how long the trend will last. And the majority of countries – above all Brazil, Argentina and Guatemala – are still travelling the opposite path, towards more complete dependence and more repressive policies.

Any general improvement in the lot of the Latin American masses thus seems almost as remote today as it did in 1969.

Chorrillos Revisited

Chorrillos Revisited

JACINTA VEGAS

The hut is difficult to find. I had remembered it as spacious and fairly well-cared-for, and it stood alone on a slope. Now the entire hill teems with hovels, surrounded by garbage and excrement, with a paralysing stench of urine. Jacinta's hut is dilapidated, in a state of collapse. When she answers, I see that she is pregnant and that she has lost two front teeth.

'Do you remember, Jacinta? We met a couple of years ago. Have there been any changes since then?'

'No, nothing's been happening here. I've cut my hair short, that's all.

'My man hasn't been able to move back home yet. They're still looking for him, for the accident. He's working somewhere in the *sierra*, on an *hacienda*, he says. He's been here twice on a visit. He comes at night, when no one can see. The last time was in October. I got pregnant.

'He brought some money with him when he came, and promised to send some more. But nothing has come. In December I caught pneumonia. Ever since then I've felt terribly tired.

'We live on my sickness benefit from the Regatta Club, two dollars 40 a week. My eldest boy has started work, that's another two dollars 40. He's employed in an engineering workshop, we are thinking of him going to night school. He's very good to me. It was him that started repairing the walls with rush matting. This place is falling down round our ears.

'The revolution? No, we haven't noticed any revolution round here.'

RINALDO RIVAS LOUDE

'Yes, I remember. A couple of years ago, wasn't it? Yes, I'm still at the same place. I still have my machine. Only it's got more difficult to find the work. This last month I haven't had anything at all. A few repairs for people round about, that's all. You can't live on that.

'The pay's the same as before, 86 cents the dozen.' (One dollar 30 has become 86 cents following the devaluation.) 'Prices have gone up, of course. The boss says nothing can be done about it. When we can't even get work, how can we ask the boss for a rise? I go without any jobs for a week, then I get a dozen or two the following week. It's very uneven. And as I said, nothing at all this past month.

'My wife goes out cleaning half the day here in Chorrillos, and makes seven to eight dollars a month. That's what we live on.

'The union? No, it never comes to anything. It's like this, we're about ten workers at the shoe factory. But most of them are young boys. They can work a day here and there, as if it was a game. But if you've got a family like me, then you want to work every day, daily, all days. To make your *centavos*. So I don't get mixed up in it. The boss says a union doesn't suit him. It's not a good time, he says. So we agree with him and say it's not a good time. He pays what he pleases. After all, he owns the factory.'

'And what happened about the asphalt and the water and the sewerage? There were a lot of people who believed in the mayor ...'

'No, it hasn't come. It hasn't come. In spite of all the

promises and propaganda. Nothing. As you see, we live just as we did. Nothing has changed.

'The water still comes in a tank truck and costs seven cents a barrel. But it only comes twice a week. And you use such a lot of water now it's summer, and it doesn't stay fresh, either. We have to buy from private sellers too, at two cents a bucket.'

'The new government, has it made any difference?'

'No, things are as usual, as you might say. Although of course, a lot of what they're doing must be very good. Take rice, for instance, which was up to 36 cents a kilo. Now you can buy it from the army trucks for 21 cents. It's not the old rice, it's a round rice, a Chinese rice. But you can eat it. What with the population going up and production standing still, no progress anywhere – obviously, we can count ourselves lucky to get Chinese rice.'

VÍCTOR LI MAU

He has moved to the Avenida Buenos Aires. His father up in Trujillo is dead, the lease of the farm has passed out of the family's hands, his brothers are looking for other work. He himself is married, they have a little boy. He is very gentle with the little boy.

'The military government hasn't meant any changes, not as far as I can see. Two important things have happened : unemployment has increased and prices have gone up. The poor have got poorer.

'Here in town, everything is the same. The old mayor went, you remember – and with him the plan for a motorway to the beach, and expensive clubs that would give the district a new source of income. I don't know if it would have worked – anyway it all came to nothing. The new mayor is honest, but he has no power.

'I don't think I'll be going on here. It's not much good collecting old clothes. You only get at the symptoms, not the causes. We're going to move up to the *sierra*, where the problems have their roots. But I don't know yet what I'm going to do there.'

'Isn't there anyone for whom things have gone really well? Someone who's better off now than two years ago?'

'Well, there's Lucía. Her uncle owns a restaurant in Nasca and is well off. He's helped her with the money to get a real house.'

LUCÍA ROJAS CENTENO

I didn't meet her, she was out washing. But the house was there, right next to the place where the old shack had stood. It was a real house with two real rooms and a real floor of cement, real glass windows, and a real wooden door.

What a victory this house in Chorrillos was in the battle of life!

I looked in through the window and saw the sewing-machine. In the shack she would never have dared have it out, for fear of thieves. Now it stood safely behind the real wooden door, fully visible through the real glass window.

ANA CASTAÑÓN ORMENO

She had moved. I found her in the dark corridor outside the door of her new house. She had locked herself out, and was sitting there waiting.

'Have things got better in any way? Well, two of the children have started school. We've been promised the electric light here, perhaps even next month. That would be an improvement.

'I live here with a friend and her children. I still do washing and cleaning. I make two dollars a day, twice a week.

'My father had to move to Chimbote. You can't do business any more here in Lima, he says. It's impossible to buy, impossible to sell. So now he deals in fish-meal and wool in Chimbote. He's some sort of agent for a firm called Multimar. One thing at least is that the change of climate did my mother good. She's up and about now. So that way I suppose you can say things have got a bit better.'

MARINA PÉREZ

The heavy, sandy slope, half a mile long, up to the house. This is in an even greater state of collapse than previously. The rush mats have rotted to pieces, there are great holes in the corrugated cardboard. Marina is pregnant. Her husband is there on a visit, lying naked on the bed, which occupies almost the entire room. He pulls on trousers and vest, and goes out.

'I never thought I would see you again. Everything's the same here. Although prices have gone up something terrible. Not like they were before. Sweet potatoes used to cost 3.50 *soles* the bag, now they're up to six *soles*.' (Fourteen cents in both cases, owing to devaluation.) 'They've moved the market and nothing's in order there yet, they keep pushing us to and fro. It wasn't worth going in today. And it's not often I have my husband here.

'Otherwise I make breakfast for the children, and go into the square at three in the morning. I get back here with what's over in the bag around twelve. Yes, I leave the children alone here. After all, the boys go to school. My oldest has started in Grade One four times now. He still goes with his little brother, who's starting for the second time.

'Otherwise nothing's happened. The pigs? We had a bit

of bad luck there. We should have eaten them, like the boys said. Only I thought that would be a waste. As it was they got sick and died. It was our neighbour that killed them. He gave them water with washing-powder in while I was at the market. You can't keep pigs round here unless you're at home to look after them.'

MIGUEL BARRANICHEA

His picture had been on the front page of the *Dagens Nyheter*, Sweden's largest daily. A reader sent him twenty dollars, which he spent on a wall of clay brick and a proper roof. The three other walls are of rush matting. But the room is quite large and furnished with a double bunk and one single bed. We sit down on the beds. His hair is water-combed and he is wearing a newly-washed blue shirt. He seems more optimistic and in better health.

'We've managed pretty well these past two years. My wife was ill for a few months, a sort of fever. I have my bad eye. But you can't get work on the building sites now anyway, there are too many people. Some of them stay until dinner-time, others stay waiting outside all day. Better not go at all.

'There was a rumour that the mayor in Callao needed 5,000 men for a big job. Several of us went. But it was all a mistake. They *would* have needed 5,000 men if there hadn't been machines. As it was they only needed 50. We stayed there and waited, but it was all done by machine. So we had to come back. I lost 70 cents on that trip.

'But we don't think of moving back to the *sierra* any more. There's been a drought there, the crops failed, and then a sudden storm. Those who've been there say there's nothing to eat. My brother's the only child of the family still there, and he wants to come to Lima.

'My wife sells cow's heart and fried potatoes, you remember. I go to the market at four in the morning and buy the raw materials. About 14 kilos of heart. We put seven dollars a day into purchasing, and make about a dollar 20, a dollar 60. On Sundays it can be over two dollars. We pay 24 cents a day tax. But it's a risky business now, in the heat of the summer – if people don't buy, what's over has to be thrown to the dogs.

'We've joined the Leasehold Association, and we're paying off the entrance fee at 48 cents a week. The Association's got 62 members. There's a lot needs to be done here. Lighting, water, sewerage, a road – it's all got to be done. There was an engineer came, we paid four dollars 80 each, all 62 of us. That was nearly 300 dollars, we were supposed to get a plan, and drawings. But the engineer went to prison, he's been inside for eight months. They're taking up a collection to get him out. I think it was a false accusation. But it was a pity we never got a receipt for the money. And, of course, we never got the plan.'

FELICITA SALVA PLÁCIDO

'Nothing ever happens here. It's the same old thing. I lock the children in and go to work. There's so much traffic outside here, the cars just scream by, you can't leave them running around. And of course while I was away Dante had to strike a match, and the top flew into Eliot's eye. And this little one turned the saucepan over and scalded her chest. The eye operation cost 12 dollars. And what with the bandages, ointment, medicine, visits to the hospital, and the travel ... These two accidents must have cost me over 60 dollars altogether.'

'And the conflict with the United States? The new government?'

'These people ... these military people I suppose you'd call them. They say they want to make improvements, they say they're going to cut prices, but we haven't seen anything of that here. Prices are still going up. Rice, potatoes ... Meat's up to a dollar 16 a kilo, for the cheapest kind. A poor person has no chance of buying meat. It's the same with sugar, it's just too expensive.'

'But don't the military sell rice from trucks, cheaply?'

'Yes, but I haven't been able to buy any. You know, some-times we don't have any money and we have to buy on credit. And we buy rice, say, half a kilo at a time. From the soldiers you have to buy 20 kilos at a time, and pay cash. We just can't do it.'

'What about your job?'

'I'm still with the same family. I'll have been there for four years soon. The pay's still the same, 12 dollars a month.' (Twenty dollars has become 12 dollars, since devaluation.) 'I've asked for a rise, but they say they haven't got the money. And then I have various benefits – I don't have to go there if the children are sick, that's one. And sometimes I make an extra dollar washing.'

'Hadn't you just got the paper on a site?'

'Oh dear, the site. .... Yes, I've got the paper. After eight years I at last got this paper in my hand. But if we don't move in and start building within two years, I shan't be allowed to keep it. And now the two years are up. We haven't been able to start building, because we haven't had the money and materials. It costs a whole mountain of money. The posts alone cost six dollars apiece. We still haven't been able to get started. I've asked for more time and hope to be able to get a few *centavos* together. But I don't know how things will work out.

'And that's it. We've had two accidents, and prices have gone up. And so we're going to lose the site. That's what our problems have been these past two years.'

*

Dante and Eliot started playing with my tape-recorder. My work was done. I had tried to get to know Latin America, and written a book.

While writing, I had often thought I must be mistaken. Had I not created a picture from my imagination, a picture of Latin America that stemmed more from personal pessimism than from reality? Perhaps my memory was at fault, my notes unreliable. Surely, surely, it could not be in reality as I was describing it.

Yes, this was how it was. Not only the day I happened to call, but every day, incessantly, the whole time. The same struggle for food, the same fear for the future, the same fragile hope. Somewhere up there a government was overthrown, a big company expropriated. Hardly an echo reached these depths. Somewhere up there, new multi-million contracts would be signed and new fortunes made. Down here, the people were all as incomprehensibly patient and submissive as I remembered them.

Nothing had altered. Felicita was wearing the same old green dress, which her mistress had discarded. The same soup was simmering in the same buckled pan on the same stones in the corner. The old pram still hung on the earthen wall, broken and rusty. I sat on the bed like last time. Everything was the same. It had just gone on. And would go on.

For how long?

Bibliography

I did not wish to burden a book of this kind - a combined journalistic report and social analysis - with a cumbersome apparatus of notes. The following list gives some of the works I have used; only in exceptional cases does it include books already mentioned in the notes. The North American literature is over-represented, since the majority of Latin American books are available only in their country of origin - if there.

General

Claudio Véliz (ed.): Latin America and the Caribbean, A Handbook, London 1968.

Howell Davies (ed.): The South American Handbook, London. Annual.

J. P. Cole: Latin America, An Economic and Social Geography, London 1965.

Martin C. Needler (ed.): Political Systems of Latin America, New York 1964.

D. B. Heath et al. (ed.): Contemporary Cultures and Societies of Latin America, New York 1965.

Joseph A. Kahl: La industrialización en América Latina, Mexico 1965.

History

John Edwin Fagg: Latin America, A General History, New York 1963.

Lewis Hanke: History of Latin American Civilization, I–II, Boston 1967.

R. A. Humphreys: Latin American History, A Guide to the Literature in English, Oxford University 1958.

Michael Rheta Martin et al. (ed.): Encyclopedia of Latin American History, New York 1968.

Political and social problems

James Pctras et al. (ed.): Latin America, Reform or Revolution?, New York 1968.

Claudio Véliz (ed.): Obstacles to Change in Latin America, Oxford University 1965; The Politics of Conformity in Latin America, Oxford University 1967.

Seymour Martin Lipset et al. (ed.): Élites in Latin America, Oxford University 1967.

Richard Adamas et al.: Social Change in Latin America Today, New York 1960.

John J. Johnson (ed.): Continuity and Change in Latin America, Stanford University 1964; Political Change in Latin America, The Emergence of the Middle Sectors, Stanford University 1958.

Jacques Lambert: Latin America, Social Structures and Political Institutions, University of California 1967.

André Gunder Frank: Capitalism and Underdevelopment, New York 1967.

José Luis de Imaz: Los que mandan, Buenos Aires 1964.

Luis Mercier Vega: Mécanismes du pouvoir en Amérique latine, Paris 1967.

Jorge Graciarena: Poder y clases sociales en el desarrollo de America Latina, Buenos Aires 1967.

The military

Edwin Lieuwen: Arms and Politics in Latin America, Praeger paperback 1961.

John J. Johnson: The Military and Society in Latin America, Stanford University 1964.

William H. Brill: Military Intervention in Bolivia, Institute for the Comparative Study of Political Systems, 1967.

Víctor Villaueva: El militarismo en el Perú, Lima 1962; Un ano bajo el sable, Lima 1963.

The Church

J. Lloyd Mecham: Church and State in Latin America, University of North Carolina 1966.

William V. D'Antonio et al. (ed.): Religion, Revolution and Reform, New York 1964.

Edward J. Williams: Latin American Christian Democratic Parties, University of Tennessee 1967.

Gustavo Jiménez Cadena: The Role of the Rural Parish Priest as an Agent of Social Change in Central Colombia, University of Wisconsin 1965.

CELAM: Directorio Católico Latinamericano, Bogotá 1968.

Oswaldo Albornoz: Historia de la acción clerical en el Ecuador, Quito 1963.

B. Castro Villagrana et al.: La iglesia, el subdesarrollo y la revolución, Mexico 1968.

Émile Pin: Elementos para una sociología del catolicismo latino-americano, Bogotá 1963.

D. Helder Cámara: Revolucão dentro da Paz, Rio de Janeiro 1968.

Márcio Moreira Alves: O Christo do povo, Rio de Janeiro 1968; Paz e Terra, No. 6, 1968.

The towns

Glenn H. Beyer (ed.): *The Urban Explosion in Latin America*, Cornell University 1967.

Bruce H. Herrick: *Urban Migration and Economic Development in Chile*, Cambridge 1965.

Oliver Oldman *et al.*: *Financing Urban Development in Mexico City*, Harvard University 1967.

Peter W. Aamato: *An Analysis of the Changing Patterns of Elite Residential Areas in Bogotá, Colombia*, Cornell University 1968.

W. Mangin: 'Mental Health and Migration to Cities, A Peruvian Case', *Annals of the New York Academy of Sciences*, 1960.

Reforms

Pan American Union: *The Alliance for Progress and Latin American Development Prospects, A Five-year Review 1961–65*, Baltimore 1967.

Herbert K. May: *Problems and Prospects of the Alliance for Progress*, New York 1968.

Social Progress Trust Fund: 'Socio-economic Progress in Latin America', *Annual Report*, Inter-American Development Bank, Washington.

On tax reform

R. M. Sommerfeld: *Tax Reform and the Alliance for Progress*, University of Texas 1966.

Milton C. Taylor: *Fiscal Survey of Colombia*, Joint Tax Program of the Organization of American States and the Inter-American Development Bank, Baltimore 1965; *Problems of Tax Administration in Latin America*, Joint Tax Program, Baltimore 1965.

R. Bird *et al.* (ed.): *Readings on Taxation in Developing Countries*, Baltimore 1964.

Harley H. Hinrichs: *Una teoría general del cambio de la estructura tributaria durante el desarrollo*, Centro de Estudios Monetarios Latinamericanos, Mexico 1967.

On land reform

CIDA: *Tenencia de la tierra y desarrollo socio-económico del sector agrícola 1–6*, Washington 1965. (The six volumes cover the Argentine, Brazil, Chile, Colombia, Ecuador, Guatemala and Peru.)

Oscar Delgado (ed.): *Reformas agrarias en la America Latina*, Mexico 1965.

William C. Thiesenhusen: *Chile's Experiments in Agrarian Reform*, University of Wisconsin 1966.

Albert O. Hirschman: *Journeys toward Progress*, New York 1965, Chapter 2.

Sergio Aranda: *La revolución agraria en Cuba*, Mexico 1968.

Revolution

Richard Gott: *La experiencia guerrilla en Bolivia*, Estudios Internacionales, No. I, 1968, Santiago de Chile.

Luis E. Aguilar: *Marxism in Latin America*, New York 1968.

Rollie Poppino: *International Communism in Latin America*, New York 1964.

Orlando Fals Borda: *La subversión en Colombia, El cambio social en la historia*, National University of Colombia 1967.

Camilo Torres: *Liberación o muerte*, Havana 1967.

Germán Guzmán: *Camilo, El cura guerrillero*, Bogotá 1967.

Carlos H. Pareja: *El padre Camilo, El cura guerrillero*, Mexico 1967.

Fabricio Ojeda: *Hacia el poder revolucionario*, Havana 1967. (Venezuela.)

Venezuela en Armas, Havana.

Gonzalo Ani Castillo: *Historia secreta de las guerrillas,* Lima 1967.

Rogger Mercado: *Las guerrillas del Perú,* Lima 1967.

Mario A. Malpica: *Biografía de la Revolución,* Lima 1967, Chapter 12.

Ministerio de Guerra: *Las guerrillas en el Perú y su represión,* Lima 1966.

Glauco Carneiro: *Historia das revoluçones brasileiras,* Rio de Janeiro 1965.

Mines and oil

BOLIVIA:

Guillermo Bedregal: *Monopolios contra países pobres, La crisis mundial del estaño,* Mexico 1967.

Sergio Almaraz Paz: *El poder y la caída,* La Paz 1967.

CHILE:

Markos Malmakis *et al.*: *Essays on the Chilean Economy,* Yale University 1965.

Mario Vela Valenzuela: *La política económica del cobre en Chile,* University of Chile 1961; *Un política definitiva para nuestras riquezas básicas,* Santiago de Chile 1964; *La encrucijada del cobre,* Santiago de Chile 1965.

MEXICO:

Marvin D. Bernstein: *The Mexican Mining Industry 1890–1950,* New York 1964.

Miguel S. Wionczek: *El nacionalismo mexicano y la inversión extranjera,* Mexico 1967.

Lorenzo Meyer: *México y Estados Unidos en el conflicto petrolero,* Mexico 1968.

VENEZUELA:

Robert Engler: *The Politics of Oil, A Study of Private Power and Democratic Directions,* Chicago University 1961.

Rómulo Betancourt: *Venezuela, política y petróleo,* Caracas 1967.

Héctor Malave Mata: *Petróleo, y desarrollo económico de Venezuela,* Caracas 1962.

Some countries

THE ARGENTINE:

Aldo Ferrez: *The Argentine Economy*, University of California 1967.

Tómas Roberto Fillol: *Social Factors in Economic Development, The Argentine Case*, Cambridge 1961.

George Pendle: *Argentina*, Oxford University. Numerous editions. (The same series, published by the Royal Institute of International Affairs, includes monographs on the majority of Latin American countries.)

BRAZIL:

Department of the Army: *U.S. Army Area Handbook*, Washington 1964. (Similar works are available for most Latin American countries. Very useful. Can be obtained from the U.S. Printing Office, Washington D.C. 20402, U.S.A.)

Celso Furtado: *The Economic Growth of Brazil*, University of California 1965.

Thomas E. Skidmore: *Politics in Brazil 1930–64*, Oxford University 1967.

Irving Louis Horowitz: *Revolution in Brazil*, New York 1964.

Jean-Claude Bernadet *et al.*: *Brasil hoy*, Mexico 1968.

MEXICO:

Stanley R. Ross (ed.): *Is the Mexican Revolution Dead?*, New York 1966.

Raymond Vernon (ed.): *Public Policy and Private Enterprise in Mexico*, Harvard University 1964.

William P. Glade *et al.*: *The Political Economy of Mexico*, University of Wisconsin 1968.

Joe C. Ashby: *Organized Labour and the Mexican Revolution under Lázardo Cárdenas*, University of North Carolina 1963.

Howard E. Cline: *Mexico, Revolution to Evolution 1940–60*, Oxford University 1963; *The United States and Mexico*, New York 1963.

Diego G. López Rosado: *Problemas económicos de México*, National University of Mexico 1966.

PERU:

François Bourricaud: *Pouvoir et société dans le Pérou contemporain*, Paris 1967.

José Matos Mar *et al.*: *Perú problema*, Lima 1968.

Virgilio Roel: *La plantificación económica en el Perú*, Lima 1968.

Emilio Romero: *Historia económica del Perú*, Buenos Aires 1949.

VENEZUELA:

Robert J. Alexander: *The Venezuelan Democratic Revolution*, Rutgers University 1964.

John Friedmann: *Regional Development Policy, A Case Study of Venezuela*, Cambridge 1966.

International Bank of Reconstruction and Development: *The Economic Development of Venezuela*, Baltimore 1961.

D. F. Maza Zavala: *Venezuela una economía dependiente*, Central University of Venezuela 1964.

CENDES: *Estudio de conflictos y consenso*, 1–15, Central University of Venezuela 1967 onwards.

These books are often based on the research of others: publications from various university institutions, official hand-outs, stencils, brochures and other documents. I myself have used large quantities of such material. The above list includes only works that there should be at least some chance of obtaining.